D1475604

STUDIES IN CLASSICAL LITERATURE, **1**

Imprimi potest:

Most Rev. Augustine Sépinski, O.F.M.
(Minister General)
Very Rev. Donald Hoag, O.F.M.
(Minister Provincial)

Nihil obstat:

Rt. Rev. Patrick W. Skehan
(Censor Deputatus)

Imprimatur:

† Patrick A. O'Boyle
(Archbishop of Washington)
August 12, 1964

The *nihil obstat* and *imprimatur* are official declarations that a book or pamphlet is free of doctrinal or moral error. No implication is contained therein that those who have granted the *nihil obstat* and the *imprimatur* agree with the content, opinions or statements expressed.

THE HEBREW TEXT OF SIRACH

A TEXT-CRITICAL AND HISTORICAL STUDY

by

ALEXANDER A. DI LELLA, O.F.M.

Holy Name College

1966

MOUTON & CO.

LONDON · THE HAGUE · PARIS

Printed by J. J. Augustin, Printers, Glückstadt (bei Hamburg), Germany

To

My Father and Mother

ὁ γὰρ Κύριος ἐδόξασεν πατέρα ἐπὶ τέκνοις,
καὶ κρίσιν μητρὸς ἐστερέωσεν ἐφ' υἱοῖς.

(Sir 3, 2)

PREFACE

This book began as a Ph.D. dissertation in Semitic Languages and Literatures at the Catholic University of America, Washington, D.C. It bore a slightly different title – *A Text-Critical and Historical Study of the Hebrew Text of Sirach* (Washington, 1962) – and was published in 1963 by University Microfilms, Inc., Ann Arbor, Michigan. Parts of the work also appeared in two articles: "Qumrân and the Geniza Fragments of Sirach", *CBQ*, 24 (1962), 245–267; and "Authenticity of the Geniza Fragments of Sirach", *Bib*, 44 (1963), 171–200. What I offer in the present book is a revised and augmented edition of the dissertation, with a general bibliography on Sirach.

Writing a dissertation is not an easy task. Indeed in moments of difficulty and fatigue the neophyte scholar is vividly reminded of and is tempted to endorse wholeheartedly Coheleth's keen, if somewhat cynical, remark: "Of the making of many books there is no end, and in much study there is weariness for the flesh" (Eccl 12,12). But when one investigates a subject that is more interesting than was originally expected, then such a one is truly fortunate. For the long hours of research spent in dusty libraries and in one's study, and the tedious labor of presenting results in a unified and readable fashion, become pleasant and rewarding experiences.

The present writer considers himself among those fortunate ones. Almost from the time that Prof. (Rt. Rev. Msgr.) Patrick W. Skehan, who was my major professor, suggested that I study the Cairo Geniza MSS of Sirach, I have been enthusiastic about the subject, despite initial misgivings. That enthusiasm still remains. This is a tribute, of course, to the skillful guidance that I received from

Prof. Skehan first of all, and also from Prof. Louis F. Hartman, C.Ss.R., and Prof. Roland E. Murphy, O.Carm., who were the other readers of the dissertation. For the many useful suggestions and for the encouragement and help that I received from these three scholars, I am sincerely grateful.

When I began graduate studies at the Catholic University of America, Very Rev. Celsus R. Wheeler, O.F.M., was Minister Provincial of the Province of the Most Holy Name (New York), of which I am a member. To him and to his successor, Very Rev. Donald Hoag, O.F.M., I offer special thanks for granting me the opportunity of pursuing higher studies in Semitic Languages and Literatures.

The publication of this book has been made possible through grants – for which I am sincerely grateful – from Holy Name College, Washington, D. C., and the Catholic Biblical Association of America.

It is my pleasant duty to express my gratitude also to the librarians and staffs of the Catholic University of America, the Library of Congress (Washington), the New York Public Library, Columbia University, the Zionist Archives and Library (New York), the British Museum, the Cambridge University Library, the Bodleian Library (Oxford), the École Biblique (Jerusalem, Jordan), the Studium Biblicum Franciscanum (Jerusalem, Jordan), the Hebrew University (Jerusalem, Israel), the Pontifical Biblical Institute (Rome), the Pontificium Athenaeum Antonianum (Rome), and the Vatican Library.

Finally, I thank the publishers, Mouton and Co., for including this work in their series, *Studies in Classical Literature*.

Holy Name College
Washington, D.C.

ALEXANDER A. DI LELLA, O.F.M.

CONTENTS

LIST OF ABBREVIATIONS

Books of the Old Testament: Gn, Ex, Lv, Nm, Dt, Jos, Jgs, Ru, 1 Sm, 2 Sm, 3 Kgs, 4 Kgs, 1 Par, 2 Par, Ezr, Neh, Tb, Jdt, Est, Jb, Ps, Prv, Eccl, Ct, Wis, Sir, Is, Jer, Lam, Bar, Ez, Dn, Os, Jl, Am, Abd, Jon, Mi, Na, Hb, So, Ag, Za, Mal, 1 Mc, 2 Mc.

A	Codex Alexandrinus of the LXX.
AER	*American Ecclesiastical Review.*
AJSLL	*American Journal of Semitic Languages and Literatures.*
Anton	*Antonianum.*
B	Codex Vaticanus of the LXX.
BA	*Biblical Archaeologist.*
BASOR	*Bulletin of the American Schools of Oriental Research.*
Bib	*Biblica.*
BZ	*Biblische Zeitschrift.*
C	Codex Ephraemi rescriptus of the LXX.
CBQ	*Catholic Biblical Quarterly.*
CCD	The Holy Bible Translated from the Original Languages with Critical Use of All the Ancient Sources by Members of the Catholic Biblical Association of America.
EstEc	*Estudios Eclesiasticos.*
ExpT	*Expository Times.*
HarvTR	*Harvard Theological Review.*
HPR	*Homiletic and Pastoral Review.*
HUCA	*Hebrew Union College Annual.*
JAOS	*Journal of the American Oriental Society.*
JBL	*Journal of Biblical Literature.*
JCS	*Journal of Cuneiform Studies.*
JJS	*Journal of Jewish Studies.*
JNES	*Journal of Near Eastern Studies.*
JQR	*Jewish Quarterly Review.*
JTS	*Journal of Theological Studies.*
l(l).	line(s).
LXX	The Septuagint.
NRT	*Nouvelle Revue Théologique.*
PG	*Patrologia Graeca*, ed. by Migne.
PL	*Patrologia Latina*, ed. by Migne.
RB	*Revue Biblique.*

REJ	*Revue des Études Juives.*
RevBén	*Revue Bénédictine.*
S	Codex Sinaiticus of the LXX.
S*	Codex Sinaiticus of the LXX, first hand.
$S^{c.a}$	Codex Sinaiticus of the LXX, second hand.
ST	*Studia Theologica.*
TLZ	*Theologische Literaturzeitung.*
TPQ	*Theologisch-Praktische Quartalschrift.*
TQ	*Theologische Quartalschrift.*
TZ	*Theologische Zeitschrift.*
v(v).	verse(s).
VD	*Verbum Domini.*
VDBS	Vigouroux, *Dictionnaire de la Bible, Supplément.*
VieSp	*Vie Spirituelle.*
VT	*Vetus Testamentum.*
WZKM	*Wiener Zeitschrift für die Kunde des Morgenlandes.*
ZAW	*Zeitschrift für die Alttestamentliche Wissenschaft.*
ZDMG	*Zeitschrift der deutschen morgenländischen Gesellschaft.*
ZKT	*Zeitschrift für Katholische Theologie.*
ZNW	*Zeitschrift für die neutestamentliche Wissenschaft.*

INTRODUCTION

In 1896, S. Schechter, professor of Talmudic Hebrew at Cambridge University, examined a leaf of an old MS and immediately recognized it to be a portion of Sir in Hebrew. The leaf had been recovered from the Geniza of the Qaraite Synagogue in Old Cairo.[1] Prior to Schechter's discovery, Sir was known in Hebrew through only a few generally inexact quotations found in the rabbinical literature. The Greek and Syriac versions, from which all other translations were made, had been the basic sources of our knowledge of the Book.

Between 1896 and 1900, many more fragments of Sir in Hebrew were identified among the vast materials recovered from the Cairo Geniza. These fragments fell into four distinct groups, generally called MSS A, B, C, and D,[2] and were dated from the ninth to the twelfth century.

In 1931, J. Marcus discovered a new leaf of Sir in Hebrew among the fragments contained in the Adler Geniza collection in the library of the Jewish Theological Seminary of America. This leaf was designated MS E.[3] It added 34 new distichs – by distich we mean two "hemistichs" or one Hebrew poetic line – to the 1056

[1] For the details and first publication of this exciting discovery, cf. S. Schechter, "A Fragment of the Original Text of Ecclesiasticus", *Expositor*, 5th series, 4 (1896), 1–15.

[2] In the reckoning of I. Lévi, MS C is called MS D, and vice versa. Hardly any scholars, however, have followed Lévi in this respect.

[3] *The Newly Discovered Original Hebrew of Ben Sira (Ecclesiasticus xxxii, 16–xxxiv, 1): The Fifth Manuscript and a Prosodic Version of Ben Sira (Ecclesiasticus xxii, 22–xxiii, 9)* (Philadelphia, 1931). This pamphlet is a corrected reprint of the article which appeared originally in the *JQR*, n. s., 21 (1930–1931), 223–240.

previously recovered. In 1958 and 1960, J. Schirmann identified a few more leaves of MSS B and C.[4] These new finds contained 81 distichs, of which only seven and a half were not already represented in the earlier fragments. Hence, the total thus far identified is 1098 distichs, slightly more than two-thirds of the Book, which in Greek contains 1616 distichs.

The generally accepted view in the first years after the initial discovery of Hebrew Sirach was that the Cairo MSS contained a text which is independent of Greek and Syriac, and is therefore essentially authentic, even though it was disfigured by numerous scribal errors and other corruptions and by the presence of frequent glosses. During this same period, however, a few scholars were suspicious of the Hebrew fragments, and consequently evolved elaborate, and often fanciful, hypotheses that the Cairo Hebrew text of Sir had been retranslated by a clever medieval Jew from Persian, Greek, and/or Syriac. These theories were immediately refuted by the majority of scholars; hence, we could say that by 1915 the common opinion held that the Geniza text of Sir was genuine.

During the past 40 years, however, there has been a rising wave of skepticism concerning the authenticity of the Cairo Hebrew. E. J. Goodspeed, C. H. Gordon, A. Büchler, R. Storr, M. Hadas, C. C. Torrey, H. L. Ginsberg, H. Duesberg, P. Auvray, and others have questioned the value, if any, of the Geniza text of Sir.

This being the case, a reappraisal and fresh study of the Cairo text are certainly called for. In keeping with the perspicacity that is his wont, Professor P. W. Skehan suggested that I investigate the Geniza MSS of Sir independently before examining the standard commentaries and studies that have appeared during the past 65 years.[5] I did just that. The present book is the result of this investigation.

[4] "*Dap ḥādāš mittôk sēper ben-Sîrā' hā-'ibrî*", *Tarbiẕ*, 27 (1957–1958), 440 to 443; "*Dappîm nôs^{e}pîm mittôk sēper 'ben-Sîrā'*"", *Tarbiẕ*, 29 (1959–1960), 125–134. I have re-edited these leaves in "The Recently Identified Leaves of Sirach in Hebrew", *Bib*, 45 (1964), 153–167.

[5] Cf. the bibliography at the end of this book for a list of works on the Geniza text of Sir.

The first thing I did was to subject to text-critical analysis the five Geniza MSS in general, and in particular those vv. which are extant in two or three MSS at the same time,[6] comparing the Hebrew text with the Greek, Old Latin, Syriac Peshiṭta, and Syrohexaplar. This procedure led to two inescapable conclusions: (1) the text of the Cairo fragments of Sir is essentially genuine; (2) it does nevertheless contain *some* retroversions from the Syriac Peshiṭta.

I then made an historical study of the Geniza text of Sir, establishing a definite relationship between the events referred to in an important Syriac letter of Timothy I to Sergius (near the end of the eighth century A.D.) and the recent epoch-making discoveries near Khirbet Qumrân. The new evidence provided by these sources corroborates throughout the text-critical arguments in favor of the substantial authenticity of the Cairo Hebrew.

In this book I do not pretend to solve all or even most of the textual problems relating to the Book of Sirach. As I stated above, I have restricted myself to proving, on the one hand, the substantial authenticity of the Cairo Geniza text and, on the other hand, the existence of some retroversions in that text. The Greek version in two recensions – the Great Uncials and the cursive Codex 248 group – has its own peculiar problems for which I intend to give no solution. For attempted solutions the gentle reader is directed to the commentaries (especially Smend's). The expanded text of the Old Latin version which St. Jerome left untouched when he incorporated it into the Vulgate still presents many interesting problems.[7] The Syriac Peshiṭta offers few problems: its faults generally antedate our oldest MSS (Codex Ambrosianus and Br. Mus. Codex 12142 – both of the sixth century), and are repeated in the later MSS that form the bases for the Walton and Mosul editions; I have found few interesting textual variants in the Peshiṭta tradition.

[6] There are 130 such vv., of which six are extant in three MSS (B, C, and D): 36, 29. 30. 31; 37, 19. 22. 24.

[7] In passing, I should mention that I have found several passages where Old Latin agrees with the Cairo Hebrew text against the Greek tradition and the Syriac Peshiṭta.

For the text of the Geniza fragments of Sirach identified up to 1900, I made my own transcription from the generally excellent Cambridge and Oxford facsimiles.[8] I have also consulted the editions of H. L. Strack,[9] R. Smend,[10] I. Lévi,[11] and M. H. Segal.[12] For MS E I have been forced to rely, for the most part, on the transcription of J. Marcus,[13] because the facsimiles that he published are difficult and, at times, impossible to read, having been printed on cheap, dull paper instead of the usual glossy paper. Lévi[14] and Segal[15] also published MS E; I have consulted these editions too. Of the leaves of MSS B and C recently identified by J. Schirmann, I have made from the original MSS at the University Library, Cambridge, my own edition and published the same,[16] because Schirmann's transcriptions are not as accurate as they could be. When I cite a text from a leaf that is damaged, I have indicated a partial letter, whose value is virtually certain, by a semicircle over the letter (א̆). All other marks given in my transcription are found in the MS(S).

As regards the uncial tradition of the Greek version I have utilized principally the edition of H. B. Swete[17] because in it one can see at a glance which MS(S) give(s) a particular reading. For

[8] *Facsimiles of the Fragments Hitherto Recovered of the Book of Ecclesiasticus in Hebrew* (Oxford-Cambridge, 1901).

[9] *Die Sprüche Jesus', des Sohnes Sirachs* (Leipzig, 1903). This is the most convenient edition to use, but unfortunately it contains some errors.

[10] *Die Weisheit des Jesus Sirach, hebräisch und deutsch* (Berlin, 1906). This is the most reliable edition of the fragments found up to that time. I have been told that Smend is the one who smeared vaseline on the Oxford fragments of Sirach. I examined them in the summer of 1963: they are difficult to read even under ultraviolet light; hence, the vaseline damage seems to be permanent.

[11] *L'Ecclésiastique*, 2 parts (Paris, 1898, 1901); *The Hebrew Text of the Book of Ecclesiasticus* (= *Semitic Studies Series*, 3) (Leiden, 1904). Lévi's editions, particularly the latter, are not recommended, containing too many errors to be of real use. Cf. also n. 2 above.

[12] *Sēper ben-Sîrā' ha-šālēm*, 2d ed. (Jerusalem, 1958). Segal's edition is not recommended for two reasons: (1) it contains errors; (2) it is inconvenient to use.

[13] See n. 3 above.

[14] "Un nouveau fragment de Ben Sira", *REJ*, 92 (1932), 136–145.

[15] See n. 12 above.

[16] See n. 4 above.

[17] *The Old Testament in Greek*, 2, 3d ed. (Cambridge, 1907).

Greek Codex 248 I used the edition of J. H. A. Hart.[18] I consulted Holmes and Parsons[19] for the variants of the other cursive MSS.

I utilized A. M. Ceriani's beautiful facsimile edition of Codex Ambrosianus of the Syrohexaplar.[20]

It was my good fortune to be in Rome when the fine critical edition of the Vulgate (= Old Latin) text of Sirach was published a few months ago.[21] I obtained a copy of that text immediately and used it in the present work.

For the Syriac Peshiṭta I have employed Codex Ambrosianus also published in facsimile by Ceriani,[22] as well as the editions of Lagarde,[23] Walton,[24] and Mosul.[25]

[18] *Ecclesiasticus: the Greek Text of Codex 248* (Cambridge, 1909).

[19] *Vetus testamentum graecum cum variis lectionibus*, 4 (Oxford, 1827).

[20] *Codex syro-hexaplaris Ambrosianus photolithographice editus* (Milan, 1874).

[21] *Biblia sacra iuxta latinam vulgatam versionem*, 12: *Sapientia Salomonis, Liber Hiesu filii Sirach* (Rome, 1964).

[22] *Translatio Syra Pescitto veteris testamenti ex codice Ambrosiano sec. fere VI photolithographice edita*, 2, 4 (Milan, 1878).

[23] *Libri veteris testamenti apocryphi syriace* (Leipzig-London, 1861). Lagarde used Br. Mus. Codex 12142 for Sirach.

[24] *Biblia sacra polyglotta*, 4 (London, 1657); variants are contained in vol. 6, pp. 46f.

[25] *Biblia sacra juxta versionem simplicem quae dicitur Pschitta*, 2 (Beirut, 1951).

I. SURVEY OF OPINIONS CONCERNING THE CAIRO HEBREW

In this chapter we shall attempt three things: (1) to point out some of the inadequacies in the treatment of the Cairo Hebrew on the part of the proponents of the genuineness of this text; (2) to present the position of E. Nestle and I. Lévi who felt that some parts of the Cairo Hebrew represented the original of Ben Sira, whereas other parts were retroversions from Syriac and Greek; and (3) to discuss the position of the opponents of the authenticity of this text.

A. PROPONENTS OF THE AUTHENTICITY OF THE CAIRO HEBREW

In an extensive survey of scholarly views on the Geniza fragments of Sirach, E. Schürer wrote: "Für die Originalität [of the Cairo Hebrew] haben sich fast alle kompetenten Forscher mit großer Entschiedenheit erklärt."[1] This judgment correctly summarized the state of the question (as of 1909) in respect to the authenticity of the Geniza Hebrew. Our purpose here is not to restate the arguments advanced by the many scholars whom Schürer speaks of, but rather to show how these scholars as well as most others after them failed to provide an adequate solution to the problem of the doublets found in the Cairo MSS. Toward this end we shall analyze briefly the position of M. H. Segal, one of the most prolific Sirach scholars, for his views more or less reflect those espoused by other scholars before and after him.

[1] *Geschichte des jüdischen Volkes im Zeitalter Jesu Christi*, 3, 4th ed. (Leipzig, 1909), 223.

M. H. Segal

Segal attempts to prove that there existed four different Hebrew recensions of Sirach, viz. (in chronological order): (1) the *Vorlage* of Greek I (the Uncials); (2) the *Vorlage* of Greek II (Codex 248 being the best representative of the group); (3) the *Vorlage* of Syriac; and (4) the text of the Geniza fragments.[2] He claims that: "The existence of these different recensions ... eventually culminated in [the] latest form [of the Book] as represented by the Hebrew fragments and the debased text of the quotations in rabbinic literature."[3] As we hope to prove in Chapter III, the Cairo MSS, as a whole, do not contain the "latest form" of the Book, but rather an early form that existed prior to 68 A.D., for, as it will be shown, the Geniza fragments embody a text that substantially goes back to the caves of Qumrân.

Because of his misconceptions in respect to the history of our Book, Segal writes:

> A feature common to both Syr. and Heb. [= the Geniza text] is the tendency occasionally to simplify the difficult classical diction of the author and to reduce it to the easy popular diction of mishnaic Hebrew. This tendency has sometimes given rise to a duplication of the sayings of our book in two forms, one in a more or less severe classical Hebrew and the other in a simplified colloquial Hebrew. The older classical form has been preserved in Gr. and the later popular form in Syr., while Heb. has as a rule preserved the two forms side by side.[4]

Among the vv. which Segal cites as evidence of this theory are: (1) 15, 15 ותבונה לעשות רצונו אם תאמין בו גם אתה תחיה,[5] in which he claims that the second part agrees with Syriac, and the first with Greek; and (2) 16, 3 ממי שהיו לו בנים רבים [בעו]לה ומאחרית זדון, in

[2] "The Evolution of the Hebrew Text of Ben Sira", *JQR*, n. s., 25 (1934 to 1935), 148.

[3] *Ibid.*, 91 f. Cf. also his "*Sēper ben-Sîrā' beqûmrân*", *Tarbiẕ*, 33 (1963–1964), 245 f.

[4] *Art. cit.* (n. 2), 118. Cf. also Segal's *Sēper ben-Sîrā' ha-šālēm*, 2d ed. (Jerusalem, 1958), 62 f.

[5] This is the reading of MS A. A recently discovered leaf of MS B also contains the line, but in this form: ... ואמונה לעשות רצון אל·

which he states that the first part, up to [בעו]לה,[6] agrees with Syriac, and the second with Greek. From his discussion of these and other vv., Segal concludes: "... that Syr. is based upon a Hebrew text which embodied popular paraphrases of certain verses originally current orally in Jewish circles of the talmudic period."[7]

In Chapter IV we discuss in considerable detail several of the vv. which Segal alleges as proof of this theory. It is our contention that the materials that have come to light from the caves near Khirbet Qumrân[8] and the discovery of several more leaves of the Cairo Hebrew, prove conclusively that the "simplified colloquial Hebrew" that is found in some hemistichs of the Geniza text is not evidence for a "popular" Hebrew recension, but rather for retroversion of these hemistichs from Syriac.

R. Smend, A. Fuchs, N. Peters, G. H. Box, W. O. E. Oesterley

A position broadly similar to Segal's is maintained by most other scholars who uphold the authenticity of the Geniza text: for example, R. Smend,[9] A. Fuchs,[10] N. Peters,[11] G. H. Box and W. O. E. Oesterley.[12]

Such a position, however, seems incapable of providing a plausible explanation for the numerous doublets found in the Geniza Hebrew. Perhaps for this reason, some scholars, as we shall see below, rejected the authenticity of the Cairo text altogether. A careful text-critical analysis of the Geniza MSS and an historical study of materials pertinent to these MSS, have convinced the present writer that the theory of Segal *et al.* is wrong. This is not to say, however, that we agree with the opponents of the Cairo text. Quite the contrary. Rejecting the originality of most of the doublets,

[6] This reconstruction is incorrect. Cf. my discussion of this v. in Chapter IV, pp. 139–142.

[7] "The Evolution of the Hebrew Text ...", 123.

[8] See Chapter III.

[9] *Die Weisheit des Jesus Sirach erklärt* (Berlin, 1906).

[10] *Textkritische Untersuchungen zum hebräischen Ekklesiastikus* (= *Biblische Studien*, 12, 5) (Freiburg i. B., 1907).

[11] *Das Buch Jesus Sirach oder Ecclesiasticus* (Münster i. W., 1913).

[12] "Sirach", in *The Apocrypha and Pseudepigrapha of the Old Testament*, 1, ed. by R. H. Charles (Oxford, 1913), 268–517.

which we certainly do, need not imply a rejection of the rest of the text which is just as certainly genuine. It seems completely illogical for the opponents to dismiss as retroversion the entire text merely because there is undeniable evidence for retroversion of small parts of that text.

B. THE PECULIAR POSITION OF NESTLE AND LÉVI

E. Nestle

Although E. Nestle limits his discussion to only a few vv. of our Hebrew text, he is of the opinion that the Geniza fragments represent a text that is partly original and partly retroverted from Greek (MS C) and from Syriac (MS A).[13] The best argument he offers is based upon 4, 30:

MS C		MS A
אל תהי כאריה בביתך	30a	אל תהי ככלב בביתך
ומתפחז בעבודתך	30b	ומוזר ומתירא במלאכתך

30a μὴ ἴσθι ὡς λέων ἐν τῷ οἴκῳ σου,
30b καὶ φαντασιοκοπῶν ἐν τοῖς οἰκέταις σου.

ܠܐ ܬܗܘܐ ܟܠܒܐ ܒܒܝܬܟ. 30a
ܘܪܕܘܦ ܘܕܚܠ ܒܥܒܕ̈ܝܟ. 30b

Concerning this v. Nestle writes:

> Can there be any doubt that A agrees with S [= Syriac] and C with G [= LXX]? Compare especially the second clause, where S has two words, A has also two, C for one word of G has one word. What is more natural than the conclusion that A and C are not the original, but dependent upon S and G, *retranslations*, as [D.S.] Margoliouth affirmed of B? But we must not be too rash: we ask, How would a late Jewish translator hit upon מתפחז to render so obscure a word as φαντασιοκοπῶν? פחז is rare in biblical Hebrew (Gn 49[4], Jer 23[32]); it suits the context very well; it might be easily confounded with פחד 'fear,' and thus explain the rendering of S, and it is a favourite word with Sirach (see H [= Hebrew] 8[2] 19[2]

[13] "Sirach (Book of)", in *A Dictionary of the Bible*, 4, ed. by J. Hastings (New York–Edinburgh, 1902), 547ff.

41[17mg.] 42[10mg.], S 19[2] 23[4.6.16.17]); *it may therefore have preserved the original.*[14]

Retroversion from Greek is, of course, *possible*, but we think that it has not been proved by Nestle's argument. In fact, Nestle's admission that מתפחז could hardly have been translated from Greek and "*may therefore have preserved the original*", appears to refute the argument that the reading of MS C is retroverted from Greek.

We do admit, however, that the reading כאריה of MS C could have resulted from retroversion of the Syrohexaplar, which reads: ܠܐ ܬܗܘܐ ܐܝܟ ܐܪܝܐ ܒܒܝܬܟ ܘܕܚܝܠ. But if that was the case, retroversion appears to have taken place only as regards that word, for in the second half-line, MS C does not manifest any dependence at all upon the Syrohexaplar: ܘܡܬܪܕܦ ܒܡܫܡܫܢܝܟ ܩ̈ܕܡ ܒܝܬܟ ܘܕܚܝܠ.

With respect to ככלב of MS A, Nestle is correct in stating that this reading is dependent upon Syriac. It seems virtually certain that Ben Sira wrote כלביא. But the Syriac translator misread these consonants as *kalbî*', the *aleph* being otiose, as in the Qumrân orthography. Thus, he understood the word as an adjective, like יְהוּדִי or שְׁלִישִׁי. In his translation, however, he merely wrote ܟܠܒ. It is quite possible that the medieval scribe saw in his exemplar the original reading כלביא; but since he considered the image too violent, he changed the word to ככלב under the influence of Syriac.

Nestle's other arguments for retroversion from Greek are also open to question.[15] But with respect to the relationship of Hebrew to Syriac, we agree with Nestle that some parts of the Geniza text are retroverted from Syriac, as Chapter IV will prove.

[14] *Ibid.*, 547. W. R. Taylor, *The Originality of the Hebrew Text of Ben Sira in the Light of the Vocabulary and the Versions* (Toronto, 1910), defends a theory similar to Nestle's; Taylor writes (p. 24): "In conclusion, we may say that while H. [= Hebrew text] contains some of the remains of an original text, it has become so corrupt that for purposes of criticism it has little value in addition to that of the versions. In most instances where the versions have become corrupt or reflect a corrupt original, H. gives us no help. The many lacunae in H. have been filled by translations from the versions. Emendations have been made on the basis of the versions. The marginal notes are often the readings of equally corrupt texts; e.g. cp. the relations of B. and C. The text represents an attempted restoration of the original on the basis of some faulty remains and the versions."

[15] Cf. Box and Oesterley, *op. cit.*, 276.

I. Lévi

Between 1896 and 1901, I. Lévi shifted his opinion several times as regards the authenticity of the Cairo Hebrew of Sirach. In 1896, after examining the first and (up to that time) only leaf of Sirach in Hebrew (39, 15–40, 6), he questioned Schechter's judgment that the fragment contained the original of Ben Sira.[16] Then in 1897 and 1898, after studying other portions of the Geniza text that had recently come to light, Lévi maintained that the Hebrew was certainly original.[17] In 1899, he attempted to prove that the Hebrew fragments discovered up to that point represented a text that in great measure was retroverted from Syriac and partially from Greek.[18] In 1900, he again favored the authenticity of at least part of the Geniza text.[19] And in the introduction to the second part of his commentary on the Hebrew MSS (published in 1901), Lévi humbly retracted his views of 1899 when he had rejected the essential genuineness of the Hebrew text.[20] Thus, Lévi again favored the authenticity of the Cairo text.

[16] "Découverte d'un fragment d'une version hébraïque de l'Ecclésiastique de Jésus fils de Sirach", *REJ*, 32 (1896), 303f.

[17] "... Le text hébreu est bien l'original .... L'hébreu n'est pas une *retraduction* du grec ni du latin, qui procède du grec, mais qu'au contraire, le grec ne s'explique que par l'hébreu .... Même opération pour le syriaque." So writes Lévi in "La Sagesse de Jésus, fils de Sirach: découverte d'un fragment de l'original hébreu", *REJ*, 34 (1897), 4. Similar ideas are expressed in his *L'Ecclésiastique*, part 1 (Paris, 1898), XVIII.

[18] "Les nouveaux fragments hébreux de l'Ecclésiastique de Jésus fils de Sira", *REJ*, 39 (1899), 15: "... Les nouveaux fragments [30, 11–31, 11; 32, 1–33, 3; 35, 9–36, 21; 37, 27–38, 27; 49, 12–51, 30; 3, 6–7, 29; 11, 34–16, 26] portent la trace visible qu'ils ne sont – au moins pour un certain nombre de chapitres – qu'une retraduction en hébreu d'une version syriaque." See also *ibid.*, 177–190.

[19] "Fragments de deux nouveaux manuscrits hébreux de l'Ecclésiastique", *REJ*, 40 (1900), 24: "Ces chapitres [36, 26–40, 1 of MS D (= Lévi's MS C)] sont donc bien, sinon l'original pur, du moins une copie assez fidèle de l'original."

[20] *L'Ecclésiastique*, part 2 (Paris, 1901), XXf.: "Bientôt après paraissaient les nouveaux morceaux de B. et de A. découverte par M. Schechter, et ce fut une amère déception pour quelques personnes, dont nous fûmes: ils donnaient raison, en partie, a l'invraisemblable affirmation du professeur d'Oxford [D. S. Margoliouth]. Nos fragments n'étaient pas une traduction du persan, mais du syriaque et, en certains points, du grec. Loyalement, avec un zèle trop impatient, nous nous empressâmes de faire connaître notre désillusion et notre

In brief, Lévi's final opinion is that the Cairo Hebrew is substantially authentic, but contains nevertheless some retroversions from Syriac. Thus he writes:

> In many places [of MSS A and B] the same verse appears in two forms, of which one generally agrees with the Greek and the other with the Syriac. But what is more, the doublet which agrees with the Syriac contains matter lacking sense which can only be explained as a *false interpretation of the Syriac*; and in that case the sentence is conspicuous by the platitude and late character of the language and syntax, as well as by the rupture of the parallelism, to which the author evidently held. One is therefore constrained to admit that these verses are *retranslations of the Syriac*. The same must be said of certain fragmentary verses .... With these reservations the fact remains nevertheless that the body of the book is really the original, the very work of Ben Sira. This is sufficiently proven by the numerous errors of countersense committed by the translator which can be explained only as a wrong reading or interpretation of the Hebrew. But as has happened with all the texts of antiquity, ours has suffered at the hands of the scribes.[21]

Lévi holds the same views in his article on Sirach in *The Jewish Encyclopedia*.[22]

We are in broad agreement with Lévi's final position. Since Lévi's time, however, the textual history of the Geniza fragments has undergone a profound change, thanks to a Syriac letter written about 800 A.D. by Timothy I, the Nestorian Patriarch of Seleucia, and the highly probable connection of certain events narrated therein with the epoch-making discoveries at Khirbet Qumrân (see Chapter III).

---

conviction, au risque de nous attirer des brocarts de toute sorte. Nous ne fûmes pas seul à exprimer cette opinion; M. Bickell, entre autres, tint le même langage, indépendamment de nous."

[21] *The Hebrew Text of the Book of Ecclesiasticus* (= *Semitic Study Series*, 3) (Leiden, 1904), Xf.

[22] "Sirach, The Wisdom of Jesus, the Son of", *The Jewish Encyclopedia*, 11 (New York, 1905), 393f.

C. OPPONENTS OF THE AUTHENTICITY OF THE GENIZA HEBREW

In this section we shall state briefly the position of those scholars who reject the complete text of the Cairo MSS on the grounds that it is a generally poor example of retranslation by some medieval Jew who used as basis a Persian, Greek, and/or Syriac version of the Book.

D. S. Margoliouth

Among the first to call into question the genuineness of the Geniza text was D. S. Margoliouth, who wrote a twenty page pamphlet[23] on the subject. Interestingly enough, Margoliouth's essay won virtually no adherents to the bizarre retroversion hypothesis he had proposed; rather, he engendered immediate and almost universal opposition. The reason for this reaction is not difficult to discern, as we shall see forthwith from select quotations out of this pamphlet.

Margoliouth writes: "The appearance of many of the pages of the MS[24] is not unlike that which would be presented by the rough copies of retranslations of Ecclesiasticus such as many scholars must at different times have made."[25] On the existence of some Persian glosses found in the margins of MS B, Margoliouth bases his whole theory. He alleges several vv. as proof that the Cairo fragments represent a retranslation in part from Persian, but confesses in all candor: "I attach little importance to several of the Persian conjectures; some three, I think, are certain."[26] Even if Margoliouth's three Persian conjectures were correct (all three are, however, open to serious question), it would seem methodologically incorrect, as well as illogical, to throw out the entire text of the Hebrew fragments merely because there was some evidence for partial retroversion.

[23] *The Origin of the 'Original Hebrew' of Ecclesiasticus* (London-Oxford, 1899). In an earlier article, "Observations on the Fragment of the Original of Ecclesiasticus Edited by Mr. Schechter", *Expositor*, 5th series, 4 (1896), 140–151, Margoliouth was of the opinion that the Cairo Hebrew was original.

[24] Margoliouth had at his disposal only MS B when he wrote his pamphlet.

[25] *The Origin of the 'Original Hebrew'* . . ., 4.

[26] *Ibid.*, 12.

Margoliouth concludes his essay with a short "history" of the medieval Persian Jew who was responsible for the text contained in the Cairo MSS. This "history" is so astounding that it deserves full quotation.

> And now before we part from him, let us learn something of the history of this remarkable man, who some centuries ago set himself the task of reconstructing Ecclesiasticus out of a Syriac and a Persian translation. We have had to criticize his work severely; but for him we have nothing but admiration. He lived after 1000 A.D., for the Persian which he knew was already mixed with Arabic words and phrases to overflowing; but his native language was Arabic, for he uses that for his stop-gap words. He was taught Hebrew by a Jew who had a pronunciation similar to that of the Christians of Urmi; else why should he mis-spell *dōr*, 'generation,' as דבר in xvi. 5? He was no great grammarian, else how could he make such a mistake as גיפת in xl. 16.... It was over a bargain then, perhaps at Baghdad, that some Christian quoted Ben-Sira to him – probably the verse which says that a dealer is a knave; and he learned to his astonishment that the proverbs of Ben-Sira, of which he had heard, were preserved in the Christian scriptures, though lost to the Jews. And fired with the thought that he too might do something for the dear Hebrew language and the honour of his race, he makes haste to procure a copy, and presently engages a teacher to help him to read it. And talking of languages, as teachers will, his tutor mentions casually that he has a friend who knows a tongue of which they both are ignorant; one who for the love of Christ and His Apostles has learned the language in which their Gospel was composed. And when the Grecian is introduced, he takes some interest in the Ben-Sira project, but regrets (not without ostentation) that the worthy Jew should base his work on the Syriac, when the Greek in his possession is so much fuller and better. And when he has proved this by examples, which he could easily do, the Jew tells him that if he will translate the Greek into Persian, he, the Jew, will reward him well. And presently the materials are all collected; he can read Syriac,

> and has a complete copy of the Persian; and he collects the Old Testament parallels, and tries to think what the Hebrew can have been. And indeed he does some things well; he even restores the original felicitously once or twice where both versions are misleading; but he makes – as what pioneer does not? – a number of mistakes, and cannot satisfy himself in a variety of passages. And so, desirous of doing well the task which has been given him, he collates and corrects and revises and transcribes till death overtakes him before the work is finished. And then his MS. falls into the hands of a pedant, who knows Hebrew better than the master did, but knows nothing else; and he scores a few poor and worthless emendations on the margin (xli. 5 is an example), and has fair copies made, and sells some, but not many; for the Jews like to get good value for their coin.
>
> This is the only account that I can excogitate of this extraordinary book. And having read it over many times I regard it as the true one.[27]

As could be expected, Margoliouth's weird and unbelievable theory was quickly and forcefully refuted. There is no need of repeating here the arguments which completely undermined Margoliouth's fanciful construction. S. Schechter and C. Taylor,[28] W. Bacher,[29] T. Nöldeke,[30] E. König,[31] I. Lévi,[32] C. H. Toy,[33] and J. Touzard[34] adequately confronted and supplied convincing answers to Margoliouth's unfounded objections to the Cairo Hebrew.[35]

[27] *Ibid.*, 19f.

[28] *The Wisdom of Ben Sira: Portions of the Book Ecclesiasticus from Hebrew Manuscripts in the Cairo Genizah Collection Presented to the University of Cambridge by the Editors* (Cambridge, 1899), LXX–LXXV.

[29] "An Hypothesis about the Hebrew Fragments of Sirach", *JQR*, 12 (1899 to 1900), 92–108.

[30] "Bemerkungen zum hebräischen Ben Sīrā", *ZAW*, 20 (1900), 93f.

[31] "Professor Margoliouth and the 'Original Hebrew' of Ecclesiasticus", *ExpT*, 10 (1898–1899), 512–516; 564ff.; 11 (1899–1900), 31f.

[32] *Op. cit.*, part 2, pp. XIXf.

[33] "Ecclesiasticus", in *Encyclopaedia Biblica* (London, 1904), 1168.

[34] "Nouveaux fragments hébreux de l'Ecclésiastique", *RB*, 9 (1900), 541–552.

[35] The controversy over Margoliouth's pamphlet caused some bitter exchanges. Cf. various notes entitled "The Hebrew Ecclesiasticus", *ExpT*, 10 (1898–1899), 528 (Margoliouth); 567f. (Margoliouth); on p. 568, Schechter

G. Bickell

Another early opponent of the Geniza text of Sirach was G. Bickell.[36] He argued that the text of the alphabetic canticle in chap. 51 (vv. 13–30) "folgt hier überall sklavisch dem syrischen, hat dieselben Lücken und Zusätze; nirgends zeigt sich eine Spur von Benutzung des griechischen Textes."[37] Then as regards "das Hexastich 12, 10–11", he writes:

> Hier folgt der Hebräer im Ganzen genau dem Syrer; nur am Ende des zweiten Stichos verläßt er diesen, welcher durch Verwechslung von רֹעוֹ mit רֵעוֹ den Sinn verfehlt hatte, um sich dem Griechen anzuschließen .... Für den Kairiner Text hier Ursprünglichkeit an zunehmen, erscheint unmöglich.[38]

The final canticle and the "Hexastich" are indeed in poor textual condition. But even if Bickell's contention with respect to these two portions of the Cairo text were true, his general conclusion that

---

felt constrained to write: "I have 'tasted the delights of authorship' long before the Laudian Professor [Margoliouth] began his famous career of literary failures, both in Aryan and Semitic languages. In my youth I even enjoyed a controversy, when conducted on gentlemanly lines, but I must decline any further correspondence against Professor Margoliouth, whose methods do not recommend themselves to me as either gentlemanly or scholarly." Schechter in his "Review of *The Origin of the 'Original Hebrew' of Ecclesiasticus*", *The Critical Review*, 9 (1899), 387, also made this appropriate comment: "Professor Margoliouth in his pamphlet entitled *The Origin of the "Original Hebrew" of Ecclesiasticus* has supplied a certain need. No discovery of any vital interest was ever made without some ingenious person challenging either its importance or its genuineness. A lacuna would have remained in the history of the Ben Sira discoveries had their authenticity been allowed to pass uncontested." (Reading these words today, one is immediately reminded of S. Zeitlin and his untenable views regarding the authorship and date of the Qumrân materials, concerning which cf. Chapter III.) Margoliouth, however, was not convinced by the barrage of articles and reviews that had been aimed at his pamphlet. In "The Destruction of the Original of Ecclesiasticus", *ExpT*, 16 (1904–1905), 26–29, he tries to prove that גנז means "to destroy" not "to hide away/conceal/remove out of sight". Schechter immediately answered Margoliouth's latest fanciful theory in the same vol. of *ExpT*, pp. 185f.; on pp. 236f. Bacher also adds his refutation of Margoliouth's article.

[36] "Der hebräische Sirachtext eine Rückübersetzung", *WZKM*, 13 (1899), 251–256.

[37] *Ibid.*, 254.

[38] *Ibid.*, 255f.

the *entire* Hebrew text is not genuine[39] appears methodologically unsound. We do not, however, agree with Bickell that the "Hexastich" is substantially dependent on Syriac. A text-critical examination of only one half-line will prove that Bickell overstated his case.

Sir 12, 10b:

MS A: כי כנחשת רועו יחליא

ὡς γὰρ ὁ χαλκὸς ἰοῦται, οὕτως ἡ πονηρία αὐτοῦ.

Syrohexaplar: ܐܝܟ ܓܝܪ ܕܢܚܫܐ ܡܫܚܬ ܗܟܢܐ ܒܝܫܘܬܐ ܕܝܠܗ

Peshiṭta: ܡܛܠ ܕܐܝܟ ܢܚܫܐ ܗܘ ܕܡܚܒܠ ܠܚܒܪܗ

Translations:

Hebrew: "For like bronze, his wickedness corrodes (i.e. is a source of corrosion)."

Greek and Syrohexaplar: "For as bronze corrodes, so does his wickedness."

Syriac: "For he is like bronze which corrupts its neighbor."

Bickell does confess that רועו was not retranslated from Syriac, but shows rather a dependence upon Greek. If ever there was an *ad hoc* solution, this is one. Bickell could, of course, have been consistent in his theory, if he claimed that רועו derived from ܒܝܫܘܬܐ of the Syrohexaplar. But, in any case, that is not so. For Hebrew is certainly original. The reading רועו is the common basis of both Syriac's mistranslation, ܚܒܪܗ (the Syriac translator misread *yod* for *waw* as the second consonant in his *Vorlage*; this phenomenon is explained in detail in Chapter III), and for Greek's correct ἡ πονηρία αὐτοῦ. Moreover, יחליא could in no way have been occasioned by Syriac's ܡܚܒܠ "to defile/profane/pollute", which is much less colorful than "to corrode". MS A could have been influenced here

[39] *Ibid.*, 251: "Der Eindruck, welchen ich schon beim Erscheinen der ersten hebräischen Sirachpublikation durch NEUBAUER und COWLEY empfangen hatte, daß wir es hier nicht mit einem Originaltexte zu thun haben, ist mir durch die von SCHECHTER und TAYLOR veröffentlichte zweite Blätterserie zur Gewißheit geworden. Um diese Überzeugung vor den Fachgenossen zu begründen, mögen einstweilen zwei, wie ich glaube, entscheidende Beweise genügen, da mir durch besondere Gefälligkeit der Redaktion gestattet ist, diesen Aufsatz noch in dem vorliegenden, eigentlich bereits abgeschlossenen, Hefte erscheinen zu lassen, und ich daher möglichst wenig Raum zu beanspruchen wünsche." For some comments on Bickell's article, cf. E. Nestle, "Ecclus. xii. 10, 11", *ExpT*, 11 (1899–1900), 143.

by the Syrohexaplar, which Bickell does not even bring into the discussion, but it is virtually impossible, at any rate, that the poetical conciseness of the Hebrew hemistich was derived from the Syrohexaplar, which is an awkward, word-for-word rendering of Greek.

E. J. Goodspeed

Despite the generally convincing arguments in favor of the authenticity of the Cairo Hebrew that have been adduced by scholars in the first quarter of this century, there has arisen in the last twenty years a swelling wave of skepticism in regard to this text. Although the recent opponents of the Cairo text are, for the most part, scholars of no mean rank, one could be thoroughly disillusioned by the unscientific offhandedness with which our text in its entirety has been spurned. Thus, the late E. J. Goodspeed wrote:

> (Ben Sira) wrote of course in Hebrew, but the original Hebrew of the book no longer exists. The considerable Hebrew portions of Ecclesiasticus, amounting to about two-thirds of the whole, that have come to light in recent years in medieval manuscripts are probably retranslations of it from Greek back into its original tongue, not genuine remains of the original Hebrew.[40]

The famed Bible translator offers in support of this judgment no evidence whatever! He does not even refer to any scholarly works where the reader could find such a theory argued out.

M. Hadas

In a similar manner, M. Hadas states categorically: "Hebrew fragments of the book found in the present century are not the original but a retranslation from the Greek."[41]

C. C. Torrey

In his book, *The Apocryphal Literature*,[42] C. C. Torrey objects strongly to the Geniza text:

[40] *The Story of the Apocrypha* (Chicago, 1939), 25.

[41] *The Apocrypha*, trans. by E. J. Goodspeed, introduction by M. Hadas (New York, 1959), 222.

[42] New Haven, 1945, 97.

> It is possible to see back of the Greek version a powerful and original Hebrew text, the work of a master of the literary language. In the Cairo Hebrew this impression is not maintained. What we read in a multitude of passages is commonplace, flabby, and distinctly second rate. It is customary to excuse much of this as "late Hebrew." The trouble is not with the character of the language, however, but with the lack of literary taste and skill. It is exactly what would be expected of a well-equipped writer of (say) the eighth or ninth century who should undertake, without any profound study, to reproduce the text of Ecclesiasticus, basing his work mainly on the Syriac version. The question cannot be discussed here.

Torrey offers no proof for his blanket condemnation of the Cairo text. Perhaps he thought the last sentence above excused him from providing evidence for his sweeping conclusions.

When we read Torrey's essay, "The Hebrew of the Geniza Sirach",[43] we find the same bias against the Cairo text, and very little evidence (most of it open to very serious question) to justify his views. Since, as far as the present writer could discover, no one has answered Torrey's article,[44] we shall examine the main objections he offers against our text, to determine whether or not they are sufficiently weighty to warrant the conclusion that this text does not represent substantially the work of Ben Sira.

But first we should note that Torrey commits the decidedly unscholarly fault of gravely misrepresenting the opinion of an important Sirach scholar. He quotes[45] from I. Lévi's article in *The Jewish Encyclopedia* (vol. 11, p. 394 – Torrey erroneously assigns this volume to the year 1899, but it was actually published in 1905) these words: "It may safely be said that in the main the work of Ben Sira has been preserved just as it left his hands." In a footnote concerning this quotation, Torrey writes:

> This he retracted in the following year; and in the second volume (1901) of his *L'Ecclésiastique ou la Sagesse de Jesus*

[43] Found in *Alexander Marx Jubilee Volume* (New York, 1950), 585–602.
[44] One could be tempted to suppose that the scholarly world politely ignored the article because of its lack of objectivity and critical sense, as we shall see.
[45] *Art. cit.*, 586.

> [sic] *fils de Sira* he proved conclusively that Ben Sira's acrostic poem in Chap. 51 is a translation from the Syriac. (It was not made clear why the translation should have been confined to this one portion of the book!)[46]

Since, oddly enough, Torrey supplies no references, it is difficult to determine precisely in which article or book Lévi supposedly retracted the judgment quoted above with respect to the authenticity of the Geniza Hebrew text. Because Torrey mistakenly gives 1899 as the date of Lévi's 1905 article in *The Jewish Encyclopedia*, presumably 1900 is "the following year" in which the retraction took place. But there was no retraction in 1900. As we saw above, Lévi did change his mind regarding the genuineness of our Hebrew text, but that took place in 1899. In any case, Lévi never retracted the view expressed in *The Jewish Encyclopedia*, which view is his final opinion concerning the Cairo text. Finally, Lévi did not confine retroversion from Syriac to only Chap. 51, as Torrey charges.

As regards the relationship of the Geniza text to the grandson's Greek, Torrey writes:

> The two texts were found to agree extensively in material content, and yet there were very great and important differences. The Greek could not have been obtained from any Hebrew resembling this, nor could the Hebrew have been derived from the Greek. The two traditions were perfectly distinct . . .[47]

Evidence for this all-embracing conclusion? None at all. One is almost led to suspect that Torrey did not bother to examine much of the Hebrew text in the light of the Greek.

It seems that one sweeping statement deserves another, for further on in his article, Torrey asserts:

> It is not simply that the Greek and the Hebrew do not correspond closely, in some such way as text and version correspond in every other Old Testament writing of which the original has been preserved; *the two are thoroughly diverse from each other in every part of the book*. Generally speaking, the material is the same and in the same order. A given verse of a given

[46] *Ibid.*

[47] *Ibid.*, 587.

> chapter in *Heb* [= the Cairo text] will usually be found to have some recognizable counterpart in the similarly numbered verse in *Grk*. When however we look for verbal agreement we rarely find it, even in those very numerous passages in which the Greek seems to show us with certainty not only the idiom but also the exact words employed by Ben Sira. If we suppose that this translation was made in the manner of the other Greek versions of which we have knowledge, we are obliged to conclude that it was made from another Hebrew text. There are not half a dozen consecutive verses in our Greek, in any part of the whole book, which could possibly have been derived by translation from the Cairo Hebrew or from any Hebrew closely resembling it.[48]

In that declaration there are at least two errors. First, as regards the arrangement of the materials, the order of chapters and verses is not the same in Hebrew and in Greek.[49] It is amazing that Torrey did not seem to notice this fact, or if he did, that he did not call attention to it, for it is certainly significant in any discussion of the relationship between the Hebrew text and Greek. Secondly, Torrey's first and last sentences are simply not true. We have found in verse after verse a very close correspondence between Greek and the Cairo text. Moreover, as we shall see in Chapter II, there are some instances where Greek becomes intelligible only after we examine the Geniza Hebrew.

Torrey questions the customary judgment that the grandson made a loose translation. Consequently, he writes: "We are ... prepared at the outset to find the rendering [of the grandson] truly faithful, according to its author's ability."[50] The crucial part of that statement is the last phrase. In an interesting article entitled "Sirach in Hebrew and in Greek",[51] L. F. Hartman proves quite satisfactorily that: "The words of [the grandson's] own Foreword, in which he apologizes 'for any apparent failures' in his work, should

[48] *Ibid.*, 588f. Emphasis is Torrey's.

[49] Cf. Chapter II below where the displacement of some chapters in the Greek is fully discussed.

[50] *Art. cit.*, 589.

[51] *CBQ*, 23 (1961), 443–451.

be taken more seriously by those who would use his version as the basis for their modern translation."[52]

Torrey finally presents us with some examples that in his opinion prove the superiority of the grandson's version (and the Hebrew *Vorlage* that it reflects) over the Cairo Hebrew text. The first example is 6, 2. To appreciate the complexity of the textual problems involved in this verse, we present the Cairo text, the Greek, Old Latin, and Syriac. In his discussion, Torrey employs the Greek text, referring only incidentally to the rest of the textual witnesses.

MS A: אל תפול ביד נפשך ותעבה חילך עליך

μὴ ἐπάρῃς σεαυτὸν ἐν βουλῇ ψυχῆς σου,
ἵνα μὴ διαρπαγῇ ὡς ταῦρος ἡ ψυχή σου.

Non te extollas in cogitatione animae tuae velut taurus ne forte elidatur virtus tua per stultitiam.

ܠܐ ܬܫܬܥܠܡ ܒܠܒܐ ܕܢܦܫܟ. ܕܠܐ ܬܐܟܘܠ ܐܝܟ ܬܘܪܐ ܚܝܠܟ.

Torrey translates the Greek line in this way: "Be not exalted in your own persuasion, lest your soul be torn in pieces like a bull; [v. 3] you will consume your own foliage and destroy your fruit and will leave yourself like a dry stem."[53] Torrey's entire argument with respect to the verse in question, which we admit is partially corrupt, is as follows:

> Evidently that which is "torn off," so that its leaves are consumed and its fruit is destroyed is a *branch* (שׂוֹךְ), not a *bull* (שׁוֹר), as the Greek has it. (Observe that *Syr* renders ὡς ταῦρος, a good example of its dependence on *Grk*.)[54]

First of all, we should note that Greek is more corrupt than Torrey indicates. The reading ἡ ψυχή σου is certainly not what the grandson wrote – it is a dittography from 2a –, for Old Latin has "virtus tua". Thus, presumably at least one Greek MS contained ἡ ἰσχύς σου, a phrase which, like Syriac's ܚܝܠܟ, bears witness to the authenticity of חילך in the Cairo Hebrew text.

Secondly, the existence of ὡς ταῦρος and ܐܝܟ ܬܘܪܐ points to *a* Hebrew *Vorlage* that contained the phrase כשור. Torrey's statement that Syriac here depends on Greek appears unwarranted. Despite

[52] *Ibid.*, 445.
[53] *Art. cit.*, 593.
[54] *Ibid.*

the fact that כשור was read by both the grandson and the Syriac translator we do not think that the phrase is original because of the following reasons:

(1) Thanks to the grandson's use of διαρπάζω again in 36, 30a, we can reconstruct with a reasonable measure of probability the original verb that Ben Sira wrote in 6, 2b. In 36, 30a we read:

MSS B, C, and D: באין גדיר (גדר) יבוער כרם

οὗ οὐκ ἔστιν φραγμός, διαρπαγήσεται (248: διαρραγήσεται) κτῆμα.

ܐܝܟ ܕܠܝܬ ܣܝ̈ܓܐ ܢܬܒܙܙܘܢ ܟܪ̈ܡܐ.

From this evidence we can legitimately conclude that 6, 2b also contained the verb בער. Instead of כשור, however, the original Hebrew most likely read בע(ו)ר, piel infinitive absolute. Thus, 6, 2b probably read originally: ותבער בע(ו)ר חילך.

(2) An early copyist transcribing this v. was reminded of Ex 22, 4 in which according to the ancient rabbinic interpretation בְּעִירֹה was understood as "grazing animal", not as "burning fire". The copyist then read בע(ו)ר as כשור probably because the last vv. of Ex 21 give legislation regarding wandering bulls.

(3) As regards the verb תעבה of the Cairo text, it is clear that the second and third consonants have exchanged places. Thus, we may rightly infer that *a* Hebrew copy of Sir contained the form תבעה, also a difficult reading. But it is a reading that could have been occasioned by the Samaritan-recension-type variant יבעה in Ex 22, 4. Presumably the Syriac translator read תבעה – ܬܒܥܐ. From Jastrow (*Dictionary*, p. 181) we learn that the rabbis of the Tosefta and the Talmud were troubled by this same variant in connection with the meaning of Ex 22, 4.

Another possible explanation of the Greek and Syriac reading is offered by Segal[55] who in accordance with the ancient rabbinic interpretation of בעיר as "grazing animal" suggests that the original Hebrew of 6, 2b read: ותבער כבעיר חילך. Thus, Segal assumes that the grandson and the Syriac translator understood בעיר as "beast" but translated the word more specifically as "bull".

From our discussion it should be clear that Torrey's use of 6, 2 is at best of questionable value for proving his untenable theory that Greek is superior to the Cairo Hebrew.

[55] *Op. cit.*, 35.

Torrey's next specimen is 38, 11b:

MS B: ערך / הונך ודשן ערו̊ך בכנפי הונ̊יך

καὶ λίπανον προσφοράν, ὡς μὴ ὑπάρχων.

Syrohexaplar: ܘܪܘܢ ܡܩܘܪܒܢܐ ܐܝܟ ܠܐ ܐܝܬܝܟ

Note: Syriac does not exist for this verse.

Again we quote Torrey's full argument:

> "Make your offering generous, as though you did not exist." Grk's ὡς μὴ ὑπάρχων is here the rendering of כְּאֵינְךָ; cf. Jer. 50: 20 (Gr. 27: 20) and Ps. 102: 16 (Heb. 103: 16). The original reading was obviously כְּאוֹנְךָ, "*according to your ability.*" (*Heb* gives the command the conclusion which is obviously necessary, and employs a late idiom.)[56]

Torrey's conjecture as to the reading of the grandson's *Vorlage* is plausible enough. Indeed, אונך provides the basis for Greek's mistranslation. The grandson read *yod* instead of *waw* (a common mistake in those days; see Chapter III) as the second consonant of the word. If that is the case, the medieval scribe substituted for און the more common word הון. Rather than the simple particle כְּ, however, the original probably read (if in fact בכנפי is corrupt) כְּפִי.

We should note here that in Torrey's theory the Cairo text is the product of retroversion from Syriac. But we now ask: how did this distich come into being? Clearly, not from Syriac which does not exist, and hardly from Greek (or the Syrohexaplar) which is evidently corrupt! The only reasonable conclusion that can be drawn from this set of circumstances is that the Geniza Hebrew is essentially original. Torrey's prejudice against our text, however, obfuscates his critical judgment to such an extent that he cites this verse in support of his untenable theory, whereas in point of fact, this verse well serves as an instance of the originality of the Cairo Hebrew.

Torrey's next argument reads:

> A case of (corrupt) transliteration will serve equally well to show that *Heb* does not give us the true text of Sirach. According to 48: 17, King Hezekiah in order to benefit

[56] *Art. cit.*, 593f.

> Jerusalem brought in *Gog*. That which he actually brought in, according to 2 Chron. 32: 30, was the water of Gihon, גִּיחוֹן, thus written by Sirach, and by his grandson transliterated Γιων, which in careless copying became Γιωγ, with a confusion of the two letters not uncommon in cursive Greek.[57]

The term "cursive" could be ambiguous. Although most scholars use it as a synonym of "minuscule",[58] of which the earliest specimen dates from 835 A.D.,[59] Torrey obviously does not. Perhaps he had in mind what V. Gardthausen calls "Majuskelcursive",[60] which was used from the late third century B.C. to the early fourth century A.D. But an examination of *gamma* and *nu* in Gardthausen's Table 4a, which gives typical forms of this script, failed to convince the present writer that these two letters could be easily confused. Be that as it may, even if these letters could be commonly confused in some kind of early "cursive" script, Torrey's explanation assumes that the two uncial Codices B and C, the only MSS that contain the reading ΓΩΓ, were copied from "cursive" exemplars. For Bible MSS, however, uncial writing was far more common up to 835 A.D.

It is probable that the readings τὸν γωγ (of B and C), τὸν ηωγ (of 253, 25, and S*), and τὸν ἀγωγόν (of S$^{c.a}$) are, as Box and Oesterley suggest,[61] corruptions of τὸν ὑδραγωγόν, "conduit, aqueduct" (cf. 24, 30 in Greek and 4 Kgs 18, 17 in the LXX). But even if Torrey's conjecture were correct,[62] his argument is still worthless. It is unfair too, because it does not present the complete textual situation. Had Torrey taken the trouble to consult the usual text-critical works on the LXX, he would have discovered that Codex A as well as Codex 248 and many other Cursives (together

[57] *Ibid.*, 594.

[58] Cf. F. Kenyon, *Our Bible and the Ancient Manuscripts*, revised by A. W. Adams, 5th ed. (London, 1958), 45.

[59] Cf. R. Devreesse, *Introduction à l'étude des manuscrits grecs* (Paris, 1954), 32.

[60] *Griechische Palaeographie, 2 Band: Die Schrift, Unterschriften und Chronologie im Altertum und im byzantinischen Mittelalter*, 2d ed. (Leipzig, 1913), 173 ff.

[61] *Op. cit.*, 502.

[62] J. H. A. Hart, "[Note on] Sir. xlviii 17, a, b.", *JTS*, 4 (1902–1903), 591 f., also favors the reading γιων as the original of the grandson who read in his *Vorlage* גיחון.

with Old Latin) contain the reading ὕδωρ in place of γωγ. This well attested Greek reading reflects the Cairo Hebrew's מים; Syriac's ܡܝܐ also agrees with Hebrew.

Torrey repudiates the Geniza text of 48, 17d:

MS B: ויחסום הרים מקוה

καὶ ᾠκοδόμησεν κρήνας εἰς ὕδατα.

He suggests that:

> Ben Sira's Hebrew was וַיִּבֶן לַמַּיִם בְּרֵכוֹת, "and he constructed pools for the water," which is precisely what Hezekiah did, 2 Chron. 32: 3–5, 30; the former passage understood to include the making of an eastern pool between the two walls .... The grandson's translation-Greek was quite correct. Here also, as so often elsewhere, in place of the interesting text which Ben Sira wrote we have in *Heb* a poor substitute.[63]

The Cairo text seems, at least to the present writer, much more "interesting" than the prosaic Greek of this hemistich. But if we assume for the moment that the Geniza text is a retranslation (from the Syriac, as Torrey maintains), we would be then forced to admit quite a marvel in respect to this half-line. For, first of all, we find the rare word יחסום in our Hebrew text; a retroverter would hardly have chosen this word. Secondly, Syriac does not even have this hemistich! Therefore, either we must postulate a "creatio ex nihilo" or we must turn to Greek for the basis of the "poor substitute" we find in our Cairo Hebrew! It is, however, inconceivable that our Hebrew was based upon this Greek; in fact, Torrey's attempt at retranslation from the Greek proves this fact beyond a doubt. But Greek could and indeed did have as its basis a text like that of the Geniza Hebrew, difficult as it is. For κρήνας εἰς ὕδατα is a fair enough translation of מקוה, and as regards the grandson's ᾠκοδόμησεν for יחסום, we can see a parallel in the LXX's περιοικοδομήσουσιν for חֹסֶמֶת in Ez 39, 11.

Torrey's next argument against the Cairo text is this:

> At the very beginning of the new Hebrew text, notice is served that it is *not* the original. The first Genizah fragment begins

[63] *Art. cit.*, 594.

> with the closing words of 3: 6, a verse dealing with the son who honors his father. *Heb* has only the closing words, "honors his mother." Grk, however, has ἀναπαύσει μητέρα αὐτοῦ, showing that Sirach wrote יָנִיחַ אִמּוֹ, "will bring peace to his mother," cf. Prov. 29: 17.[64]

We must again call attention to Torrey's failure to provide the complete textual picture. Although ἀναπαύσει has the backing of the best witnesses in the Greek tradition, Codices 55 and 254 have instead τιμήσει. It is true, however, that the arrangement of the fragmentary Hebrew text fails to convey the original thought of Ben Sira. The reading מכבד of 6b most likely resulted from a switch or repetition of the participle in vv. 6 and 7, of which the latter is missing in Hebrew. A similar repetition took place in Codices 55 and 254: the τιμήσει (πατέρα) of 7a was put into 6b: τιμήσει μητέρα αὐτοῦ. The original of 6b probably read מְנַחֵם (cf. Gn 5, 29), not יָנִיחַ, as Torrey suggests.

From the text itself the final objections that Torrey offers against the authenticity of the Cairo Hebrew are as follows:

> Verse 8 [of chap. 3] is spoiled by the weak citation of Deut. 28: 2 in place of Ben Sira's most fitting conclusion. Observe also that the latter makes the connection with the following verse which is lost in *Heb*. The original figure of building in verse 9 is changed to planting in *Heb*. The five-fold repetition of כבד in the Hebrew of verses 10–12 can hardly be charged to Ben Sira, and no one of these three verses as they appear in *Heb* can stand comparison with the text which *Grk* represents.[65]

Though we concede that parts of the Cairo Hebrew in vv. 10–12 are corrupt, we disagree most emphatically with Torrey's conclusion that our Hebrew text is completely secondary. In particular, as regards v. 9 in the Geniza text and in Greek, Hartman provides a perfect answer to Torrey's misgivings:

> The beautiful Hebrew verse that has come down to us in MS A is unquestionably original: *birkat ʾāb tᵉyassed šōreš* / *wᵉqillat ʾēm tintōš nāṭaʿ*, which CCD (3, 9) renders as: "For a

[64] *Ibid.*
[65] *Ibid.*, 594f.

> father's blessing gives a family firm roots, / but a mother's curse uproots the growing plant." By giving a free rendition of the verse, the Greek translator moved the family from its Palestinian farm into an Alexandrian tenement house.[66]

From an examination of the text-critical arguments in Chapter II and of the historical arguments in Chapter III, it will become clear that the Cairo Hebrew is *substantially* genuine. There exist, however, a number of retroversions in this text (some of these are discussed in Chapter IV); but these retroversions, which unfortunately most commentators disallow, do not justify Torrey's sweeping conclusion: "That which has survived to the present day is a Syriac text of the Ben Sira proverbs and a Hebrew version which is based upon it. Neither of the two has been rightly understood."[67]

H. L. Ginsberg

One of the latest opponents of the Cairo Hebrew is the eminent scholar H. L. Ginsberg, who wrote an unbelievable article[68] about our text. Only full quotation does justice to the astounding remarks that he makes:

> It is no favorable reflection upon our guild that the following facts (they are nothing less) still have to beg for recognition:
>
> 1. The Greek version of Ben Sira (G) is an about 90% literal rendering of a smooth, pleasing Hebrew.
>
> 2. The Peshitta (S) of this Book is clearly a very free rendering of a Hebrew text which diverged but little from that which served G as archetype.

[66] *Art. cit.*, 449.

[67] *Art. cit.*, 602. C. H. Gordon, "Review of *Publications of the Alexander Kohut Memorial Foundation*, Vol. VIII", *JBL*, 56 (1937), 415, is also a proponent of the complete retroversion hypothesis; he writes: "The statement that Ben Sira is now known in the original Hebrew is hardly warranted though widely accepted. The Geniza text is probably a back-translation from an Aramaic-Syriac version." Other opponents of the Cairo Hebrew are A. Büchler, "Ben Sira's Conception of Sin and Atonement", *JQR*, n. s., 13 (1922–1923), 303–335; 461–502; 14 (1923–1924), 53–83; and R. Storr, "Einige Bedenken gegen die Echtheit des hebräischen Jesus Sirach", *TQ*, 106 (1925), 203–231.

[68] "The Original Hebrew of Ben Sira 12 10–14", *JBL*, 74 (1955), 93ff.

3. The Genizah Hebrew text (H) is composed in an idiom which (a) is for the most part hideous, (b) is rarely presupposed by G, and (c) for the most part alternates between execrably literal reproduction of S and substitution of biblical (or other) flourishes which only vaguely suggest the general thought of S. In addition to S, the Syrohexaplar Version (S^h) was occasionally consulted by the producer or producers of H.

All of which being so, who would recover some semblance of the real Hebrew original must reconstruct it, as best he can, primarily from G. But we must gratefully accept any aid which S^h may offer us for the recovery of G, and any help which may be forthcoming from S in deciding between two or more possible Hebrew originals of a Greek rendering.

It is reported that fragments of a Hebrew Ben Sira have been discovered in the Wilderness of Judah. Since, however, the site is not Khirbet Qumran, the fragments may not be so old as the Khirbet Qumran scrolls; in that case they may be of the same character as H. But if they are at least pre-Arab, it is probable that

1. They will be found to be as unlike H as imaginable.

2. They will be found to be very similar to the approximation to the original of 12 10–14 which is reconstructed below.[69]

Ginsberg then proceeds to reconstruct "the real Hebrew original" "as best he can".

Such a procedure for as eminent a scholar as Ginsberg is truly amazing. For he offers not a single shred of evidence in support of these irresponsible claims. Perhaps he expects his readers to compare for themselves his retranslation of 12, 10–14 with the Geniza Hebrew so that they may obtain a glimpse, however brief, of what the original of Ben Sira must have looked like! Needless to say,

[69] *Ibid.*, 93. With respect to Ginsberg's statement, "Since ... the site is not Khirbet Qumran, the fragments may not be so old as the Khirbet Qumran scrolls", we should note that even though Cave II is some distance from the main settlement at Qumrân, scholars generally refer to this cave as a Qumrân cave. In any case, the materials from Cave II antedate 68 A.D. That the Cairo Hebrew is a complete retroversion was held by Ginsberg for years; cf. his short note in *ZAW*, N.F., 14 (1937), 309.

retroversion is a precarious operation at best; at worst, it is presumptuous. To take one example, we shall examine Ginsberg's reconstruction of the "original" of 12, 10b. Ginsberg: כי כנחש תחלד רעתו. His translation of his retranslation: "For his malice burrows like a snake." (For the Cairo Hebrew and the versions of this hemistich, see the discussion offered in our treatment of Bickell's theory, above, p. 31.) Ginsberg explains the history of this half-line in this way:

> Because חלד can mean (in post-biblical Hebrew) both "to burrow" and "to rust," an unwary scribe or translator might easily think of the latter meaning first and consequently read the ת at the end of the first word instead of the beginning of the second, thus making the former mean "copper" instead of "serpent." Hence the renderings of G and S. For this to happen, נחש had to be followed, in the original Hebrew, immediately by תחלד, and as a matter of fact the equivalent of נחשת is still followed immediately by the equivalent of חלד in G and S. But in retroverting S into Hebrew, the maker(s) of H separated the two words in question, and so strayed still further from the original Hebrew ...[70]

Ginsberg's creation is gratuitous, and his explanation as to what happened to Greek and Syriac is sheer fancy. Against the clear evidence of both Greek and Syriac, Ginsberg completely changes the metaphor contained in this half-line. The image found in the Cairo Hebrew, and reflected in Greek and Syriac, is certainly what Ben Sira wished to convey (cf. p. 31 above). Furthermore, Cairo Hebrew's רועו – the basis both of the grandson's ἡ πονηρία αὐτοῦ and of Syriac's mistranslation ܥܒܕ̈ܘܗܝ – is perfectly good Hebrew. Ginsberg's רעתו is completely uncalled for, and could not possibly be the starting point of Syriac's ܥܒܕ̈ܘܗܝ.

Chapters II and III will provide a fuller answer to Ginsberg's blanket condemnation of the Cairo text; we call attention especially to the section in Chapter III that deals with the Qumrân Cave II fragments of Sirach, which antedate 68 A.D. and consequently are pre-Arab!

[70] "The Original Hebrew of Ben Sira ....", 94.

H. Duesberg, P. Auvray

H. Duesberg and P. Auvray, authors of the fascicle on Sirach[71] for the famed *Bible de Jérusalem*, also take rather strong exception to the Geniza MSS. They write: "Non seulement ce sont en général des manuscrits peu soignés, contenant nombre de négligences et d'erreurs, mais le texte même qu'ils présentent est subjet à caution."[72] True, as every Sirach scholar would acknowledge, caution is the order of the day when one deals with the Cairo Hebrew. For, as our French authors explain: "De nombreux passages sont manifestement corrompus."[73]

The conclusion they draw from these observations is, however, quite mystifying: "Des doublets, voire des triplets de maints versets, et de fréquentes notes marginales dénotent l'incertitude de la transcription."[74] As we hope to prove in Chapter IV, the doublets in general result not from "l'incertitude de la transcription", but from retroversion, concerning which our French scholars are aware, but which, strangely enough, they do not connect with the doublets!

They then make this very questionable statement: "Enfin la qualité même de la langue et certaines comparaisons avec les versions grecque et syriaque ont fait parler, pour certains fragments du moins, d'une retraduction."[75] Hartman justly remarks that the "du moins" in their sentence is "positively misleading".[76] We think that the entire sentence is completely unfounded. No one has proved (nor is likely to prove) that any one of the Geniza fragments, *as a whole*, is the product of retroversion from Syriac or Greek (or Persian).

The next statement of the French scholars is grossly unfair: "Bref, si l'on peut dire avec certitude que l'hébreu est la langue originale de l'Ecclésiastique, on ne peut affirmer que le texte hébreu récemment retrouvé représente l'état primitif du livre."[77] Surely,

[71] *Le livre de l'Ecclésiastique (La Sainte Bible de Jérusalem)*, 2d ed. (Paris, 1958).

[72] *Ibid.*, 19.

[73] *Ibid.*

[74] *Ibid.*, 19f.

[75] *Ibid.*, 20.

[76] *Art. cit.*, 444.

[77] *Op. cit.*, 20.

not even the staunchest defender of the authenticity of the text of the Cairo MSS would be foolish enough to claim that the text in all its parts represents the primitive state of the Book. But, if we employ the same logic and criterion as Duesberg and Auvray, we should reject the Hebrew text of Ez which likewise hardly represents "l'état primitif du livre".

Finally, our French authors write: "C'est tout au plus une recension assez tardive et passablement corrompue à laquelle il est permis de préférer le texte grec."[78] With respect to the debatable procedure of basing a translation upon the Greek version, we refer our readers to Hartman's instructive article.[79] In Chapter III we will attempt to prove that what is genuine in the Geniza fragments is not "une recension assez tardive", but rather a text which antedates 68 A.D. Consequently, this text gives us what is essentially Ben Sira's original or something very close to it.

[78] *Ibid.*

[79] *Art. cit.*, 447–451, especially. For the well-known *Bonner Bible*, A. Eberharter, *Das Buch Jesus Sirach oder Ecclesiasticus* (= *Die Heilige Schrift des Alten Testamentes übersetzt und erklärt in Verbindung mit Fachgelehrten*, 6, 5) (Bonn, 1925) also translates Sirach from Greek, but for a practical reason, not because he thought the Hebrew was hopeless or secondary. He explains his position in the *Vorwort:* "Den griechischen, und nicht den hebräische Text als Vorlage zu verwenden, empfahl sich vor allem deshalb, weil der hebräische Text des Buches nur zu dreifünftel Teilen erhalten ist, und dieser Umstand den Übergang von einer Textvorlage zur andern zur notwendigen Folge gehabt hätte, wodurch der einheitliche Charakter der Übersetzung beeinträchtigt worden wäre. Die textliche Beschaffenheit des Griechen gab übrigens reichlich Anlaß, den hebräischen Text, wo er vorhanden ist, heranzuziehen. Textverbesserungen nach dem Hebräischen sind ziemlich zahlreich, seltener solche nach anderen Texten." Cf. also pp. 10f.

II. AUTHENTICITY OF THE CAIRO HEBREW: TEXT-CRITICAL ARGUMENTS

In the preceding chapter we saw that the theories advanced against the substantial authenticity of the Geniza text were based upon inadequate evidence. Indeed, by their outright rejection of our text in its entirety the opponents have raised more difficulties than they have solved. Since we feel that we have provided a satisfactory answer to the objections leveled at the Cairo Hebrew, we shall present in this chapter a series of text-critical arguments that seem to make the genuineness of the Hebrew text more than a matter of opinion. Chapter III will then provide important historical witnesses for the defense of our position.

We shall marshal our arguments under three headings: (1) a study of two citations in the Geniza text which agree with the *Vorlage* of the LXX rather than with the Massoretic text; (2) the order of chapters found in Sir; (3) a critical investigation of select verses from the Cairo MSS.

A. CITATIONS AGREEING WITH *VORLAGE* OF LXX

In at least two instances the Geniza text contains Old Testament references which agree with what must have been the *Vorlage* of the LXX rather than with the *textus receptus*, as represented by the Massoretic text.

Sir 46, 19c

The first text is Sir 46, 19c:

כופר ונעלם ממ[י לקח]תי   וכל אדם לא ענה בֿו

"'From wh[om have] I [taken] a bribe or a pair of sandals?' But no one answered him." The second word should read וְנַעֲלַיִם, as is clear from Greek: χρήματα καὶ ἕως ὑποδημάτων ἀπὸ πάσης σαρκὸς οὐκ εἴληφα· καὶ οὐκ ἐνεκάλεσεν αὐτῷ ἄνθρωπος. Syriac paraphrases the second Hebrew word: ܘܟܣܦܐ ܘܦܘܪܥܢܐ ܡܢ ܐܢܫ ܠܐ ܢܣܒ. ܘܟܠ ܒܣܪ ܠܐ ܐܣܗܕ ܥܠܘܗܝ. In support of the Geniza reading, as emended, we have Am 2, 6: עַל־מִכְרָם בַּכֶּסֶף צַדִּיק וְאֶבְיוֹן בַּעֲבוּר נַעֲלָיִם; and Am 8, 6: לִקְנוֹת בַּכֶּסֶף דַּלִּים וְאֶבְיוֹן בַּעֲבוּר נַעֲלָיִם.[1]

The Cairo Hebrew is a clear reference to 1 Sm 12, 3, but in the recension that must have underlay the LXX which reads: ἢ ἐκ χειρὸς τίνος εἴληφα ἐξίλασμα καὶ ὑπόδημα; ἀποκρίθητε κατ' ἐμοῦ καὶ ἀποδώσω ὑμῖν. The Massoretic text for this passage is different: וּמִיַּד־מִי לָקַחְתִּי כֹפֶר וְאַעְלִים עֵינַי בּוֹ וְאָשִׁיב לָכֶם. For the words in question the Peshiṭta reflects the Massoretic text: ܐܘ ܡܢ ܐܝܕܐ ܕܡܢ ܢܣܒܬ ܟܘܦܪܐ. ܘܐܪܓܙܬ ܥܝܢܝ ܒܗ. ܐܡܪܘ ܠܝ. ܘܐܬܠ ܐܦܪܘܥܟܘܢ.

Sir 51, 2b

The second instance is Sir 51, 2b:

חשכת בשרי משחת

"You have spared my flesh from the pit/destruction." Both Greek and Syriac agree substantially with Hebrew: καὶ ἐλυτρώσω τὸ σῶμά μου ἐξ ἀπωλίας· ܘܦܨܝܬ ܦܓܪܝ ܡܢ ܚܒܠܐ. The Hebrew text seems to be a clear allusion to Is 38, 17,[2] in the form that must have been the basis for the LXX, which reads: εἵλου γάρ μου τὴν ψυχὴν ἵνα μὴ ἀπόληται. The verb in the Massoretic text is different: וְאַתָּה חָשַׁקְתָּ נַפְשִׁי מִשַּׁחַת בְּלִי. The Peshiṭta agrees rather with the Massoretic text: ܘܐܢܬ ܦܨܝܬ ܢܦܫܝ ܕܠܐ ܬܐܒܕ ܒܚܒܠܐ.

Over 50 years ago, I. Lévi noted that the fact that the Geniza Sir contained at least these two Old Testament citations obviously related to the *Vorlage* of the LXX rather than to the Massoretic text, is one of the conclusive proofs that our Hebrew text is genuine.[3] Lévi's argument receives emphatic confirmation from what the

[1] Cf. R. Smend, *Die Weisheit des Jesus Sirach erklärt* (Berlin, 1906), 447.

[2] The Sir text could also, but less directly, be an allusion to Jb 33, 18: יַחְשֹׂךְ נַפְשׁוֹ מִנִּי־שָׁחַת.

[3] "Sirach, The Wisdom of Jesus, the Son of", *The Jewish Encyclopedia*, 11 (New York-London, 1905), 394.

Qumrân materials have taught us about the history of the Hebrew Bible. For we know that there were at Qumrân a number of quite variable texts in current use before 68 A.D. In Cave IV, discovered in 1952, there were found many Hebrew fragments of the Pentateuch as well as of other Books. These contain texts: (1) that are closely related to the *Vorlage* of the LXX; (2) that reflect the Samaritan recension of the Pentateuch; (3) that are of mixed types; and (4) that are identical with the *textus receptus*.[4] But some time before the second Jewish Revolt, 132–135 A.D., the consonantal text was fixed in its wording, in its orthography, and in the rules for its transmission.[5] For in the MSS recovered from Wadi Murabbaat and from an unidentified site, dating from the second Jewish Revolt, we find a text that is identical with that of the Massoretes. It appears certain, therefore, from the use of at least two allusions to the *Vorlage* of the LXX that the Cairo Hebrew represents a text that for the most part antedates 68 A.D. (or 132 A.D., at the very latest). If this is so, the Geniza text must be essentially genuine.

Moreover, the hypothesis of medieval retroversion of the complete Book from Greek and/or Syriac becomes quite untenable, for it is inconceivable that a medieval Jew, who knew his Massoretic text well, would revert to a Hebrew text of an Old Testament citation or allusion that is not in keeping with the *textus receptus*, but one related to the *Vorlage* of the LXX.

B. THE ORDER OF CHAPTERS IN SIRACH

As is well known, chapters 30 to 36 of Sir have undergone a rearrangement in all the Greek MSS that are still extant,[6] and in all

[4] For details, see J. T. Milik, *Ten Years of Discovery in the Wilderness of Judaea*, trans. by J. Strugnell (London, 1959), 23–28, and the literature there cited. In addition, see P. W. Skehan, "Exodus in the Samaritan Recension from Qumran", *JBL*, 74 (1955), 182–187; *idem*, "The Period of the Biblical Texts from Khirbet Qumrân", *CBQ*, 19 (1957), 435–440; *idem*, "Qumran and the Present State of Old Testament Text Studies: The Masoretic Text", *JBL*, 78 (1959), 21–25; M. Greenberg, "The Stabilization of the Text of the Hebrew Bible, Reviewed in the Light of the Biblical Materials from the Judean Desert", *JAOS*, 76 (1956), 157–167.

[5] Milik, *op. cit.*, 29.

[6] Some scholars have erroneously stated that Codex 248 preserves the true order of chapters. See, for example, A. Edersheim, *Ecclesiasticus*, in *Apocrypha*,

the daughter translations, except the Old Latin, Armenian, and Slavonic. Among the daughter versions, we should note that the Arabic translation which was made from Greek – Sinai Arabic MS 155 – also contains the jumbled order of chapters of the Greek tradition.[7] With respect to this peculiarity, H. B. Swete writes:

> A remarkable divergence in the arrangement of the Septuagint and Old Latin versions of Ecclesiasticus xxx.–xxxvi. calls for notice here. In these chapters the Greek order fails to yield a natural sequence, whereas the Latin arrangement, which is also that of the Syriac and Armenian versions, makes excellent sense. Two sections, c.xxx. 25–xxxiii. 13ª (ὡς καλαμώμενος ... φυλὰς Ἰακώβ) and c. xxxiii. 13ᵇ–xxxvi. 16ª (λαμπρὰ καρδία ... ἔσχατος ἠγρύπνησα), have exchanged places in the Latin, and the change is justified by the result. On examination it appears that these sections are nearly equal, containing in B 154 and 159 στίχοι respectively, whilst א exhibits 160 in each. There can be little doubt that in the *exemplar* from which, so far as is certainly known, all our Greek MSS. of this book are ultimately derived the pairs of leaves on which these sections were severally written had been transposed, whereas the Latin translator, working from a MS. in which the transposition had not taken place, has preserved the true order.[8]

Because Syriac was made from the original Hebrew, it preserves the true order of the chapters in question. The Arabic version, that is, the one which was made from the Syriac (found in Walton's Polyglot), also contains, as one would expect, the correct order.

Old Latin embodies the true order of chapters, for as Swete indicates, it was made from a pre-archetype Greek text. The two

---

2, ed. by H. Wace (London, 1888), 25; C. H. Toy, "Ecclesiasticus", in *Encyclopaedia Biblica* (London, 1904), 1173; J. Hadot, "L'Ecclésiastique ou le Siracide", in *La Bible, L'Ancien Testament (= Bibliothèque de la Pléiade, 2)* (Paris, 1959), 1806; and M. H. Segal, *Sēper ben-Sîrā' ha-šālēm*, 2d ed. (Jerusalem, 1958), Introduction, p. 56.

[7] For this information we are grateful to Dr. Richard M. Frank, of the Catholic University of America, who is preparing an edition of this Arabic text.

[8] *The Old Testament in Greek*, 2, 3d ed. (Cambridge, 1907), vi–vii. Swete mentions in a note that the solution is due to O. F. Fritzsche, *Kurzgefaßtes exegetisches Handbuch zu den Apokryphen*, 5 (Leipzig, 1859), 169f.

Armenian translations likewise preserve the original order. The first Armenian version seems to follow Greek and sometimes the Syriac; the second one was made clearly from Greek, but preserves some elements of the first translation.[9] This being the case, the original order of chapters in the Armenian versions is probably to be accounted for on the basis of the influence of the Syriac, which, as already noted, has the proper arrangement of matter. The correct placement of chapters in the Slavonic translation is most likely due to the influence of Old Latin; in fact, the Slavonic occasionally agrees with Old Latin against all the extant Greek witnesses.[10]

From this evidence we can conclude that by the end of the third century or some time during the fourth century A.D., at the very latest, the displacement of the chapters in the Greek MS tradition was complete. No Greek MS with the primitive arrangement seems to have survived.

If the Geniza text of Sir were retranslated from Greek, as Goodspeed and Hadas would have it, one should expect the same displacement of chapters which is found in most of the daughter translations. But that is not the case. The Cairo Hebrew MSS preserve the original order of material. It appears hardly conceivable, therefore, that the Hebrew text depends in any substantial way upon the Greek version, at least in the form that is had in all the extant MSS. It is, of course, *possible* that for the proper arrangement of chapters the Geniza text depends upon the Old Latin, Armenian, or Slavonic versions. But, understandably enough, no one has ever advanced that theory, at least as far as we could discover.

The Syriac translation, based essentially upon the original Hebrew, however, may have been the starting-point for the true order of chapters in the Geniza text. In Chapter IV, we argue for partial retroversion of the Cairo Hebrew from Syriac, but we insist nevertheless that our Hebrew text is *substantially* genuine. In order to determine whether or not there is any dependence of the Geniza text upon Syriac for the correct arrangement of material, we shall

[9] L. Leloir, "Orientales de la Bible (Versions): II. Versions arméniennes", *VDBS*, 6 (Paris, 1960), 813.

[10] Smend, *op. cit.*, CXXXV.

examine the three places where the dislocation has taken place in the Greek tradition.

Sir 30, 24–25

Syriac		MS B
ܛܢܢܐ ܘܪܘܓܙܐ ܡܒܠܝܢ (ܡܫܠܡܝܢ) ܝܘܡܬܐ.	24a	קנאה ואף [י]קצרו ימים
ܘܪܢܝܐ ܒܠܐ ܙܒܢܗܘܢ ܡܥܒܕܐ ܚܘܪܐ ܕܣܝܒܬܐ.	24b	ובלא עת תזקין דאגה
ܠܒܐ ܛܒܐ ܣܓܝܐܝܢ ܡܐܟܘܠܬܗ.	25a	שנות לב טוב תחת מטעמים
ܘܟܠ ܕܐܟܠ ܣܠܩ ܥܠ ܦܓܪܗ.	25b	ומאכלו יעלה עליו

30, 24a ζῆλος καὶ θυμὸς ἐλαττοῦσιν ἡμέρας,
24b καὶ πρὸ καιροῦ γῆρας ἄγει μέριμνα.
33, 13b λαμπρὰ καρδία καὶ ἀγαθὴ ἐπὶ ἐδέσμασιν
13c τῶν βρωμάτων αὐτῆς ἐπιμελήσεται.

Translations:

MS B: (24) "Envy and anger shorten one's days, and anxiety makes one grow old before time. (25) (omit: The sleep[11]) (When a person with) good heart has delicacies before him, his food does him good (literally: ... goes up upon him; in colloquial English, the Hebrew idiom can be rendered accurately by: 'his food sticks to his ribs')."

Syriac: (24) "Envy and anger make one's days waste away (Codex Ambrosianus: ... bring to an end one's days), and anxiety produces white hairs before their time. (25) (When a person has) a good heart, many are the foods that he can eat, and everything he eats does his body good (literally: goes up upon his body)."

Greek: (30, 24) "Envy and anger shorten one's days, and anxiety brings in old age before time. (33, 13b–c) (A person with) a bright (i.e. cheerful) and good heart gives heed to the foods he eats (literally: to the foods of its [the heart's] eating)."

As is clear from a comparison of these texts, the Cairo Hebrew could not conceivably be derived from Syriac (or from Greek, for

[11] As Lévi suggests, *L'Ecclésiastique*, part 2 (Paris, 1901), p. 135, שנות may be a subtitle for a new section, "On Sleep", for the following verses deal with sleep. Cf. 31, 20; Prv 6, 10; 24, 33; 15, 15. D. W. Thomas in "The LXX's Rendering of שנות לב טוב in Ecclus. XXXIII 13", *VT*, 10 (1960), 456, suggests that λαμπρά "bright, radiant" represents שנות (from שנה = سنى in the sense of "became high, exalted in rank"; the "Arabic root means also 'shone, gleamed'").

that matter). The verb קצר in 30, 24a would never have been used to render ܒܠܐ (Lagarde, Walton, Mosul) or ܒܛܠܘ (Codex Ambrosianus), for the roots בלה and בטל both exist in Hebrew and presumably would have been used by one who was retranslating from Syriac. In 30, 24b, תזקין דאגה could scarcely have as basis ܡܕܡܐ ܚܘ̈ܪܐ ܕܦܬܐ. In 30, 25, there are so many differences between the texts that one would be unreasonable in assuming a dependence of Hebrew upon Syriac. On the contrary, however, it is apparent that Hebrew forms the common basis of both Greek and Syriac.

Sir 33, 16–17

Syriac		MS E
ܘܐܦ (ܐܦ) ܐܢܐ ܐܚܪܝܬ ܐܬܝܬ.	16a	וגם אני אחרון[12] שקדתי
ܐܝܟ ܡܥܒܪܢܐ ܕܟܪܡܐ ܒܬܪ ܡܩ̈ܛܦܐ	16b	וכמו עולל אח[ר הבוצרים]
ܘܒܒܘܪ̈ܟܬܗ ܕܐܠܗܐ ܐܢܐ ܩܕܡܬ.	17a	ב[ברכ]ת אל גם אני קדמתי
ܘܐܝܟ ܡܩܛܦܐ ܡܠܝܬ ܡܥܨܪܬܝ.	17b	וכבוצר מלאתי [יקבי]

36, 16a κἀγὼ ἔσχατος ἠγρύπνησα,
30, 25a ὡς καλαμώμενος ὀπίσω τρυγητῶν·
25b ἐν εὐλογίᾳ κυρίου ἔφθασα,
25c καὶ ὡς τρυγῶν ἐπλήρωσα (248: ἔπλησα) ληνόν.

Translations:

MS E: (16) "And also I was the last to keep watch, (and) like a gleaner af[ter the grapegatherers]. (17) By the b[lessing] of God I also was out front, and like the grapegatherer I filled [my winepress]."

Syriac: (16) "(Walton, Mosul: And) at last I too arrived, like a gleaner of the vineyard after the grapegatherers. (17) And by the

[12] J. Marcus, *The Newly Discovered Original Hebrew of Ben Sira (Ecclesiasticus xxxii, 16–xxxiv, 1): The Fifth Manuscript and a Prosodic Version of Ben Sira (Ecclesiasticus xxii, 22–xxiii, 9)* (Philadelphia, 1931) 18 (this pamphlet is a corrected reprint of the article which appeared originally in the *JQR*, n. s., 21 [1930–1931], 223–240); and Lévi, "Un nouveau fragment de Ben Sira", *REJ*, 92 (1932), 140f., read here אחריו. But with Segal, *op. cit.*, 207, 212, we read אחרון, which of course could have been misread as אחריו (see our discussion of confusion between *waw* and *yod* in Chapter III).

benevolence of God I stood up, and like the grapegatherer I filled my winepress."

Greek: (36, 16a) "And I was the last to keep watch, (30, 25) like a gleaner after the grapegatherers. By the blessing of the Lord I was out front, and like a grapegatherer I filled the winepress."

Here again the Cairo Hebrew is certainly original, except for the first *waw* of 16b which is most likely a dittography (see the first word of 17b), and could hardly be dependent in any way upon Syriac. In 16a, for example, we note that שקדתי, the authenticity of which is attested to by the grandson's ἠγρύπνησα – a word used in the LXX for שׁקד in Ezr 8, 29; Jb 21, 32; Ps 101 (102), 8; Ps 126 (127), 1; Prv 8, 24; and Dn 9, 14 – could never be the result of retroversion of ܐܬܝܬ. And in 16b, the addition of ܕܒܪ̈ܡܐ makes it extremely improbable that Hebrew is influenced by Syriac. In 17a the verb ܩܡܬ, which makes little sense, could not serve as basis of קדמתי. In fact, the Syriac translator misread קדמתי as קמתי; hence, the poor reading ܩܡܬ. Finally, we call attention again to the fact that a text like that recovered from the Cairo Geniza, though it is fragmentary, certainly was the common denominator of both Greek and Syriac.

Sir 36, 13a–b

Syriac		MS B
ܟܢܘܫ ܟܘܠܗܘܢ ܫܒ̈ܛܘܗܝ ܕܝܥܩܘܒ.	13a	אסוף כל שבטי יעקב
ܘܢܐܪܬܘܢ ܐܚܣܢܐ ܕܐܡܪܬ ܡܢ ܩܘܕܡܬܐ ܡܝܘ̈ܡܬܐ.	13b	ויתנחלו כימי קדם

33, 13a σύναγε πάσας φυλὰς Ἰακώβ,
36, 16b καὶ κατεκληρονόμησα (read: κατακληρονομήσεις[13]) αὐτοὺς καθὼς ἀπ' ἀρχῆς.

Translations:

MS B: "Gather all the tribes of Jacob, so that they may possess their inheritance as in the days of old."

Syriac: "Gather all the tribes of Jacob, so that they may take their possession as you have said from the ancient days."

[13] Old Latin has "haereditabis". The reason why we find κατεκληρονόμησα is that 36, 16b is out of place. In order to suit the context of its wrong position, κατακληρονομήσεις was changed to κατεκληρονόμησα.

Greek: (33, 13a) "Gather all the tribes of Jacob, (36, 16b) and (you shall) give them their inheritance (or: and [you shall] make them your possession) as from the beginning."

It is only in 36, 13b that we can comment about the relationship between Syriac and Hebrew, for 13a is identical in Hebrew, Syriac, and Greek, and can prove nothing with respect to the independence of Hebrew or its dependence upon Syriac. But the Geniza text of 13b could scarcely be based upon Syriac. First of all, it does not seem the least bit likely that a medieval Jewish translator would employ the verb נחל to render ܚܣܢ when the root ירש would be a perfectly good Hebrew equivalent of the Syriac verb. Secondly, there is nothing in the Cairo Hebrew to match ܐܡܪܐ. Thirdly, an unreasonable measure of good will is required to see a dependence of כימי קדם upon ܡܢ ܩܘܕܡܬܐ ܡܩܕܡܝܬܐ. The Hebrew text, however, clearly forms the basis of both Syriac and Greek; in fact, only a text like the Geniza Hebrew could be the point of departure for these versions, whereas neither one of them could explain the divergencies that exist between Hebrew, Greek, and Syriac. This phenomenon will be stressed again and again in this chapter, because it is one of the most cogent arguments for the authenticity of our Hebrew text.

From the discussion of the above three passages, we can legitimately conclude that the Cairo Hebrew depends in no way whatever upon Syriac with respect to the proper arrangement of chapters. That being the case, it appears implausible that Hebrew is derived *essentially* from Syriac.

C. CRITICAL EXAMINATION OF SELECT VERSES FROM THE CAIRO MSS

It is not our intention, nor is it indeed necessary, to analyze in detail all the passages which prove that the Cairo Hebrew must be original. Nor will we repeat or catalogue the opinions found in the various commentaries with respect to the genuineness of our text.[14]

[14] In addition to the commentaries listed in our bibliography, cf. A. Vaccari's recent article, "Ecclesiastico, 37, 10. 11: critica ed esegesi", *EstEc*, 34

Rather, as a result of our independent study of the Cairo MSS, we have chosen for analysis typical examples from each of the five MSS. Together with the other evidence offered in this and the following chapters, these examples are sufficient to establish that the Geniza text enjoys the presumption of authenticity. Only when serious and weighty reasons can be adduced against this text (as, for example, in those cases of retroversion which are demonstrated in Chapter IV) can we legitimately consider it secondary.

Sir 7, 20

MS C		MS A
אל תרע עבד עובד אמת	20a	אל תדע באמת עובד אמת
וכן שכיר נותן נפשו	20b	וכן שוכר נותן נפשו

20a μὴ κακώσῃς οἰκέτην ἐργαζόμενον ἐν ἀληθείᾳ,
20b μηδὲ μίσθιον διδόντα (248: τὴν) ψυχὴν αὐτοῦ.

20a ܠܐ ܬܪܦܐ ܠܥܒܕܐ ܕܦܠܚ ܒܩܘܫܬܐ.
20b ܐܦܠܐ (Walton, Mosul: ܘܐܦܠܐ) ܠܐ ܠܐܓܝܪܐ ܕܡܠܗܐ ܢܦܫܗ.

Translations:

MS A: "Do not recognize in truth one who works faithfully, and in like manner one who hires one who gives of himself."

MS C: "Do not mistreat a slave who works faithfully, or a hired laborer who devotes himself completely to his work (literally: who gives of himself)."

Greek: "Do not mistreat a household slave who works faithfully, or a hired laborer who devotes his life completely to his work (literally: who gives his life)."

Syriac: "Neither strike repeatedly/mistreat a slave who works faithfully, nor a hired laborer who wearies himself."

Commentary:

MS A is evidently corrupt: תדע is an easily understandable mistake (paleographically speaking) for תרע; באמת is a dittography of

(1960), 705–713, especially pp. 712f. In passing, we should note that the venerable Vaccari says that, as far as he knows, there are only five modern translations of Sir from the original Hebrew: those of Smend, Peters, Box and Oesterley, and Hamp, and his own. He could have mentioned that the CCD translation was also based upon the Cairo MSS.

the last word in the hemistich. In 20b, שוכר is most likely to be explained as an instance of a word in which *waw* and *yod* were confused due to the great similarity between these letters in the exemplars employed by the medieval copyists;[15] that is to say, the scribe saw שכיר but misread the *yod* as a *waw*, thus necessitating the transposition of the *waw* from the third to the second position in the word.

This verse is a parade example that graphically illustrates two important facts: (1) a text like the one recovered from the Geniza (MS C in the case at hand) must have been the common denominator of both Greek and Syriac; (2) neither of these two versions can account for the idiomatic Hebrew found in the Cairo MSS.

Since the ideas contained in κακώσῃς ("do evil") and ܬܬܟܬܫ ("strike/buffet repeatedly; treat roughly") can be obtained from תרע, it is perfectly logical and normal to assume that the Hebrew verb was present in the *Vorlage* of both ancient translations. The last word of 20a, אמת, can be used as an adverb in standard Biblical Hebrew (cf. Jer 10, 10); the grandson and the Syriac translator, however, add the preposition "in", thus giving us an adverbial phrase. If Hebrew were retranslated from either Greek or Syriac, one would expect באמת[16] in place of simply אמת.

As regards the second half-line there is no reason at all to suspect retroversion from either Syriac or Greek, or from any other version. Hebrew (MS C) makes perfectly good sense and must have been the original that the grandson and the Syriac translator rendered. In particular, it is virtually impossible that נותן was retroverted from ܡܟܡܟܠ. On the contrary, however, it takes little good will to see that Syriac's free translation could proceed from נותן.

Sir 7, 25

MS C		MS A
הוצי]א ב[ת ויצא עסק	25a	הוצא בת ויצא עסק
ואל ג]בר[נבון זבדה	25b	ואל נבון גבר חברה

[15] Cf. Chapter III, where this feature of the Cairo MSS is discussed at length.

[16] Indeed, Smend, *op. cit.*, 69, thinks both MSS A and C originally read this word.

25a ἔκδου θυγατέρα, καὶ ἔσῃ τετελεκὼς ἔργον μέγα,
25b καὶ ἀνδρὶ συνετῷ δώρησαι αὐτήν.
ܐܦܩ ܒܪܬܐ ܘܢܦܘܩ ܒܣܘܣܬܐ. 25a
ܘܠܓܒܪܐ ܕܝܢ ܚܟܝܡ (ܠܚܟܝܡܐ) ܗܒܝܗ. 25b

Translations:

MS A: "Give away a daughter in marriage and an important task is done with (literally: make a daughter depart and a task/worry departs), but have her marry one who is understanding, among men."

MS C: "Gi[ve] away a [daugh]ter in marriage and an important task is done with, but present her to a m[an] with understanding."

Greek: "Give away a daughter in marriage and you will have completed an important task, and present her to a man with understanding."

Syriac: "Give away a daughter in marriage and a calumny/false witness (?) departs, but present her to a man who is wise (Walton: to a wise man)."

Commentary:

Here again in the Geniza text we find a vigorous and concise bit of Hebrew poetry that could not conceivably be descended from either Greek or Syriac.

The copyist of MS A has accidentally switched the position of the second and third words of 25b; the reading of MS C is almost certainly to be preferred.

In regard to the last word of 25b, it appears that MS C's זבד, a rare word (occurring once as a noun and once as a verb in Biblical Hebrew: Gn 30, 20), is original, for this verb provides a common source for Greek and Syriac. We should note that in Sir 36, 24 (MSS C and B margin) and 40, 29 (MS B margin), זבד occurs also as a noun. MS A's חבר, which is more common in the Hebrew Bible, is probably to be accounted for as a scribal substitution for, or as a simple copyist's error of, זבד. Be that as it may, it seems difficult to imagine how זבד, or even חבר for that matter, could with any degree of probability be the result of retroversion from Greek or Syriac.

The fact that עסק in 25a is not found at all in Biblical Hebrew is no argument against the genuineness of the word.[17] This noun occurs several other times in Sir: 3, 22; 38, 24; 40, 1; in 11, 10, it is spelled עשק. It means "work, business; misery; worry". In any event, it is most improbable that עסק was retranslated from ἔργον μέγα or ܛܘܠܡܐ. However, עסק/עשק can be the common denominator both of the grandson's correct interpretation and of the Syriac translator's misunderstanding. For ἔργον μέγα is a fair enough rendering of עסק, and ܛܘܠܡܐ most likely resulted from a misreading of the עשק orthography as עֹשֶׁק,[18] "oppression, extortion, wrong", a good biblical word. If that is so, then עסק/עשק must be genuine.

We should note that ויצא shows no dependence upon ἔσῃ τετελεκώς. But the reverse could indeed be true; that is to say, the grandson freely translated his grandfather's clever use of the hifil[19] and qal of the same verb. Syriac proves that the Cairo Hebrew is original in this respect.

In the second hemistich, retroversion is almost certainly to be ruled out because it seems very unlikely that a medieval writer would choose the rare word זבד to render δώρησαι or ܗܒ; and if חבר is original, the case for retroversion is even worse, for חבר has no associations whatever of "giving". Furthermore, it is quite improbable that ܠܓܒܪܐ ܚܟܝܡܐ (Walton) or ܠܓܒܪܐ ܕܚܟܝܡ (Codex Ambrosianus, Lagarde, Mosul) provided the basis for גבר

[17] Cf. S. Liebermann, "Ben Sira à la lumière du Yerouchalmi", *REJ*, 97 (1934–1935), 53.

[18] Segal, *op. cit.*, 49, has a similar explanation. Smend, *op. cit.*, 70, also seems to allow this possibility.

[19] In an attempt to argue against the authenticity of the Cairo Hebrew of this v., D. S. Margoliouth employs some extraordinary "logic". In his article, "Note on Ecclus. vii. 25", *ExpT*, 23 (1911–1912), 234, he asserts: "The verb הוציא in Rabbinic means 'to turn a wife out,' i.e. divorce her; it is most unlikely that a father who gave his daughter in marriage could be said to do the same, 'turn her out.' No one (one would fancy) ever uses such an expression in this context." True, no one would use the verb "to divorce" in the present context. But the very use of הוציא argues *against*, *not for*, retroversion, because a medieval scribe, realizing that הוציא does have "to divorce" as one of its usual meanings, would scarcely choose this verb to render the thought that Greek and Syriac convey. Therefore, we can conclude that הוציא is the product of Ben Sira's pen, not of a medieval retroverter's.

נבון, because a retranslator from Syriac presumably would have employed the good Hebrew adjective חכם to render ܚܟܝܡܐ/ܚܟܝܡ.

Sir 10, 19

MS B		MS A
	19a	זרע נכבד מה זרע לאנוש
	19b	[זרע נכבד ירא ײי]
זרע נקלה מה זרע לאנוש	19c	
זרע נקלה עובר מצוה	19d	זרע נקלה עובר מצוה

Uncials:

19a σπέρμα ἔντιμον ποῖον; σπέρμα ἀνθρώπου·
19b σπέρμα ἔντιμον ποῖον; οἱ φοβούμενοι τὸν κύριον.
19c σπέρμα ἄτιμον ποῖον; σπέρμα ἀνθρώπου·
19d σπέρμα ἄτιμον ποῖον; οἱ παραβαίνοντες ἐντολάς.

248:

19a σπέρμα ἀσφαλείας οἱ φοβούμενοι κύριον.
19b καὶ ἔντιμον φύτευμα οἱ ἀγαπῶντες αὐτόν.
19c σπέρμα ἀτιμίας οἱ μὴ προσέχοντες τῷ νόμῳ.
19d σπέρμα πλανήσεως οἱ παραβαίνοντες ἐντολάς.

Old Latin: Semen hominum honorabitur hoc quod timet dominum; semen autem hoc exhonorabitur hominum (omitted by many MSS and the editions) quod praeterit mandata domini.

Syrohexaplar:
ܙܪܥܐ ܡܝܩܪܐ ܐܝܢܐ. ܙܪܥܐ ܕܒܪܢܫܐ. 19a
ܙܪܥܐ ܡܝܩܪܐ ܐܝܠܝܢ ܕܕܚܠܝܢ ܡܢ ܡܪܝܐ. 19b
ܙܪܥܐ ܡܨܥܪܐ ܐܝܢܐ. ܙܪܥܐ ܕܒܪܢܫܐ. 19c
ܐܦ ܙܪܥܐ ܕܨܥܪܐ ܐܝܠܝܢ ܕܥܒܪܝܢ ܦܘܩܕܢܐ. 19d

Syriac Peshiṭta:
ܙܪܥܐ ܡܝܩܪܐ ܗܘ ܕܕܚܠ ܠܐܠܗܐ. 19a
ܙܪܥܐ ܡܝܩܪܐ ܡܢ ܕܕܚܠ ܠܐܠܗܐ. 19b
ܙܪܥܐ ܡܝܩܪܐ ܡܢ ܕܢܛܪ ܦܘܩܕܢܐ (ܦܘܩܕܢܐ). 19c
ܙܪܥܐ ܨܥܝܪܐ ܗܘ ܕܕܚܠ ܠܐܠܗܐ. 19d
ܙܪܥܐ ܨܥܝܪܐ ܡܢ ܕܠܐ ܢܛܪ ܦܘܩܕܢܐ (ܢܛܪ ܦܘܩܕܢܐ) 19e

Translations:

Hebrew: (MS A) "What can be an honorable seed? The seed of man. [The honorable seed is the one that fears Yahweh]. (MS B)

What can be a dishonorable seed? The seed of man. (MSS A and B) The dishonorable seed is the one that transgresses the commandment."

Uncials: "What can be an honorable seed? The seed of man. What is an honorable seed? Those who fear the Lord. What can be a dishonorable seed? The seed of man. What is a dishonorable seed? Those who break the commandments."

248: "Those who fear the Lord are a stable/firm seed, and those who love Him are an honorable plant. Those who do not pay heed to the Law are a dishonorable seed; those who break the commandments are an unstable/erring seed."

Old Latin: "That seed of men will be honored that fears the Lord, but that seed of men will be dishonored that breaks the commandments of the Lord."

Syrohexaplar: "What can be an honorable seed? The seed of man. Those who fear the Lord are an honorable seed. What can be a dishonorable seed? The seed of man. Also those who transgress the commandments are an unstable/erring seed."

Syriac Peshiṭta: "An honorable seed is that which is sown by man; an honorable seed is whoever fears God; an honorable seed is whoever keeps the commandment(s: Codex Ambrosianus, Lagarde). A dishonorable seed is that which is sown by man; a dishonorable seed is whoever does not keep the commandment(s)."

Commentary:

These hemistichs are very instructive with respect to the theories of the opponents of the Cairo Hebrew text who charge that it is retranslated from Syriac (Bickell, Torrey, Ginsberg) or from Greek (Goodspeed, Hadas) or at times from the Syrohexaplar (Ginsberg). For in all the various textual traditions – Hebrew, Greek, Syriac, and the daughter versions of the last two – this v. has undergone more than one of the errors that copyists are wont to commit.

Starting with the Greek tradition, we notice no small discrepancy between the Uncials and Codex 248 (70 also has the reading of 248). Our task here is not to attempt to explain how this difference came a out, but merely to point out that the Geniza Hebrew could in no way have as its source either the uncial or cursive Greek.

In the Uncials, we find four questions and four answers, one of each per half-line. This arrangement does not appear original. The development of thought is better preserved in the Cairo Hebrew, of which the second hemistich has been restored by us on the basis of the parallelism to 19d and the versions. In fact, the Syrohexaplar and the Ethiopic version (based upon Greek) omit the second and fourth ποῖον, while S* leaves out only the fourth one. In any event, what needs to be stressed here is that the Geniza Hebrew could scarcely have originated by way of retroversion from either the uncial or the cursive tradition. The Cursives 248 and 70 contain no questions at all, whereas the Uncials contain too many questions. The two questions we find in the Cairo text are almost certainly the only ones that Ben Sira wrote.

But what about retroversion from the Syrohexaplar, which Ginsberg maintains "was occasionally consulted by the producer or producers of H"?[20] For after all, like the Hebrew it too has only two questions. There are three textual arguments against assuming retroversion from this version: (1) before the translation of the fourth σπέρμα, it adds the word ܐܦ, which does not appear in Hebrew; (2) נקלה could not conceivably have been occasioned by ܠܛܥܝܘܬܐ, which accurately renders πλανήσεως (found in 248 and 70); (3) the last two words of the v. are plural in the Syrohexaplar but singular in Hebrew; if a medieval Jew were retranslating from this version, he would surely have given us עוברים and the perfectly good plural form מצות.

Old Latin contains only the second and fourth hemistichs, the first and third being omitted because of homoioarchton. Either they dropped out of the text in the course of transmission or they were never translated in the first place.

Syriac is interesting in that it has no questions in any of its half-lines. Either the Syriac translator misunderstood the original Hebrew (which would not be unusual), or he decided to give a prosaic rendering of his *Vorlage*. In place of ܕܙܢܝܢ of 19a and c, Codex Pocockianus has ܕܙܢܢ, a reading found also in Codex Usserianus but in 19a only. The earliest and best Syriac MSS, however, provide the reading given at the beginning of this section.

[20] Cf. Chapter I, p. 43.

Instead of the original four hemistichs, Syriac gives five, the third being a gloss or expansion occasioned by the words of the concluding half-line of this verse. The third and fourth hemistichs are omitted in Codex Usserianus; the first and fourth in Codex S. Hardy. Thus, while we can readily see how a text like the Cairo Hebrew (19b being restored as suggested above) must certainly have been the source of Syriac, the reverse could hardly have been the case.

As regards the Geniza text, we now possess three instead of only two of the four hemistichs, thanks to Schirmann's discovery of a new leaf of MS B in 1960.[21] MS A has suffered from homoioarchton, omitting 19b–c. MS B may also have been the victim of this same scribal error; but it is just as likely, if indeed not more so, that this MS contained 19a–b. Since 19c–d are the first two hemistichs on *side a* of the newly discovered leaf, it is quite probable that 19a–b were the last two hemistichs on *side b* of the previous leaf, which is not extant.

The restoration of 19b offered above is virtually certain. Because the Cairo Hebrew with 19b restored is the only text to preserve the proper parallelism, we must conclude that it represents faithfully the very words written by Ben Sira. If we were to assume for the moment, however, that a medieval author retranslating from Greek or Syrohexaplar or Syriac – all of which are corrupt – happily hit upon the very words that Ben Sira originally wrote, we would be forced to admit a literary miracle. As in theology, so in textual criticism (if we may adjust Ockham's razor a little), "miracula non sunt multiplicanda."

Sir 15, 19

MS B		MS A
[עיני אל יראו]ו מעשיו	19a	עיני אל יראו מעשיו
והוא יכיר כל מפעל אנוש	19b	והו יכיר עָׄלׄ כל מפעל איש

19a καὶ οἱ ὀφθαλμοὶ αὐτοῦ ἐπὶ τοὺς φοβουμένους αὐτόν,
19b καὶ αὐτὸς ἐπιγνώσεται πᾶν ἔργον ἀνθρώπου·

ܘܥܠܡܕܡ ܕܕܚܠܘܗܝ ܚܙܝܢ. 19a
ܘܚܟܡ ܒܟܠܗܘܢ ܠܥܒܕ̈ܘܗܝ ܕܒ̈ܢܝ ܐܢܫܐ. 19b

[21] "*Dappîm nôs^epîm mittôk sēper 'ben-Sîrā'*", *Tarbiẕ*, 29 (1959–1960), 125 to 134. I re-edited this leaf in *Bib*, 45 (1964), 156; cf. Introduction above, p. 16.

Translations:

MS A: "The eyes of God see His (*h*is?) works, and He knows man's every deed."

MS B: "[The eyes of God se]e His works, and He knows man's every deed."

Greek: "And His eyes (are) upon those who fear Him, and He knows man's every deed."

Syriac: "And His eyes see everything, and He understands all the minds/opinions/doctrines of men."

Commentary:

From the size of the lacuna[22] it seems certain that MS B contained the same reading as MS A. In MS A, 19b, the word הו is a copyist's error for הוא; a similar mistake is found also in the margin at 32, 3 (MS B). The dots above and below על denote deletion.

In 19a Greek is corrupt. Old Latin offers us little help: "oculi dei (some MSS and the editions: *domini*) ad timentes eum." It seems that the trouble with the Greek translation did not stem from the Hebrew *Vorlage* but rather from the grandson's recollection of Ps 33, 18, which in the LXX reads: ἰδοὺ οἱ ὀφθαλμοὶ κυρίου ἐπὶ τοὺς φοβουμένους αὐτόν. Thus, the Hebrew behind the grandson's Greek would be: וְעֵינָיו אֶל יְרֵאָיו, a reading which could hardly be original in view of the parallelism. Since the grandson misread אל as the preposition instead of the noun, "God", he was forced to add to the first word, עיני, either the third person singular masculine suffix or a noun. He chose the former. As the third word of the hemistich he read יְרֵאָיו in place of the obviously correct יראו, imperfect, third person plural of ראה, "to see". Then he had to ignore the last word, מעשיו, for it could make no sense in the Hebrew as understood by him. But Ben Sira certainly wrote מעשיו, because the word suits the context admirably and is weakly reflected by Syriac's ܦܠܚܝܗܘܢ. In any case, the point being argued here is that Greek could not conceivably be the basis of the Geniza Hebrew, but the reverse

[22] See the facsimile of this leaf published by us, "The Recently Identified Leaves of Sirach in Hebrew", *Bib*, 45 (1964), TAB. IV, between pp. 154 and 155.

is indeed true. In 19b, Greek accurately reflects the Hebrew original as represented in the Cairo text.

As regards Syriac, we should note that in 19a its word order is completely different from that of the Hebrew. Syriac understands יראו correctly, but like Greek, it puts the third person singular masculine suffix on the word for "eyes". Finally, the expression ܟܠܗܘܢ is a poor equivalent for מעשיו. In 19b, Syriac substitutes ܬܪ̈ܥܝܬܐ, "minds, opinions, doctrines", for the patently original מפעל , which is reflected by Greek's ἔργον.

Since, therefore, Syriac differs so considerably from Hebrew in both 19a and b, it appears unthinkable that the former is the starting-point for the latter.

Hence, neither Greek nor Syriac can explain the Cairo text. But Hebrew does provide a common denominator for these two versions. Therefore, we can conclude that the Geniza text represents the original or something very close to the original of Ben Sira. One can hardly agree with Smend's conjecture that the original read: ועיני ייי אל יראיו or ועין ייי אל יראיו or ועיני אל אל יראיו.[23] He attempts to justify his emendation on the basis of Greek and Ps 33, 18, and Ps 34, 16.[24] But because the parallelism in the two psalm passages is completely different from that found in Sir 15, 19, his conjectures appear uncalled for. The parallelism contained in the untouched Cairo Hebrew seems quite natural and needs no improvement.[25] Most commentators agree with this judgment.[26]

Sir 32, 20

MS E		MS B
[בדרך מוקשת] אל תלך	20a	בדרך מוקשת אל תלך
ואל תתקל בדרך פעמים	20b	ואל תתקל בנגף פעמים

[23] *Die Weisheit des Jesus Sirach, hebräisch und deutsch* (Berlin, 1906), 19.

[24] *Die Weisheit des Jesus Sirach erklärt*, 144.

[25] Cf. Jb 31, 4; Prv 15, 3.

[26] Cf. Lévi, *L'Ecclésiastique*, part 2, p. 112; N. Peters, *Das Buch Jesus Sirach oder Ecclesiasticus* (= *Exegetisches Handbuch zum Alten Testament*, 25) (Münster i. W., 1913), 130f.; G. H. Box-W. O. E. Oesterley, "Sirach", in *The Apocrypha and Pseudepigrapha of the Old Testament*, ed. by R. H. Charles, 1 (Oxford 1913), 371; and Segal, *op. cit.*, 98.

35, 20a ἐν ὁδῷ ἀντιπτώματος μὴ πορεύου,
20b καὶ μὴ προσκόψῃς ἐν λιθώδεσιν.

20a ܒܐܘܪܚܐ ܕܡܫܘܪܬܐ ܠܐ ܬܐܙܠ.
20b ܕܠܡܐ ܬܬܬܩܠ ܒܟܐܦܐ ܕܬܪ̈ܬܝܢ ܙܒ̈ܢܝܢ.

Translations:

MS B: "On a path beset with snares do not walk, and do not stumble twice on the (same) obstacle."

MS E: "[On a path beset with snares] do not walk, and do not stumble twice on the (same) path."

Greek: "On a path on which you may fall (literally: on a path of stumbling/resistance) do not walk, and do not stumble upon rocky places."

Syriac: "On a path which is stony do not travel, lest you stumble twice on the rock."

Commentary:

Greek is corrupt in 20b. As Hart plausibly suggests,[27] instead of λιθώδεσιν, the grandson most likely wrote λίθῳ δίς, which would agree with Syriac and the sense of the Cairo Hebrew. The corruption in the Greek tradition must have antedated the Old Latin, for the latter reflects the reading found in all the extant Greek MSS: "in via ruinae non eas, et non offendes (2 MSS, first hand; all other MSS: *offendas*) in lapides."

The word ἀντιπτώματος is extremely rare in Biblical Greek.[28] Apparently, the word is rare in classical Greek too.[29] The meaning of the word, however, seems clear enough: "resistance; stumbling". But the point at issue here is that מוקשת, "snares, bird-traps", could not be a retroversion of this Greek word, as it would have to be in the theory of Goodspeed and Hadas.

With respect to 20b, we have seen that λιθώδεσιν is corrupt. This being so, it appears virtually inconceivable that the words נגף פעמים (as a noun, the first word occurs only seven times in the Hebrew

[27] *Ecclesiasticus: the Greek Text of Codex 248* (Cambridge, 1909), 184.

[28] The only other occurrence in the entire Greek Bible is Sir 31, 29.

[29] Cf. H. G. Liddell-R. Scott-H. S. Jones-R. McKenzie, *A Greek-English Lexicon* (Oxford, 1953), 162.

canon) would have been retranslated by a medieval writer from this Greek word. Even if the assumed retranslator had the critical acumen to perceive the mistake in Greek and to reconstruct as the grandson's original λίθῳ δίς, he would hardly have chosen נגף to render λίθῳ. Consequently, the Cairo Hebrew could not have Greek as its source. On the contrary, however, it takes little imagination to see that a Hebrew text like that recovered from the Geniza was the *Vorlage* of the grandson.

As regards Syriac we find many serious objections to the hypothesis that it served as basis for this Hebrew distich. If we assume for the present that the Cairo text was retroverted from Syriac, it seems odd that the medieval author did not employ ארח to render ܐܘܪܚܐ. And it would take a vivid imagination, divorced from reality, to see מוקשת as a retroversion of the adjectival phrase ܕܦܣܘܪܬܐ. In the second hemistich of Syriac, we find the subordinating conjunction ܕܠܡܐ, which introduces a negative purpose clause; in the Cairo Hebrew, the second clause is introduced by the coordinating conjunction "and", which seems to be original because Greek has the same construction. Concerning the last three words of Syriac the same observation made with respect to λίθῳ δίς is equally valid.

Now we are willing to concede that תתקל may not be original, the reason being that תקל seems to be a Mishnaic/Talmudic word which does not occur in the Hebrew canon, nor in the non-biblical literature from Khirbet Qumrân published up to 1960.[30] If that is the case, Ben Sira's original probably read תכשל which was then changed (only the two middle consonants needing alteration) to תתקל under the influence of Syriac's ܬܬܩܠ. But if that is so, the Cairo Hebrew is nevertheless *substantially* genuine. It is this contention that we wish to prove in this book. Of course, it is not absolutely necessary to admit that תתקל is not original. (The verb תקל is found also in 13, 23 and 15, 12.) Just because the word does not occur in the Hebrew canon, we are not entitled to conclude that it is a comparatively late borrowing from Aramaic. This verb may have come into Hebrew in the days of Ben Sira.

[30] K. G. Kuhn, *Konkordanz zu den Qumrantexten* (Göttingen, 1960), does not list the word.

The reading בדרך of 20b in MS E is most likely a dittography of the same phrase presumably found at the beginning of 20a, as in MS B.

Sir 36, 31

MS C		MSS B and D
מי יאמין בצ̆בא גדוד	31a	מי יאמין בגדוד צבא
המדלג מעיר א̆ל ע[י]ר	31b	המדלג מעיר אל עיר

MS C		MS B	
כ̆ן איש אשר אין לו קין	31c	כן איש אשר°לא קן	[א]שר אין לו
המרגיע כאשר יסביב	31d	המרגיע באשר יערב	

MS D: 31c–d כן איש אשר אין לו קן המרגיע באשר יערב

31a τίς γὰρ πιστεύσει εὐζώνῳ λῃστῇ
31b σφαλλομένῳ (S, A: ἀφαλλομένῳ;
248: ἐφαλλομένῳ) ἐκ πόλεως εἰς πόλιν;
31c οὕτως ἀνθρώπῳ μὴ ἔχοντι νοσσιὰν
31d καὶ καταλύοντι οὗ ἐὰν ὀψίσῃ.

31a ܡܢܘ ܓܝܪ ܢܗܝܡܢ ܠܓܝܣܐ ܕܙܪܝܙܐ ܠܡܗܠܟܘ.
31b ܕܗܘ ܫܘܪ ܡܢ ܡܕܝܢܬܐ ܠܡܕܝܢܬܐ.
31c ܘܗܟܢܐ ܓܒܪܐ ܕܠܝܬ ܠܗ ܐܬܪܐ.
31d ܐܝܟܐ ܕܢܚܫܟ ܫܪܐ.

Translations:

MSS B (margin) and D: "Who will trust a band of armed men that bounds from city to city? In like manner, (who will trust) a man who has no nest, who takes his rest in the place where evening comes upon him (literally: where it becomes evening)?"

MS C: "Who will trust the armed men of a band (or: armed men who have gathered together) that (who) bound(s) from city to city. In like manner, (who will trust) a man who has no nest, who takes his rest when he . . . (?) . .?"

Greek: "For who will trust a well-girded/well-equipped/active robber who staggers (S, A, 248: who bounds) from city to city? In like manner, (who will trust) a man who has no nest, and who takes up his quarters in the place where evening comes upon him (literally: where it becomes evening)?"

Syriac: "For who will trust the young man [10 to 18 years of age] who is like a gazelle which bounds from city to city? In like manner, (who will trust) a man who has no wife? In the place where he happens to be he dies."

Commentary:

The expression, גדוד צבא (MSS B and D), which is to be preferred over the arrangement of the words in MS C, is perfectly good Hebrew.[31] In 31c of MS B, we have translated the marginal reading, because the main text is corrupt, as is obvious from the correct reading provided by MSS C and D. The last word of MS C is corrupt. In 31c, קין of MS C is a typical example of the expanded orthography of the medieval (and modern) period.

The Cairo MSS despite the few corruptions already noted have preserved the original text of these hemistichs. For it does not appear at all plausible that the diction, poetic balance, and beautiful imagery of the Geniza text could have resulted from retroversion of Greek (or Syrohexaplar) or Syriac.

Except for the first half-line, Greek presents us with a faithful reflection of Ben Sira's thought. But it is precisely that half-line which provides conclusive evidence against retroversion. By no stretch of the scholarly imagination could גדוד צבא be based upon εὐζώνῳ λῃστῇ or upon ܠܓܝܣܐ ܕܠܝܠܐ, the slavish translation of the Greek expression in the Syrohexaplar.[32] Moreover, the conjunction γάρ has no counterpart in Hebrew. In 31b, the reading of Codices S and A, or of 248 (also 155 and 106) is superior to that found in Codices B and 308.

Syriac is a more eloquent witness, albeit in an indirect way, for the genuineness of the Cairo text. For it is altogether impossible for Syriac to be the source of this Hebrew; on the contrary, however, it seems certain that the mistake found in Syriac could be explained only on the basis of a text like that found in the Cairo Geniza. The word ܓܕܘܕܐ, for example, was employed by the Syriac translator because he thought that the Hebrew noun con-

[31] Cf. גְּדוּדֵי צְבָא מִלְחָמָה in 1 Par 7, 4.

[32] We should recall that Ginsberg thinks that the Syrohexaplar was occasionally consulted by the assumed retranslator(s) of the Cairo Hebrew.

taining the same consonants meant "young man". This error made him think that צבא must be understood as "gazelle";[33] hence, Syriac's ܛܒܝܐ, which is the Aramaic consonantal equivalent of Hebrew צבי.[34] Given these two blunders, the Syriac translator had to add the phrase "ܕܕܡܐ ܠ in order to connect the two words. This being the case, it would be nothing short of a stupendous marvel for a medieval author, retranslating from Syriac, to produce what we find in the Geniza text.

In 31c, all the Syriac MSS and editions consulted, except of course the Syrohexaplar which slavishly reproduces Greek, have "wife" instead of "nest"; the latter is a reading whose originality is attested to by both Hebrew (all three MSS) and Greek. And in 31d, Syriac has ܢܬܠܒܫ ܢܦܘܐ in place of the evidently correct "come to rest; repose; lodge" and "it becomes evening" of Hebrew and Greek. As Smend suggests,[35] ܢܦܘܐ apparently is an inner Syriac mistake for ܢܒܘܐ, "lodge; pass the night", which would then be a dim reflection of יערב. In any case, the Cairo Hebrew could hardly be derived from the Syriac we now possess. That the medieval Jews had a Syriac text different from the one we now have would be an assumption for which there is not a single shred of evidence.

Sir 37, 1

	MS B	MS D
1a	°כל אומר אמר אהבתי	כל אוהב אומר אהבתי
Margin 1a	כל אוהב אומר אהבתי	
Margin 1b	אך יש אוהב שם אוהב	אך יש אהב שם אהב

1a πᾶς φίλος ἐρεῖ ἐφιλίασα (B: αὐτῷ) κἀγώ·
1b ἀλλ' ἔστιν φίλος ὀνόματι μόνον φίλος.

1a ܘܟܠ ܪܚܡܘܗܝ ܐܡܪ ܕܪܚܡܬ.
1b ܒܪܡ ܐܝܬ ܪܚܡܐ ܕܫܡܗ ܪܚܡܐ.

[33] Cf. 1 Par 12, 9, where we find the orthography צְבָאִים instead of the more usual צְבָיִם, "gazelles".

[34] The initial consonant of this root in proto-Semitic would be ẓ, which in Hebrew becomes צ and in Aramaic ; Arabic and Ugaritic, however, preserve the original morpheme, ظَبْيٌ, ẓby.

[35] *Op. cit.* (n. 1), 326.

Translations:

MSS B (margin) and D: "Every friend says: 'I am a friend.' But there is a friend who in name (only) is a friend."

Greek: "Every friend will say: 'I am indeed a friend.' But there is a friend who in name only is a friend."

Syriac: "And to one's friend one says: 'I am a friend.' But there is a friend whose name is friend."

Commentary:

This verse illustrates two important characteristics of the Geniza Sir: (1) the copyist's errors often found in the MSS;[36] (2) the authenticity of the Hebrew text.

The first scribe of MS B wrote אומר by mistake (it is a dittography of the following word) instead of the clearly correct אוהב, and then left out the entire second hemistich. In its place he put v. 2, writing the last few words in smaller than usual letters so that the entire v. could be fitted into the left-hand side of the page. A second scribe, who made many corrections in this calligraphically beautiful but error-filled MS, obviously had before him a copy of a text either identical with or very similar to that of MS D;[37] he added in the margin the correct text which corresponds to MS D. The word שם is correct; the preposition ב״ְ was left out (most likely by Ben Sira himself) in order to avoid the repetition of ב after אוהב.

With respect to Greek, we should note first of all that a future tense verb is employed where Hebrew has a participle. If Hebrew were retroverted from Greek, one would expect the imperfect of אמר. Secondly, κἀγώ has no counterpart in Hebrew, and presumably a retranslator would have rendered the word. Thirdly, the grandson expanded the poetically concise Hebrew of the second half-line; the addition of μόνον is justifiable, of course, for it is the translator's task to convey the sense of the original. Thus, to assert that Hebrew here depends upon Greek is to go beyond the evidence

36 For a list of scribal errors found in the Geniza MSS of Sir, cf. Peters, *Der jüngst wiederaufgefundene hebräische Text des Buches Ecclesiasticus untersucht, herausgegeben, übersetzt und mit kritischen Noten versehen* (Freiburg i. B., 1902), 31ff.

37 This can be proved from many of the marginal readings of MS B which agree with MS D.

into the realm of improbable speculation. On the contrary, however, it appears reasonable to affirm that the grandson had before him a text like that found in the Geniza MSS. The αὐτῷ found in Codex B is a dittography of κἀγώ, as Smend suggests.[38]

It is even more unlikely that Syriac can explain the poetic balance and thought of the Cairo text. For in the first hemistich, Syriac is clearly corrupt. It may be that the Syriac translator himself wrote ܟܠ ܪܘܫܡ which was later incorrectly transcribed as ܡܠܪܘܫܡ (a mistake not difficult to visualize in the Estrangela script).[39] Given this reading, a copyist then added the third person singular masculine suffix to the word in an attempt to make the text more intelligible. Because this poor reading is found in all the Syriac MSS and editions available, it seems that the error was made in their archetype. Whatever the case, the Geniza Hebrew scarcely reflects Syriac as we know it.

In the second half-line, the Syriac translator also endeavored to provide his readers with the sense of the original Hebrew. But he was much less fortunate in his effort than was Ben Sira's grandson. At any rate, it is evident enough: (1) that Syriac had as *Vorlage* a text like the one we find in the Cairo MSS; (2) that Hebrew could not have as its origin the present Syriac.

We can reasonably conclude, therefore, that the *casus pendens* present in 1b of Hebrew could in no way be derived from Greek or Syriac, and consequently must be original.

Sir 37, 2

MS D		MS B	
2a הלא דין מגיע עד מות		הלא דין מגיע אל מות	על
2b ריע כנפש נהפך לצר		רע כנפשך נהפך לצר	כנפש

2a οὐχὶ λύπη ἔνι (248: μένει) ἕως θανάτου
2b ἑταῖρος καὶ φίλος τρεπόμενος εἰς ἔχθραν (A: ἔχθρον);

ܘܠܐ (ܕܠܐ) ܡܛܠܬܐ ܕܡܛܐ ܠܡܘܬܐ. 2a
ܘܚܒܪܐ ܕܫܦܝܪܐ ܐܝܟ ܢܦܫܟ ܗܘܐ ܠܟ. 2b

[38] *Op. cit.* (n. 1), 326.

[39] Lévi, *op. cit.* (n. 11), 178, has a similar explanation. Cf. V. Ryssel, "Die Sprüche Jesus', des Sohnes Sirachs", in *Die Apokryphen und Pseudepigraphen des alten Testaments*, ed. by E. Kautzsch, 1 (Tübingen, 1921), 411.

Translations:

MSS B (margin) and D: "Is it not a judgment [read: דָוֹן, sorrow] touching upon death when a companion who is like oneself turns into an enemy?"

Greek: "Is it not a sorrow that exists (248: that remains) till death when a companion and friend turns toward hatred (A and many Cursives: into an enemy)?"

Syriac: "And he does not last (Codex Ambrosianus, Walton, Mosul: Who does not last) till death. May you have a steadfast friend who is like yourself."

Commentary:

As was the case with the examples we have considered thus far, this v. also proves that the Cairo Hebrew is essentially independent of both Greek and Syriac (and any other version, *pace* Ginsberg), and therefore is genuine.

The word דין found in MSS B (text and margin) and D is a mistake for דָוֹן,[40] which means "sorrow, grief".[41] This same error is found in 14, 1; 30, 21. 23; and 38, 18. As we will show, the misreading of *yod* for *waw* or vice versa is not uncommon in the Geniza fragments of Sir (and in other documents recovered from the Geniza; see Chapter III, pp. 97–101, for complete details). This phenomenon seems to prove that the exemplars from which the medieval copyists transcribed their texts made no unmistakable distinction between these two letters. The most plausible explanation for this is, as we shall see, that the text of these exemplars was at one time in the caves near Khirbet Qumrân.

A comparison between Hebrew and Greek makes it sufficiently apparent that the former depends in no way upon the latter. Neither Greek verb in 2a – μένει or ἔνι – would prompt a retranslator to

[40] The critical note in the CCD translation incorrectly reads "*dāyôn*" instead of "*dāwôn*".

[41] Concerning this word which is an Aramaism, cf. S. Schechter-C. Taylor, *The Wisdom of Ben Sira: Portions of the Book Ecclesiasticus from Hebrew Manuscripts in the Cairo Genizah Collection Presented to the University of Cambridge by the Editors* (Cambridge, 1899), XXXVI and 54, and Smend, *op. cit.* (n. 1), 130.

think of מגיע. In 2b, ἑταῖρος καὶ φίλος could scarcely be the source of רע כנפש which appears original, being reflected by Syriac's ܐܝܟ ܢܦܫܟ. The words καὶ φίλος could be, as Segal suggests,[42] a translation of (וְ)אֹהֵב which the grandson may have taken from v. 1.

Since the Syriac translator completely misunderstood his *Vorlage* or failed to render all the words, it would be sheer folly to insist that the Cairo text descended from Syriac. The first hemistich does not even make sense in Syriac; the second is completely different from Hebrew.

With respect to the Cairo text, the preposition עד (MS D) seems preferable to אל and על, for it is evidently the basis of ἕως and ܥܕܡܐ.[43] In 2b, כנפש (MSS D and B margin) perhaps is better than כנפשך found in the body of MS B, the reason being that a second person reference is not necessary. We should note that in Dt 13, 7 (רֵעֲךָ אֲשֶׁר כְּנַפְשְׁךָ), and in 1 Sm 18, 1 (וַיֶּאֱהָבֵהוּ [Qᵉre] יְהוֹנָתָן כְּנַפְשׁוֹ) and 3 (בְּאַהֲבָתוֹ אֹתוֹ כְּנַפְשׁוֹ), כנפש has a suffix because there is in the immediate context another suffix of the same person. But in our present text, since רע has no suffix, כנפש needs none either.

Sir 37, 6

MS D		MS B	
אל תשכח חבר בְּקֶרֶב	6a	אל תשכח חביר בקרב°	תכחש / בקבר
ואל תעזבהו בשללך	6b	ואל תעזבהו בשללך	

6a μὴ ἐπιλάθῃ (A, 248: ἐπιλαθοῦ) φίλου ἐν τῇ ψυχῇ σου,
6b καὶ μὴ ἀμνημονήσῃς (S*, 248: μνημονεύσῃς) αὐτοῦ ἐν χρήμασίν σου.

6a ܠܐ ܬܛܥܝܗ ܪܚܡܐ (ܪܚܡܟ) ܒܩܘܪܒܐ.
6b ܘܠܐ ܬܫܬܠܛܘܢܝ ܒܩܢܝܢܟ.

Translations:

MS B: "Do not forget (margin: deny/disavow) a comrade during the battle (margin: in the grave), and do not neglect him when you are distributing the booty."

[42] *Op. cit.*, 235.
[43] Cf. Segal, *loc. cit.*

MS D: "Do not forget a comrade in (your) heart, and do not neglect him when you are distributing the booty."

Greek: "Do not forget a friend in your soul/heart, and do not be unmindful of (S* and 248: do not remember [*sic*]) him in your wealth."

Syriac: "Do not praise a friend (Codex Ambrosianus, Walton, Mosul: your friend) when he is nearby (literally: in the vicinity), and do not put him in charge over your house."

Commentary:

The last word of 6a in MS D is so pointed in the MS. The right hand margin of MS B has בקבר, "in the grave", a reading that may have been occasioned by the thought of 7, 33b: וגם ממת אל תמנע חסד. In the left-hand margin MS B contains these words: אל תכחש חבר בקרב ונגד ערים יחזיק צנה.

Since the second part is a repetition of 37, 5b, it need not enter into the discussion here. The first part means: "Do not deny/disavow a friend in the battle." The reading תכחש does not apdear original – the *shin* has been trans posed from the second to the fourth position.

The pointing of בְּקֶרֶב is clearly a mistake. The word should be read as בַּקְרָב, "in the battle/fight", a meaning demanded by the context. The grandson made the same mistake as the copyist of MS D: ἐν τῇ ψυχῇ is a good translation of בְּקֶרֶב; the grandson also added the possessive second person singular pronoun to the phrase in order to make it more intelligible. Thus, Greek is without doubt dependent upon a Hebrew text identical with or at least very similar to that recovered from the Cairo Geniza. Now בקרב, in the sense of "in the battle", could not possibly be derived from Greek. If, however, we were to affirm for the moment that the grandson preserved the true meaning of Ben Sira's original and that the Cairo text is retranslated from Greek (Goodspeed, Hadas) or from the Syrohexaplar (Ginsberg), then we would be forced to admit the virtually inadmissible, viz. that בקרב, in the sense of "in the inner part (of the body)", would be called upon to render the phrase ἐν τῇ ψυχῇ σου. Quite patently, such an admission is out of touch with reality, for any self-respecting Jew retranslating that Greek phrase would have written בנפשך.

The reading ἐπιλαθοῦ (aorist imperative) of Codices A and 248 is inferior to ἐπιλάθῃ (aorist subjunctive, second person singular) found in most of the Uncials, for the aorist subjunctive is used to express prohibitions, the aorist imperative being rarely so used.[44] In 6b, Codices S* and 248 have dropped from ἀμνημονήσῃς the *alpha privativum*, thus giving a bad reading.

In the second hemistich, the grandson's ἀμνημονήσῃς is an explanation rather than a translation of תעזב. His explanation is, however, a good one, and need cause us no undue concern.[45] At any rate, the point at issue here concerns the possibility of retroversion of the Geniza text from Greek. By no stretch of the imagination would a retranslator hit upon תעזבהו to render ἀμνημονήσῃς αὐτοῦ. Furthermore, בשללך, which conveys the only correct sense for the context at hand, could in no plausible manner derive from ἐν χρήμασίν σου. But the Greek phrase did indeed result from a misreading of Hebrew, viz. from בשלך (בְּ+שֶׁל+ךָ), for in 33, 20a (30, 28c in the Greek order), the grandson translates the phrase בשלך (MS E) by τὰ χρήματά σου.[46]

It is quite evident, therefore, that in 6a–b the grandson had as his *Vorlage* a text like that of the Cairo Hebrew. Hence, this Hebrew could scarcely have Greek as its source.

The authenticity of Hebrew becomes unmistakably clear also from a critical analysis of Syriac. In 6a, ܠܡܫܒܚ originated from a misreading of ב for כ in תשכח. The last word of the hemistich, ܒܩܘܪܒܐ, attests to the genuineness of בקרב, even though the Syriac translator, like Ben Sira's grandson before him, failed to grasp the meaning of the Hebrew phrase. Hence, while we can see through

[44] Cf. H. W. Smyth, *Greek Grammar*, rev. by G. M. Messing (Cambridge, Mass., 1956), 409, par. 1840; F. Blass-A. Debrunner, *A Greek Grammar of the New Testament and Other Early Christian Literature*, trans. by R. W. Funk (Chicago, 1961), 184, par. 364.

[45] Segal suggests, *op. cit.*, 236, that instead of the more common תעזבהו, the original of Ben Sira contained תְּשַׁשֵּׁהוּ, which the grandson then may have misread as הִשֵּׁתוּ, "(do not) forget". Such an explanation is purely gratuitous.

[46] Some years before MS E was discovered, Peters, *op. cit.* (n. 26), 301, correctly suggested that the grandson may have misread בשללך as בשלך.

Syriac to the original Hebrew, we could not with any degree of plausibility arrive at the Cairo text by way of retroversion from Syriac.

In 6b, the Syriac translator did something not completely atypical. Instead of rendering 6b of Hebrew,[47] he provides us with a slight variation of the idea contained in 33, 20b and 21b (33, 19b and 20b in Lagarde's edition of Syriac): (33, 20a: Either a son or wife, brother[48] or friend, ...)

Syriac		MS E
ܠܐ ܬܫܠܛܟ ܟܕ ܒܚܝܝܟ	33, 20b (30, 28)	אל תמשיל בחייך
ܠܐ ܬܫܠܛܟ ܟܕ ܟܠ ܒܣܪܟ	33, 21b (30, 29)	אל תשלט בך כל [בשר]

The similarity of thought content in 33, 20–24 and 37, 1–6 is most likely what prompted the Syriac translator to do what he did. Be that as it may, neither בשללך nor תעזבהו could result from retroversion of ܒܚܝܠܟ or ܬܫܠܛܘܗܝ, respectively.

From our textual analysis of this verse, it has become apparent on the one hand that the Cairo Hebrew is independent of Greek and Syriac, and on the other hand that these two ancient versions find their common origin only in a text like the one that fortunately was found in the Cairo Geniza.[49]

47 Because Segal assumes that the original verb here was תִּטֹּשׁ ו (see n. 45), he thinks, *op. cit.*, 236, that the Syriac translator perhaps misread those consonants as תשליטהו. Such an account is somewhat strained and, in view of the evidence provided by 33, 20b and 21b, completely uncalled for.

48 MS E reads here אהב, but this is patently a copyist's error for אח, a reading whose originality is attested to by both Greek and Syriac.

49 Years before the discovery of the Geniza MSS of Sir, Edersheim (*op. cit.*, 27) called attention to the last word of 4, 15a in Greek (ἔθνη) and Syriac (ܫܪ̈ܪܐ), noting that only a supposed Hebrew original of אמת could be the common basis of both versions: Ben Sira's grandson read the consonants as אֻמֹּת (cf. Gn 25, 16) whereas the Syriac translator read them as אֱמֶת. The Cairo Hebrew text has indeed Ben Sira's original אמת. This example is analogous to בקרב that we have been considering in this section.

III. AUTHENTICITY OF THE CAIRO HEBREW: HISTORICAL ARGUMENTS

In this chapter we shall attempt to prove that the Cairo Geniza fragments of Sir were copied from exemplars which represent a text that ultimately goes back to the caves near Khirbet Qumrân. None of the arguments is in itself conclusive, but the convergence and sum of all the arguments seem to make this hypothesis more than probable. If the Cairo Hebrew fragments were based on a text that was at one time in the Essene library, they must be to that extent genuine, for it is inconceivable that one would defend a retroversion hypothesis for a text which comes from so early a date (68 A.D. at the very latest).

A. QUMRÂN CAVE II FRAGMENTS OF SIRACH

Among the many fragments recovered from Cave II near Qumrân, M. Baillet has found two pieces of hide on which were written portions of the original Hebrew text of Sir.[1] The script is transitional Hasmonaean-Herodian, similar to that of 1QIs^{b} but with more archaic forms of ה and ט, and can be dated to the second half of the first century B.C. The smaller of the two pieces contains only five letters – two certain (ת, on the first line, and א, on the second line)

[1] For the preliminary report, cf. "Le travail d'édition des fragments manuscrits de Qumrân. Communication de M. Baillet", *RB*, 63 (1956), 54; cf. also J. T. Milik, *Ten Years of Discovery in the Wilderness of Judaea*, trans. by J. Strugnell (London, 1959), 32; and M. R. Lehmann, "Ben Sira and the Qumran Literature", *Revue de Qumran*, 3 (1961), 104. Baillet gives a fine edition and discussion of the texts in *Les 'Petites Grottes' de Qumrân* (= *Discoveries in the Judaean Desert of Jordan*, 3) (Oxford, 1962), ⋆ *Textes* (pp. 75ff.) ⋆⋆ *Planches* (Plate XV).

and three doubtful. Baillet suggests that the two lines belonged to either Sir 6, 14–15 or 1, 19–20. The larger piece contains the final letters of successive units of Sir. Although, unfortunately, there are merely 30 letters present (only four words are complete), the text belongs definitely to Sir 6, 20–31. The text of 2QSir 6, 20–31 is virtually identical with that of Geniza MS A (6, 28 is extant also in the florilegium-like text of MS C: in this v. MSS A and C are identical except for the first word of 28 b where MS C has the better reading, ותהפך, while MS A has ונהפך) and is stichometrically arranged like MSS B and E from Cairo. Thus we have conclusive proof that the Qumrân sect had at least part of Sir in Hebrew, if not the complete Book; and that the stichometric writing of the Book antedates the beginning of the Christian era and consequently was not introduced by the medieval scribes of MSS B and E. It is more than probable, as we shall see in the following arguments, that the text of the MS(S) which the medieval scribes employed as basis for the Geniza MSS goes back ultimately to the caves near Qumrân.

We should note that M. H. Segal criticizes Baillet (*Les 'Petites Grottes' de Qumrân*, 75) for stating that the stichometric arrangement of the text of 2QSir supports the hypothesis that the Cairo MSS were copied from Qumrân MSS found in the eighth century A.D.[2] Segal takes a poke also at P. Kahle ("The Age of the Scrolls", *VT*, 1, 1951, 45–48) and me ("Qumrân and the Geniza Fragments of Sirach", *CBQ*, 24, 1962, 245–267 [Segal misspells my name]) for defending the same hypothesis. Segal believes that historical facts refute the theory that Hebrew Sir was lost and unknown to the Jews during the many centuries that elapsed from the time of the Qumrân sect to the eighth century.

> The Geniza MSS and also the original Hebrew text underlying the Syriac version contain numerous verses composed in Mishnaic Hebrew as distinguished from the biblical Hebrew of the same verses in the Greek version, and from the usual biblical style of the rest of the book. These Mishnaic verses obviously belong to a later stage in the development of the

[2] "*Sēper ben-Sîrā' beqûmrân*", *Tarbiẓ*, 33 (1963–1964), 245f.

text which proves the existence and the spread of the book in Talmudic times.[3]

The historical *facts* that Segal has in mind are not altogether clear. One obvious "fact" is the Mishnaic diction of numerous verses in the Geniza MSS and in the *Vorlage* of the Syriac version as opposed to the biblical Hebrew of the same verses in the *Vorlage* of Greek. As we noted above (p. 22) and as we shall see below in Chapter IV, the present writer questions Segal's interpretation of that "fact". True, Mishnaic diction can be found in some verses of the Cairo text, but that *fact* of itself does not prove that the verses result from a later recension of Ben Sira's original. The Syriac translator(s) may have had and probably did use a later recension of Sir. But to equate Syriac's *Vorlage* with the Mishnaic-flavored parts of the Geniza text is something Segal proved neither 30 years ago nor in 1964. In Chapter IV we hope to demonstrate that the Mishnaic parts of the Cairo MSS are retroversions from Syriac which were made by the medieval scribes of the MSS themselves or by other Jews before them.

Oddly enough, Segal does not consider the mass of evidence that Kahle and the present writer have accumulated to support the hypothesis which, Segal claims, is refuted by historical "facts".

We conclude this part by calling attention to two other recent discoveries of pre-Christian fragments of Sir in Hebrew. Each of these fragments is of great importance, but because they have not yet been published we have not been able to study their relationship to the Cairo Hebrew text. However, from the published report of one of the discoveries we have reason to feel confident that the new fragments will not weaken the theories we are defending with respect to the general authenticity and partial retroversion of the Geniza text of Sir.

The first fragment was discovered by Y. Yadin at Massada. Here is the report as given in *The Jerusalem Post Weekly*, vol. 6, no. 239 (May 8, 1964), p. V:

[3] *Ibid.*, English summary, p. III. Segal expressed the same ideas 30 years ago: "The Evolution of the Hebrew Text of Ben Sira", *JQR*, n. s. 25 (1934–1935), 91–149. Cf. above, Chapter I, pp. 21–22.

> Fragments of Yehoshua Ben-Sirah's apocryphal Book of Ecclesiastics [*sic*], written in Hebrew in a style which dates it to the first century B.C.E., were found in Zealot living quarters on the eastern casement [*sic*] wall of Massada. Giving the news to the season's final press conference, Professor Yigael Yadin, the expedition's leader, showed a photograph of a fragment containing about four hundred words .... The scroll, discovered at Massada, written not later than 50 B.C.E., is identical with 'style B' of the Cairo Geniza version. The variations are the same as those recorded in the margins of the latter. As well as being the earliest copy of Ecclesiasticus ever discovered, this discovery at Massada proves that the Cairo Geniza version was from the Hebrew original and was not a later retranslation.

Qumrân Cave XI has produced the second fragment of Hebrew Sir: part of the acrostic canticle of chapter 51. Although the text has yet to be published (it will appear in the near future), we have been assured by competent Qumrân scholars that the fragment is unquestionably authentic and contains as far as it goes the arrangement of the lines in their proper alphabetic order.

B. DISCOVERY OF MSS IN A CAVE NEAR JERICHO

A question which comes to mind immediately and naturally is this: how did the medieval Jews come by a text that had a stichometric arrangement? In the rest of this chapter we will attempt to provide a satisfactory answer to that question.

The Letter of Timothy I

Some years ago J. Fück came across a letter, published in 1901, that seemed to have some bearing on the sensational discoveries made at Khirbet Qumrân in 1947. He brought this letter to the attention of O. Eissfeldt who then wrote an article[4] concerning the events narrated in the letter and the possible connection of these events with the Dead Sea Scrolls. The letter in question was written

[4] "Der gegenwärtige Stand der Erforschung der in Palästina neu gefundenen hebräischen Handschriften", *TLZ*, 74 (1949), 595–600.

in Syriac by Timothy I (727/728–823),[5] the Nestorian Patriarch of Seleucia, to Sergius, the Metropolitan of Elam. After Eissfeldt's article appeared, many other scholars took notice of this important letter.[6]

The letter itself is not dated, but R. S. Bidawid argues for a date in either 796 or 797.[7] The following translation was made from the Syriac text published by O. Braun.[8]

After mentioning in detail the troubles he had undergone in having the Hexapla of the entire Old Testament copied,[9] Timothy writes:

> We have learned from trustworthy Jews, who just recently had been instructed as converts to Christianity, that ten years ago books were found in a cave [literally, a mountain-house] in the vicinity of Jericho. Here is the incident as they reported it. The dog of a certain Arab who was hunting, climbed into a cave in pursuit of some animal and did not return. When the master went to look for the dog, he came upon a small

[5] There is some discrepancy among scholars as to the dates of Timothy's birth and death. The most recent study – R. S. Bidawid, *Les lettres du Patriarche nestorien, Timothée I* (= *Studi e Testi*, 187), (Vatican City, 1956) 1, 5 – argues for the dates given above. Others give the dates 726–819; so O. Braun, "Der Katholikos Timotheos I und seine Briefe", *Oriens Christianus*, 1 (1901), 138, 146. Cf. Bidawid, *op. cit.*, 1, n. 2 and p. 5, n. 6, for further references, and pp. 1–5 for a brief biography of Timothy.

[6] Cf. R. de Vaux, "A propos des manuscrits de la Mer Morte", *RB*, 57 (1950), 417–429; P. Kahle, "The Age of the Scrolls", *VT*, 1 (1951), 44f.; *idem*, *The Cairo Geniza*, 2d ed. (Oxford, 1959), 16f.; F. V. Filson, "Some Recent Study of the Dead Sea Scrolls", *BA*, 13 (1950), 96–99; G. Lambert, "Les manuscrits du désert de Juda: IV, Tient-on un nouveau chapitre de l'histoire de la grotte?", *NRT*, 72 (1950), 199–202; G. R. Driver, "New Hebrew Manuscripts", *JQR*, n. s., 40 (1949–1950), 368; J. L. Teicher, "The Dead Sea Scrolls – Documents of the Jewish-Christian Sect of Ebionites", *JJS*, 2 (1951), 89–93; H. H. Rowley, *The Zadokite Fragments and the Dead Sea Scrolls* (Oxford, 1952), 22ff.; D. Barthélemy-J. T. Milik, *Qumran Cave I* (= *Discoveries in the Judaean Desert*, 1) (Oxford, 1955) 88; S. W. Baron, *A Social and Religious History of the Jews*, 5, 2d ed. (New York, 1957), 378, n. 50; Milik, *Ten Years* ..., 19, n. 2; Baillet, *Les 'Petites Grottes' de Qumrân*, 75.

[7] *Op. cit.*, 71; cf. also de Vaux, *art. cit.*, 419.

[8] "Ein Brief des Katholikos Timotheos I über biblische Studien des 9 Jahrhunderts", *Oriens Christianus*, 1 (1901), 299–313; Braun also provides a translation into German. De Vaux, *art. cit.*, 417f., gives a French translation of a portion of Timothy's letter.

[9] Braun, "Ein Brief des Katholikos Timotheos I...", 300–305.

> hollow [literally, a small house] inside the rocks, and many books were in it. The hunter then went up to Jerusalem and informed the Jews about this matter. Consequently, a large number of them came (from Jerusalem) and discovered books of the Old Testament as well as others written in the Hebrew script. Since the one who reported this incident to me was well-versed in literary matters, I asked him about various texts of our New Testament which are supposed to be drawn from the Old Testament, but which are not even mentioned in the Old Testament, neither in our Christian text nor in their Jewish text. And he told me that there are such texts, and that they can be found in those books which have been discovered (in the cave). After I heard the account from this catechumen, I went to the trouble of asking others besides him, and I received the very same story without variation.[10]

The above incident has striking similarities with the events that took place near Khirbet Qumrân in 1947:

> A shepherd, Moḥammad ed-Di'b (Mohammed the Wolf), was looking for a goat that had wandered off among the rocky slopes of the cliff, but, being rather weary, he sat down in the shade of a hollow in the rock. To amuse himself, he threw a stone into a hole in the cliff-face in front of him. A sound of something breaking came from inside and he took to his heels in fright. But curiosity was stronger than fear, and the next day he returned to the spot with his cousin, Aḥmad Moḥammad. The two Bedouins wormed their way through the hole into the cave and found it to be a narrow cavern, its floor strewn with potsherds. At the back stood a row of eight unbroken jars with their lids still on. These were empty, however, all but one out of which they took three rolls, one large and two smaller ones.[11]

It is not unlikely, as de Vaux[12] and Kahle[13] suggest, and as we hope to prove below, that the cave found in about the year 800

[10] *Ibid.*, 304 and 306.
[11] Milik, *Ten Years* ...., 11f.
[12] *Art. cit.*, 419f.
[13] *Cairo Geniza*, 16f.

was one of those discovered anew since 1947 at Qumrân. In fact, de Vaux even offers the conjecture that Cave XXIX is the cave spoken of in Timothy's letter. Cave XXIX contained fragments of 12 jars and 17 jar lids, of which seven were intact and stored in a pile against the wall. This arrangement of the debris together with the complete absence of written fragments seems to point, in the opinion of de Vaux, to an ancient ransacking of the cave.[14]

As to the credibility of the events narrated by Timothy, we can safely say that there is no reason to doubt the good faith of the venerable Patriarch. He was convinced that the story he was telling was true.[15]

Jaʿqūb al-Qirqisānī

The famous Qaraite scholar, Jaʿqūb al-Qirqisānī (flourished in the first half of the 10th century), in his *Kitāb al-Anwār wal-Marāqib* ("The Book of Lights and Watch-Towers"), written in 937–938,[16] mentions some significant details that add to the credibility of Timothy's letter.[17] A. de Harkavy, who in 1894 published part of "The Book of Lights ...", states that the treatise is one of the earliest and most trustworthy of all the accounts of the Jewish sects of Saadia's time.[18] Nemoy adds that it is also the most detailed and accurate.[19]

In enumerating the old Jewish sects, Qirqisānī mentions after the Samaritans, Pharisees, and Sadducees, but before the Christians, a Jewish sect about which he writes:

[14] "Exploration de la région de Qumrân", *RB*, 60 (1953), 560. Kahle, *Cairo Geniza*, 16f., thinks it probable that Qumrân Cave I is the cave that Timothy refers to.

[15] Cf. de Vaux, "A propos des manuscrits de la Mer Morte", 419.

[16] Baron, *op. cit.*, 398, n. 27. For a recent history of the Qaraites, cf. *ibid.*, 209–285.

[17] D. Barthélemy brought Qirqisānī's interesting comments to the attention of de Vaux; the latter then became the first to show the relevance of Qirqisānī's witness to the events narrated by Timothy; cf. de Vaux, "A propos des manuscrits ...", 421f. Cf. also Kahle, *Cairo Geniza*, 24f.

[18] Cited by L. Nemoy, "Al-Qirqisānī's Account of the Jewish Sects and Christianity", *HUCA*, 7 (1930), 317; cf. *idem*, "Kirkisani, Jacob", *Universal Jewish Encyclopedia*, 6 (New York, 1942), 397.

[19] *Ibid.*

> Thereupon appeared the teaching of a sect called Maġarians [al-maġārīya]; they were called so because their (sacred) books were found in a cave [maġār]. One of them is the Alexandrian[20] whose book is famous and (widely) known; it is the most important of the books of the Maġarians. Next to it (in importance) is a small booklet entitled "The Book of Yaddua," also a fine work. As of the rest of the Maġarian books, most of them are of no value and resemble mere tales.[21]

In other passages of "The Book of Lights ...", Qirqisānī also mentions the Maġarians or "Cave People". For example, he writes:

> The Maġarians fix the beginning of months by the appearance of the new [*sic*] moon. They adduce certain reasons in support of this (method); we shall mention them when we come to the discourse on the beginning of months and its indications. It is said that there are among them some who think that laughter is unlawful. Their interpretations of some passages in the Scriptures are altogether improbable and resemble foolish talk. Daūd ibn Marwān al-Muqammiṣ says in one of his books that the Sadducees ascribe corporeality to God and understand all the Scriptural descriptions of Him which imply anthropomorphism in their literal sense. The Maġarians are said to be opposed to this, i.e., they do not profess anthropomorphism; yet they also do not take these descriptions (of God) out of their literal meaning, but assert instead that these descriptions refer to one of the angels, namely to the one

[20] The identification of this Alexandrian is problematical. W. Bacher, "Qirqisānī, the Karaite, and His Work on Jewish Sects", *JQR*, 7 (1894–1895), 703, agrees with Harkavy in thinking that this is Philo. S. Poznanski, "Philon dans l'ancienne littérature judéo-arabe", *REJ*, 50 (1905), 10–31, also defends this identification. But Nemoy, "Al-Qirqisānī's Account ...", 327, n. 24, rejects the identification with Philo in these words: "... Philo wrote more than one book, and his works were hardly 'famous and widely known' among Arabic speaking Jews in Western Persia; we have nothing to show that an Arabic translation of any of Philo's works was ever made." De Vaux, "A propos des manuscrits ...", 425, also argues against the identification with Philo.

[21] Translation by Nemoy, "Al-Qirqisānī's Account ...", 326f.; cf. *ibid.*, 327, n. 26, for comments on "The Book of Yaddua". A partial translation into French can be found in Poznanski, *art. cit.*, 14; for a full French translation, see de Vaux, "A propos des manuscrits ...", 421.

> who created the world. This (opinion) is similar to the view of Benjamin al-Nahāwandī[22] which we shall explain later.[23]

Near the end of his account of the Jewish sects, Qirqisānī writes:

> These are all the doctrines of the dissenters who appeared (among the Jews) down to the present time, according to the information which we have received. Some of these sects have disappeared, e.g., the Maġarians and the Sadducees ....[24]

Later in "The Book of Lights ..." Qirqisānī gives more information which he promised in one of the quotations above:

> (The Maġarians) think that God, may his praise be glorious, created all material beings perfect and entire in the first moments of creation, as, for example, Adam and Eve, and other animals. For He created each one complete in its body; so also plants, trees, and the like. He created the body of each of the two luminaries, namely, the sun and the moon, along with all the stars, according to the ultimate degree of their possible perfection. And (the Maġarians) offer as proof that the moon was created perfect and entire the text: "As the moon remains forever ..." [Ps 89, 38]. And so when the world was created perfect and complete, the moon also was created perfect at the moment when it was created. Moreover, they say that the Bible names the two luminaries at the moment of their creation, "the large ones" [Gn 1, 16]. This (creation) took place on a Wednesday, and there is no doubt that this was the first day of the month, and that they [the sun and the moon] were created at the limit of their magnitude, since He calls them the two large ones. When the moon is full, it is largest and greatest; and we know that when it is full, that day is the first day of the month.[25]

[22] See Nemoy, "Al-Qirqisānī's Account...", 386f., for the details of Nahāwandī's teachings.

[23] *Ibid.*, 363f. Nemoy's translation of the phrase, *'idā 'abdara l-hilāl* ("when the crescent becomes full"), is wrong. The French translations of Poznanski, *art. cit.*, 14, and of de Vaux, "A propos des manuscrits ...", 421, correctly employ the translation "full moon" in place of "new moon".

[24] Translation by Nemoy, "Al-Qirqisānī's Account ...", 391.

[25] Nemoy (ed.), *Ya'qūb al-Qirqisānī, Kitāb al-Anwār wal-Marāqib*, 4 (New York, 1942), 796f. The writer is grateful to Dr. Richard M. Frank of the Catholic University of America for assistance in translating this passage as well

Another Jew, Hadassi by name, who lived in the twelfth century, also mentions the "men of the caves", but he has as his source Qirqisānī; hence, his witness is secondary and of little value.[26]

Shahrastānī

Now two Moslem authors lend considerable support to the testimony given above. The first is Shahrastānī (1076–1153), the principal scholar of the history of religions in the Middle Ages.[27] In the famous work, *Kitāb al-Milal wan-Niḥal* ("The Book of Religions and Sects"), which was composed in 1127,[28] he writes:

> But one sect of the Maqāriba [vocalized muqāriba by Badrān] claims that God spoke to the prophets, may peace be upon them, through the agency of an angel whom He had elected and whom He had given precedence over all creatures and had appointed viceroy over them. They say: "Every description of God in the Torah and in the rest of the Books is an account (given) on the authority of this angel. For otherwise it would not be possible to describe God in any way at all." They also say: "Furthermore, he who addressed Moses, may peace be upon him, is that angel. And God the exalted One is too exalted to address in human fashion mortal man ...." And it is stated that when Arius [died 336 A.D.] says that the Messiah is God and is the most perfect one in the world, he takes this statement from the (Maqāriba); they preceded Arius by 400 years. They were men of asceticism and mortification.[29]

as the texts of Shahrastānī and al-Bīrūnī given below. A French translation of most of this material can be found in de Vaux, "A propos des manuscrits ...", 422; de Vaux incorrectly gives Gn 1, 14 as the citation from Genesis.

26 Poznanski, *art. cit.*, 14; cf. also de Vaux, "A propos des manuscrits ...", 422.

27 B. Carra de Vaux, "Al Shahrastānī, Muḥammad b. ʿAbd al-Karīm", *Encyclopédie de l'Islām*, 4 (Leiden-Paris, 1934), 272.

28 *Ibid.*

29 Translated from the Arabic text in M. Badrān (ed.), *Kitāb al-Milal wan-Niḥal*, 1 (Cairo, 1910), 510ff. The Arabic text can also be found in W. Cureton (ed.), *Book of Religions and Philosophical Sects, by Muhammad al-Sharastani*, part 1 (London, 1892), 169. Badrān's edition is, however, superior to Cureton's. For French translations cf. Poznanski, *art. cit.*, 15f., and R. de Vaux, "A propos des manuscrits ...", 422.

al-Bīrūnī

The second Moslem author is al-Bīrūnī (973–1050?),[30] "one of the greatest scholars of mediaeval Islam, and certainly the most original and profound."[31] In his great work, *Āṯār al-Bākiya* ("The Chronology of the Past"), composed in about the year 1000, he writes:

> 'Abū-ʿĪsā al-Warrāq [died about the end of the ninth century] reports in his *Kitāb al-Maqālāt*[32] of a type of Jews, called the Maġāriba [variant: Maqāriba], who allege that feasts are not licit, save when the moon rises full on a Wednesday night, namely, the night following Tuesday's sunset, in the land of the Israelites. This is the beginning of the new year. From (the full moon) are calculated days and months; and according to it, the feasts follow on a cycle. For God the exalted One created the two major luminaries on a Wednesday. (The Maġāriba) likewise do not allow the Passover except on a Wednesday, nor do they impose the obligations and customs thereof, save upon one who dwells in the land of the Israelites.[33]

As is clear from simply reading the texts quoted above, Qirqisānī, Shahrastānī, and al-Bīrūnī are all referring to the same Jewish sect. The various orthographies of the sect's name can be easily accounted for on the basis of misreading the Arabic consonants in question. Qirqisānī's *al-maġārīya* is certainly the correct spelling,

[30] The date of al-Bīrūnī's death is usually fixed at 1048, but actually he must have died after 1050; for details, cf. D. J. Boilot, "Al-Bīrūnī (Bērūnī) Abu'l-Rayḥān Muḥammad b. Aḥmad", *The Encyclopaedia of Islam*, 1, new ed. (Leiden-London, 1960), 1236.

[31] *Ibid.*

[32] C. Brockelmann, *Geschichte der arabischen Literatur, Supplement*, 1 (Leiden, 1937), 341f., lists no MSS or editions of this work. It is, however, 'Abū ʿĪsā's main work, which served as an important source for many Islamic writers; for details, cf. S. M. Stern, "Abū ʿĪsā Muḥammad b. Hārūn al-Warrāḳ", *The Encyclopaedia of Islam*, 1, 130.

[33] Translated from the Arabic text found in C. E. Sachau (ed.), *Chronologie orientalischer Völker von Albērūnī* (Leipzig, 1876–1878), 284. An English translation is likewise provided by Sachau in *The Chronology of Ancient Nations. An English Version of the Arabic Text of the Athār-ul-Bâkiya of Albīrūnī* (London, 1879), 278; but since Sachau's translation is, in the opinion of the present writer, inconsistent in parts, it was decided to make a fresh translation from the Arabic. Poznanski, *art. cit.*, 16f., and R. de Vaux, "A propos des manuscrits ...", 423, give French translations of this passage.

for as he explains, the "Cave People" were so called because their sacred books were found in a *maġār*, a cave.

In Shahrastānī's *maqāriba*, the *ġain* was incorrectly read as a *qāf*, and the *yā* as a *bā*: two mistakes that are not difficult to make, since medial *ġain* and *qāf* are so alike in shape, and medial (and initial) *yā* and *bā* differ only in the diacritical marks. Al-Bīrūnī's *maġāriba* with its variant, *maqāriba*, is to be explained in like manner.[34]

Both Qirqisānī and Shahrastānī state explicitly that the sect of the "Cave People" existed in the pre- or early Christian era: Qirqisānī places the sect, as we noted above, after the Sadducees but before the Christians and states that it was extinct in his own time; Shahrastānī says that the sect preceded Arius by 400 years.

Qirqisānī relates that the books of the sect were found in a cave. Could this statement be a reference to the discovery of books in a cave that Timothy speaks of? R. de Vaux,[35] Rowley,[36] and Kahle[37] think it quite likely. And the present writer agrees. The fact that Qirqisānī makes no allusion to any biblical MSS that were found in the cave, whereas Timothy was interested only in the biblical texts, is not hard to understand. The former writer discussed only the non-canonical texts for the evidence they afforded concerning the beliefs of the sect; the latter author was not concerned with the various Jewish sects and their literature, but with only biblical texts.[38] That Qirqisānī and Timothy both refer to the same discovery of books in a cave, is probable also by reason of the fact that no reference to the sect of the "Cave People" prior to the time of Timothy has thus far been produced.[39]

The evidence adduced up to this point seems to warrant the following conclusions: (1) biblical as well as non-biblical MSS written in Hebrew were recovered about 800 A.D. from a cave in the vicinity of Jericho (Timothy); (2) the non-biblical texts belonged to a

[34] Poznanski, *art. cit.*, 16, mentions that the fourth possibility, *maqārīya*, is also found in some Arabic writers.

[35] "A propos des manuscrits ...", 423f.

[36] *Op. cit.*, 23ff.

[37] *Cairo Geniza*, 24.

[38] Cf. R. de Vaux, "A propos des manuscrits ...", 423f.; Rowley, *op. cit.*, 23f.

[39] Rowley, *op. cit.*, 24.

Jewish sect which indulged in fanciful interpretations of Sacred Scripture (Qirqisānī), and practiced a rigid asceticism (Shahrastānī); (3) the sect had its own peculiar calendar which fixed on a Wednesday the beginning of the new year and the celebration of the Passover (al-Bīrūnī); (4) the sect flourished at about the beginning of the Christian era (Qirqisānī, Shahrastānī); (5) the sect was already extinct by 937 A.D. (Qirqisānī).

A question which comes to mind quite naturally at this point is this: is there any connection between the MS find of about 800 A.D. and the Qumrân discoveries dating from 1947? That there is such a connection is considered possible by Rowley,[40] probable by R. de Vaux,[41] and practically certain by Kahle.[42] We agree with Kahle. The following analysis will, it is hoped, show the reasonableness of this view.

The caves of Qumrân, only a few miles from Jericho, have produced innumerable fragments of biblical as well as non-biblical MSS written in Hebrew, Aramaic, and Greek. The cave Timothy speaks of yielded many MSS of biblical and non-biblical texts written in Hebrew.

The non-biblical MSS of Qumrân belonged to the Essenes who lived a quasi-monastic life. In its exegesis this sect at times made fantastic applications to contemporary history. This feature becomes obvious from a simple reading of the sect's commentaries on Na, Hb, Mi, and Ps 37. The non-biblical texts of Timothy's cave were said to belong to a Jewish sect whose "interpretation of some passages in the Scriptures are altogether improbable and resemble foolish talk" (Qirqisānī); the members of the sect were "men of asceticism and mortification" (Shahrastānī).

The problems of the Essene calendar are too involved[43] to merit detailed treatment here, but from the study of competent scholars two features of this calendar are certain: (1) the new year began on

[40] *Ibid.*, 22–29.

[41] "A propos des manuscrits ...", 424ff.

[42] *Cairo Geniza*, 16ff.

[43] Cf. D. Barthélemy, "Notes en marge de publications récentes sur les manuscrits de Qumrân", *RB*, 59 (1952), 199–203; F. M. Cross, *The Ancient Library of Qumran and Modern Biblical Studies* (New York, 1958), 36, and the literature cited there; also Milik, *Ten Years ...*, 107–113.

Wednesday,[44] and (2) the Passover was celebrated also on a Wednesday.[45] In the calendar of the "Cave People" sect the new year and the Passover also fell on a Wednesday (al-Bīrūnī).

The Essenes flourished in the first two centuries before Christ and became extinct some time after the turn of the Christian era.[46] The "Cave People" sect also prospered about the time of Christ (Qirqisānī, Shahrastānī) and was extinct at least by the tenth century (Qirqisānī).

In our opinion it seems inconceivable that the similarities between the Essenes and the "Cave People" result from mere coincidence. True, there are some tenets of the "Cave People" – certain aspects of their angelology (see above) – that are not found in the Qumrân fragments thus far recovered. But the teachings in question became known to the medieval Jews from the MSS discovered in 800; hence, Qumrân texts expounding doctrines of a similar nature may never come to light, if the MSS of 800 were the only copies which contained those doctrines.

Granting that the cave discovered about 800 A.D. is one of the caves near Khirbet Qumrân, and that the "Cave People" sect can plausibly be identified with the Essenes, the reader may rightly ask: what has all this to do with the authenticity of the Cairo text of Sir?

C. THE JERICHO CAVE AND THE GENIZA HEBREW OF SIRACH

It is our contention that the Geniza Hebrew of Sir came from the Jericho cave, for this text seems to have been virtually unknown in Jewish circles from shortly after the Synod of Jamnia in the last decade of the first century A.D., when the rabbis succeeded in suppressing the Book, till the ninth century, in the latter part of which Saadia Gaon employed several quotations from Sir that correspond exactly to the Geniza text. If this text came from the Jericho

[44] Barthélemy, *art. cit.*, 200; Milik, *Ten Years* . . ., 107.

[45] Barthélemy, *art. cit.*, 200; Milik, *Ten Years* . . ., 112.

[46] The origin and final outcome of the Essenes are not clear; cf. L. Marchal, "Esséniens", *VDBS*, 2 (Paris, 1934), 1111 and 1124; Cross, *op. cit.*, 90ff.; Milik, *Ten Years* . . ., 49–97. For the Essene occupation at Qumrân, Milik accepts (p. 97) as termini 150 B.C.–68 A.D., with a hiatus of about 30 years during Herod's reign.

(Qumrân) cave, then it must be authentic since it presumably antedates 68 A.D.

By assuming that the Hebrew MSS of Sir – as well as many other fragments recovered from the Cairo Geniza – were copied from texts that came to light in 800 from the cave near Jericho, and that this cave had been used centuries earlier by the Essenes of Qumrân, we can reasonably and coherently account for a series of facts that seem to defy explanation otherwise:

1. The larger Qumrân Cave II fragment of the Hebrew text of Sir, which we spoke of in a previous section, matches the wording of MS A and is stichometrically arranged like MSS B and E from the Geniza.

2. The text of portions of the *Damascus Document*, recovered from Qumrân Caves IV, V, and VI, is substantially identical with the *A* recension of that document found in the Cairo Geniza. Moreover, fragments of an Aramaic *Testament of Levi* from Qumrân Caves I and IV give a text which is the same as that found in the Geniza MSS of that same *Testament*.

3. Saadia Gaon quotes 26 hemistichs of Sir in Hebrew; these quotations coincide virtually word for word with the text of the Cairo MSS. But most of the other rabbinical citations of Sir are quite free or but slightly resemble the Cairo text.

4. The confusion of *waw* and *yod* in the Geniza copies of the *Damascus Document* and the Hebrew MSS of Sir, cannot be explained on the basis of medieval paleography which sharply distinguishes between these two letters. The confusion must have already existed in the exemplars of these texts.

5. Whether authentic or not, the short psalm between vv. 12 and 13 of chap. 51 of Sir in Hebrew dates from pre-Christian times.

We must examine in detail each of the last four items.

The Damascus Document and the Testament of Levi

The Jerusalem Jews who examined the texts recovered from the Jericho cave were largely from the sect or party of the Qaraites. Though this sect began in Babylonia a few years after the middle of the eighth century A.D., it soon won adherents in Jerusalem which before long became the spiritual center of the Qaraites.[47] J. Mann, an authority on the sect, writes: "Ḳaraism seems to have attained a commanding lead in Jerusalem in the second half of the 9th century."[48] The logical explanation of this remarkable success seems to be:

> ... the fact that the Ḳaraites had come into possession of old material which they studied eagerly and successfully, whereas the Rabbanite circles took little notice of it because it did not fit in with their teachings. This material would appear to have been the MS scrolls brought to Jerusalem about the year 800 from the cave near Jericho.[49]

Now if the MSS found in 800 have as their source the Essene community of Qumrân, we can plausibly account for the remarkable similarities that exist between the Qaraites and the Essenes. As Kahle reports,[50] M. Zucker demonstrated the influence that the *Damascus Document*, two recensions of which (*A* and *B*) were recovered from the Cairo Geniza,[51] must have had on Daniel el-Qūmisī, a prominent Qaraite who flourished in Jerusalem in the middle of the ninth century. Indeed, the *Damascus Document* was so instrumental in the evolution of Qaraite doctrine that S. Zeitlin, evaluating the evidence in reverse, attributed the document to the Qaraites who, he claimed, wished to prove for the purpose of propaganda the antiquity of their sect.[52] The pre-Christian dating of the *Damascus Document* is now, however, beyond question,

[47] Kahle, *Cairo Geniza*, 17.

[48] *Texts and Studies in Jewish History and Literature*, 2: *Ḳaraitica* (Philadelphia, 1935), 7; cf. also pp. 3–7.

[49] Kahle, *Cairo Geniza*, 17.

[50] *Ibid.*, 18.

[51] S. Schechter published the *Damascus Document* in *Fragments of a Zadokite Work* (= *Documents of Jewish Sectaries*, 1) (Cambridge, 1910), a harshly, but justly, criticized edition, which provided only two facsimiles. The latest, and by far the best, edition of the *Document* is that of C. Rabin, *The Zadokite Documents. I: The Admonition. II: The Laws*, 2d rev. ed. (Oxford, 1958); pp. xiii–xvi contain a useful bibliography.

[52] *The Zadokite Fragments. Facsimile of the Manuscripts in the Cairo Genizah Collection in the Possession of the University Library, Cambridge, England* (= *JQR Monograph Series*, 1) (Philadelphia, 1952), 23. Zeitlin is also well known for his untenable views regarding the dating of the Dead Sea Scrolls; cf. P. W. Skehan, "Communication: Professor Zeitlin and the Dead Sea Scrolls", *CBQ*, 20 (1958), 228f.

thanks to the discovery of the *Manual of Discipline*, and especially to the identification of copies of the *Damascus Document* in Caves IV, V, and VI at Qumrân. The Qumrân MSS offer a text which is substantially identical with that of the *A* recension recovered from the Cairo Geniza, although there are some noteworthy additions.[53] The oldest Qumrân copy (4QD^{b}) is to be dated between 75 and 50 B.C., according to Milik.[54]

Where did the medieval Qaraites obtain the *Damascus Document*, a text that must have remained unknown for some 700 years? The most likely source seems to be the cave spoken of by Timothy. And since the Geniza of the Qaraite Synagogue in Old Cairo yielded the Hebrew fragments of Sir as well as the *Damascus Document*, it appears probable that both works came from the Jericho (Qumrân) Cave. Indeed, Kahle writes:

> The survival of [the Zadokite fragment and the Hebrew text of Sirach] in the time of the Mishna and Talmud has been a great problem, and we are undoubtedly right in assuming that these texts of the Geniza were copies of manuscripts found in the cave near Jericho in the 8th century.[55]

Further evidence from Qumrân in support of the hypothesis that the text of the Sir fragments from Cairo was at one time in the Essene library, is furnished by fragments of an Aramaic *Testament of Levi* from Caves I and IV.[56] As is well known, the Cairo Geniza has also produced some MSS of this Aramaic *Testament*,[57] which date from the eleventh century, possibly earlier.[58] Now the text of

[53] Milik, *Ten Years* ..., 38; cf. further Baillet, "Fragments du Document de Damas. Qumrân, Grotte 6", *RB*, 63 (1956), 513–523: between pp. 512–513, facsimiles of the Cave VI fragments are supplied.

[54] *Ten Years* ..., 38f., 125; cf. also additional note 3, pp. 151f.

[55] "The Age of the Scrolls", 48.

[56] The Cave I fragments were published by Barthélemy-Milik, *Qumran Cave I*, 88–91; plate XVII provides excellent facsimiles. The Cave IV fragments were published by Milik, "Le Testament de Lévi en araméen", *RB*, 62 (1955), 400; plate IV contains the facsimiles.

[57] The Geniza MSS were published by H. L. Pass-J. Arendzen, "Fragment of an Aramaic Text of the Testament of Levi", *JQR*, 12 (1899–1900), 651–661; and by A. E. Cowley-R. H. Charles, "An Early Source of the Testaments of the Patriarchs", *JQR*, 19 (1906–1907), 569–577 (an English translation is offered on pp. 577–583). Cf. P. Grelot, "Notes sur le Testament araméen de Lévi", *RB*, 63 (1956), 391.

[58] Cowley-Charles, *art. cit.*, 566.

the Qumrân copies of the *Testament of Levi*, which copies antedate 68 A.D.,[59] is identical with that of the Geniza MSS.[60] It seems likely, therefore, that the Hebrew text of Sir from the Geniza, like the text of the Cairo *Testament of Levi*, also was at Qumrân.

Saadia Gaon

Saadia Gaon (882–942)[61] furnishes striking circumstantial evidence that the Jericho (Qumrân) cave yielded copies of the Hebrew text of Sir. In his *Sēper ha-gālûy*, written during the years of his seclusion (931–934) after he had been temporarily suspended from the gaonate by the Exilarch David ben Zakkai,[62] Saadia quotes 26 hemistichs of Sir in Hebrew. In 25 of these – Sir 3, 21–22 (4 hemistichs); 5, 5–6 (6); 6, 6–8 (6); 6, 13 (2); 11, 28c–d (2); 13, 11d (1); 16, 17 (4) – his citations are practically identical with the text of MS A; only once – Sir 13, 11c – is the quotation not literal, but merely *ad sensum*.

This fact is quite significant, for of the other rabbinical quotations of Sir only 19 hemistichs out of a total of 106 match the wording of the Geniza Hebrew, the other 87 hemistichs being very free or merely paraphrases that but slightly resemble the Cairo Hebrew.[63] It seems highly probable, therefore, that most of the rabbis before Saadia did not possess an authentic text of Sir, but for their use of the Book had to rely upon oral tradition or upon

[59] The Cave IV fragments date from the end of the second century or beginning of the first century B.C.; so Milik, *art. cit.*, 399. The Cave I fragments are probably Herodian, or in any case antedate 68 A.D.

[60] Milik, *Ten Years* ..., 34.

[61] The year 892 has been wrongly transmitted by an early historian as the date of Saadia's birth. This date has been given in many studies of Saadia; cf., for example, H. Malter, *Saadia Gaon: His Life and Works* (Philadelphia, 1921), 25; A. E. Cowley, "Seadiah, Ben Joseph", *Encyclopaedia Britannica*, 20 (Chicago, 1947), 239. From the rich materials recovered from the Cairo Geniza, "we know now that Saadia was born in 882, between the 27th of June and the 5th of July"; so A. Marx, "Rab Saadia Gaon", in *Essays in Jewish Biography* (Philadelphia, 1947), 6f. Cf. also R. Gordis, "Saadia ben Joseph", *Universal Jewish Encyclopedia*, 9 (New York, 1942), 289.

[62] Malter, *op. cit.*, 269.

[63] For the rabbinical quotations of Sir we have used the compilation which is found in A. E. Cowley-A. Neubauer, *The Original Hebrew of a Portion of Ecclesiasticus* (Oxford, 1897), xix–xxx.

badly transmitted florilegia, the reason being that the cave near Jericho had not yet been discovered.

Now we must take into account the following considerations:

1. Saadia left Egypt, where he was born, about the year 915, or perhaps earlier, and lived for some time in Palestine. What he did there and precisely how long he stayed, we cannot be certain. But there is evidence that some of his works were written in Palestine, and that he remained there at least a few years.[64] It is quite probable that during this period of his life, Saadia first came in personal contact with the Qaraites,[65] whose center was, as we have seen above, in Jerusalem. It is not impossible that at this time Saadia also received a copy of the Hebrew text of Sir from the Jerusalem Qaraites who, as we can reasonably suppose, recovered the text from the Jericho (Qumrân) cave.

2. The existence of some Persian glosses in the margins of MS B (see the margins at Sir 32, 1; 35, 26; 40, 22; and 45, 9) points "to its having been written in Bagdad or Persia".[66] Now in 928 the Exilarch David ben Zakkai, whose official seat was in Bagdad, appointed Saadia to the supreme scholastic office of gaon of the Academy in Sura (Babylonia), which is situated in southeastern Mesopotamia. Saadia held this position, except for a brief period of three years (see above), till his death in 942.[67] Thus if he did not receive a copy of the Hebrew text of Sir in Palestine, it is possible that he came in contact with part of the text represented in the Geniza fragments on one of his trips to Bagdad or during his gaonate in Sura.

3. Saadia wrote his *Sēper ha-gālûy*, of which only fragments exist, in a highly rhetorical style, divided it into verses, and vocalized and accentuated it after the manner of a biblical text.[68] The Qaraites, among others, were shocked by the arrogance and irreverence

[64] Malter, *op. cit.*, 56 and 65f.; Marx, *art. cit.*, 8; A. A. Neuman, "Saadia and His Relation to Palestine", *JQR*, n. s., 33 (1942–1943), 130f.

[65] It is not clear whether the Qaraite movement had as yet spread into Egypt. Cf. Marx, *art. cit.*, 8; Malter, *op. cit.*, 66.

[66] Cowley-Neubauer, *op. cit.*, xiii.

[67] Baron, *op. cit.*, 21.

[68] Cf. S. Schechter, *Saadyana: Geniza Fragments of Writings of R. Saadya Gaon and Others* (Cambridge, 1903), 1; on pp. 4–7 are found Hebrew fragments of Saadia's work.

evident in Saadia's imitation of the Sacred Text. Consequently, Saadia wrote another work to justify himself against the accusation of impiety leveled against him. He states that the division of his text into verses and the addition of vowel-points and accents, are merely aids to the reading and understanding of a Hebrew book. He then mentions several whom he considered post-biblical authors who did the very same thing, yet who were not censured; among these Sir is named.[69] Hence, Saadia must have possessed a copy of at least a portion of Sir that was furnished with vowels and accents.[70]

4. Many verses in the Cairo MSS of Sir also have vowel-points and accents. See, for example, the facsimiles of 9, 3–4 (MS A); 10, 2 (MS A); 11, 6–8 (MS A); and 37, 3 (MS D).

From the preceding observations as well as from his exact quotations of Sir, it seems perfectly reasonable to conclude that Saadia had before him a text of the Book which was basically the same as that of MS A from the Cairo Geniza. The most plausible explanation as to why Saadia had a correct text of Sir, whereas the other rabbis generally did not, is that the venerable Gaon received a copy of the Sir text that had been recovered from the (Qumrân) cave near Jericho in about the year 800.

Confusion of waw *and* yod

In medieval Hebrew paleography there is an unmistakable distinction between *waw* and *yod*. This fact becomes perfectly obvious from even a rapid examination of the excellent Oxford and Cambridge facsimiles[71] of Cairo MSS A, B, C, and D which date from the ninth to the twelfth century. Even the miserably poor facsimiles[72]

[69] Malter, *op. cit.*, 269f.; Marx, *art. cit.*, 21f.

[70] Cf. C. Roth, "Ecclesiasticus in the Synagogue Service", *JBL*, 71 (1952), 171.

[71] *Facsimiles of the Fragments Hitherto Recovered of the Book of Ecclesiasticus in Hebrew* (Oxford-Cambridge, 1901); for facsimiles of the latest leaves of MSS B and C, cf. Di Lella, "The Recently Identified Leaves of Sirach in Hebrew", *Bib*, 45 (1964), between pp. 154 and 155.

[72] J. Marcus, *The Newly Discovered Original Hebrew of Ben Sira (Ecclesiasticus xxxii, 16–xxxiv, 1): The Fifth Manuscript and a Prosodic Version of Ben Sira (Ecclesiasticus xxii, 22–xxiii, 9)* (Philadelphia, 1931), facing pp. 12 and 13. This work is a corrected reprint of the article which appeared originally in *JQR*, n. s., 21 (1930–1931), 223–240.

of the one leaf of MS E, dating from the same general period as the others and stichometrically written in a cursive, medium hand, show the clear difference that exists between these two letters.

With the texts recovered from the Qumrân Caves, however, the situation is otherwise. In many of these documents the shapes of *waw* and *yod* differ but slightly, if indeed at all. In describing *waw* and *yod* in the formal Hasmonaean script (150–ca. 30 B.C.) from Qumrân, F. M. Cross, one of the few authorities in Hebrew paleography, writes:

> In the late Hasmonaean script, the curled head [of *waw*] becomes an angular hook, often shaded so that a triangular effect is given. The latter development of the head of *waw* parallels the development of *yod* so that the heads of *waw* and *yod* become virtually identical in some (but not all) scripts of the early Herodian period [30 B.C.–70 A.D.]. The ligaturing of *waw* and especially *yod* with the preceding letter becomes increasingly frequent in the late Hasmonaean era, continuing on, of course, into the Herodian scripts.[73]
>
> The *yod* regularly is attached by ligatures to the preceding letter; this creates a lengthened right leg in ligatured forms, and often the ligatured form influences the independent form, so that *yod* and *waw* become easily confused, each having a fairly long right leg. In the scribe's mind, however, though often not reflected in his pen, the head or left leg (as the case may be) of *yod* extends farther to the left than in the case of *waw*.[74]

Now Schechter noted when he published the *Damascus Document* that "there is very little consistency in such letters as *waw*, *yod* . . ., the *yod* is sometimes so large as to be confused with a *waw*."[75] And Rabin in his model edition of the *Document* confesses:

> I have not always been able to distinguish with confidence between *yod* and *waw*; it seems to me that the copyist often

[73] "The Development of the Jewish Scripts", in *The Bible and the Ancient Near East* [*Essays in honor of William Foxwell Albright*], ed. by G. E. Wright (New York, 1961), 168f.

[74] *Ibid.*, 170. See also Cross's excellent hand drawings of the various scripts in question, pp. 138f.

[75] *Fragments of a Zadokite Work*, ix.

> purposely wrote something in between the two because the manuscript from which he copied (as we know now from the Dead Sea Scrolls) did not distinguish between them at all, and he was doubtful which of the two was meant.[76]

We submit the following as instances of the phenomena that Rabin speaks of, and of actual misreadings of *waw* for *yod* or vice versa, because the *Vorlage* of the medieval scribe did not clearly distinguish between these two letters; the plate numbers refer to the poor, but serviceable facsimiles given in Zeitlin's *The Zadokite Fragments*.

1. Plate II, *l.* 16, the *yod* in ועני.

2. Plate III, *l.* 5, the *waw* in להועץ. The *waw* is so much like a *yod* that both Rabin and Schechter in their respective editions transcribe it as a *yod*. But since יעץ is a verb whose primitive first radical was *waw*, as the Arabic equivalent demonstrates, the niphal infinitive construct should restore the *waw*. Hence, להועץ is the only correct orthography.

3. Plate IV, *l.* 1, the *yod* in מקדשי.

4. Plate IV, *l.* 12, the first *waw* in מצודו; compare with the *yod* of ותפצי of plate III, *l.* 15.

5. Plate IV, *l.* 12, the *waw* in החוק; compare this *waw* with the *yod* of יהודה in the line above it.

6. Plate IV, *l.* 17, the *yod* in ההין which is a mistake, for the sense obviously requires ההון.

7. Plate V, *l.* 15, כהר ביתו, which as Rabin correctly observes,[77] should be read as כהרבותו.

There is no need to multiply examples, of which there are many, for the few cited above supply enough evidence to justify the conclusion that the *Vorlage* of the medieval scribe was not clear in its distinction between *waw* and *yod*. How can we reasonably account for this? The best explanation, the writer submits, is that the text of the *Vorlage* in question came from the (Qumrân) Jericho cave. The Qumrân Cave VI fragments of the *Damascus Document*[78] pro-

[76] *The Zadokite Documents*, viii.

[77] *Ibid.*, 21.

[78] Published by Baillet, "Fragments du Document de Damas . . .", plate II facing p. 512.

vide striking confirmation for this hypothesis. In fragment 3, for example, compare the *waw* of הקודש (*l.* 4) with the *yod* of ישראל (*l.* 3) or of ברית (*l.* 5); the shapes of these two letters are virtually identical in the examples given.

What can be said of *waw* and *yod* in the *Vorlage(n)* of the Cairo MSS of Sir? In answer to that question we call attention to the following illustrative examples of confusion between *waw* and *yod* that must have existed in the *Vorlage(n)* of the Geniza fragments; for the convenience of the reader, these examples are taken from the Oxford and Cambridge facsimiles,[79] which, since they are not numbered, we shall refer to by citing the first and last verse contained in each.

1. MS A [4, 10c–5, 10a], *l.* 23 (5, 4a) has לי; MS C [4, 23.30. 31; 5, 4–5, 7b], *l.* 5 (5, 4a) reads לו instead.

2. MS A [4, 10c–5, 10a], *l.* 26 (5, 6d) has ינוח (qal); MS C [4, 23.30.31; 5, 4–5, 7b], *l.* 11 (5, 6d) reads יניח (hiphil).

3. MS B [30, 25–31, 11], *l.* 8 (31, 5a) has חרוץ (gold) in the body of the text (a reading that is certainly correct), but the margin contains instead חריץ (slice, portion of cheese or the like; or some sort of iron implement), which is just as clearly incorrect.

4. MS B [31, 22–31, 31], *l.* 8 (31, 26a) reads בוחן (prove, test, try), which the context shows to be correct, whereas the margin has ביתן (palace).

5. MS A [13, 7b–14, 11b], *l.* 21 (14, 1b); MS B [30, 11–30, 24], *l.* 14 (30, 21a) and *l.* 17 (30, 23c); MS B [36, 24–37, 9], *l.* 10 (37, 2a); MS D [36, 29–37, 12], *l.* 5 (37, 2a); and MS B [38, 13 to 38, 27b], *l.* 8 (38, 18a) – all incorrectly read דין (judgment) in place of דון (grief, sorrow), a reading that the context in each case appears to favor and that the Greek version reflects (cf. above p. 73).

6. MS B [40, 9–40, 26b], *l.* 4 (40, 13a) has מחול אל חול (from sand/shore to sand/shore), a reading followed by the CCD translation; the margin has חיל מחיל (wealth [which comes] from

[79] See note 71 of this chapter. Most of the examples given below are taken from MS B, in the margins of which at least two other hands have written variants. We have found in these margins some variants which coincide with readings given by the four other MSS. Thus from a text-critical point of view, MS B is the most valuable of the Cairo fragments, despite its numerous and, at times inexplicable, doublets (or triplets) and other corruptions.

wealth), a difficult reading, because the second word is probably corrupt; but nevertheless it is noteworthy that the text and margin of this passage differ as to the value of the consonant after *ḥet*.

7. MS B [40, 26c–41, 9], *l*. 10 (41, 2c) reads: איש כושל ינקש בכל (a man who stumbles will strike against everything), but the margin has instead איש כושל ונוקש בכל (a man who stumbles and strikes against everything), a better reading for the context. Presumably the scribe misread *yod* as the initial consonant of the word in question; hence, he read the word as an imperfect tense, a reading which necessitated the dropping out of the medial *waw*.

8. MS B [42, 11e–23b], *l*. 9 (42, 17c) reads אימץ אלהים (God gives strength); the margin has אומץ (the strength [of God]), a poorer reading than the former.

9. MS B [42, 24–43, 17b], *l*. 6 (43, 5a) contains the word גדיל (a piel?), which clearly is a mistake; the margin has instead גדול, the correct reading.

These few examples – there are more, of course – seem to prove conclusively that the medieval scribes of the Cairo MSS frequently had trouble identifying with certitude a *waw* or a *yod* in their *Vorlagen*. As in the case of the *Damascus Document*, we submit that the most reasonable explanation is to assume that the text of these *Vorlagen* was recovered in about the year 800 from the (Qumrân) cave near Jericho.

The Psalm between Sir 51, 12 and 13

Between vv. 12 and 13 of chap. 51 of Sir in Hebrew, there is a short psalm – patterned after Ps 136 – the authenticity of which has been open to question,[80] since, among other reasons, it is found in neither

[80] The authenticity of the psalm is upheld by Schechter in the *Introduction* to *The Wisdom of Ben Sira: Portions of the Book Ecclesiasticus from Hebrew Manuscripts in the Cairo Genizah Collection Presented to the University of Cambridge by the Editors*, ed. by S. Schechter-C. Taylor (Cambridge, 1899), 35; I. Abrahams, "Schechter and Taylor's *Wisdom of Ben Sira*", *JQR*, 12 (1899 — 1900), 173f.; J. Touzard, "Nouveaux fragments hébreux de l'Ecclésiastique", *RB*, 9 (1900), 52ff.; R. Smend, *Die Weisheit des Jesus Sirach erklärt* (Berlin, 1906), 503f.; T. Vargha, "De Psalmo hebraico Ecclesiastici c. 51", *Anton*, 10 (1935), 3–10; M. H. Segal, *Sēper ben-Sîrāʾ ha-šālēm*, 2d ed. (Jerusalem, 1958), 356. I. Lévi, *L'Ecclésiastique*, part 2 (Paris, 1901), XLVII–LV, claims that the psalm, while generally authentic, was reworked by the various copyists who

the Greek nor the Syriac version, nor in their daughter translations. But, as the note in the CCD translation correctly indicates: "Though not found in any versions, and therefore of doubtful authenticity, the litany seems from internal evidence to go back to the time of Sirach."

In two adjoining distichs (the eighth and ninth) we read:

> Give thanks to him who makes a horn sprout forth
> for the house of David,
> For his mercy endures forever.
> Give thanks to him who chooses the sons of Ṣadoq
> to act as priests,
> For his mercy endures forever.

The mention of a Davidic Messiah and of the "sons of Ṣadoq" argues for a pre-Christian date of at least these verses, and presumably of the entire psalm.

The doctrine of a Davidic Messiah was prevalent in Ben Sira's time, as we know from the Qumrân literature and from Sir 49, 11 (CCD translation): "How can we fittingly praise Zorobabel, who was like a signet ring on God's right hand?"[81] That the signet ring is a Messianic reference is clear from Ag 2, 23 (CCD translation):

> I will take you, Zorobabel,
> son of Salathiel, my servant, says the LORD,
> And I will set you as a signet ring;
> for I have chosen you, says the LORD of hosts.[82]

---

added some ideas and verses to Ben Sira's original. G. H. Box-W. O. E. Oesterley, "Sirach", in *The Apocrypha and Pseudepigrapha of the Old Testament*, ed. by R. H. Charles, 1 (Oxford, 1913), 514, think that some of the verses may be genuine, but the rest of the psalm was added later; cf., however, p. 277 of the same work. N. Peters, *Das Buch Jesus Sirach oder Ecclesiasticus* (Münster i.W., 1913), 414, agrees with A. Fuchs, *Textkritische Untersuchungen zum hebräischen Ekklesiastikus* (= *Biblische Studien*, 12, 5) (Freiburg i. B., 1907), 103–110, who holds that the psalm, though old, is not original, having been added to the Book before 153 B.C. C. Spicq, "L'Ecclésiastique", in *La Sainte Bible*, ed. by L. Pirot-A. Clamer, 6 (Paris, 1951), 827, maintains that the psalm is not genuine. A. Marmorstein, "Jesus Sirach 51, 12ff.", *ZAW*, 29 (1909), 287–293, thinks the psalm is older than Ben Sira.

[81] The Hebrew (MS B) of this verse is fragmentary but can be reasonably reconstructed from the Greek and from Ag 2, 23.

[82] The CCD note on this verse reads: "This promise to Zorobabel, reversing the punishment of his grandfather (Jer 22, 24), is a continuation of the Messianic hope; cf. Za 6, 11f." Cf. also R. T. Siebeneck, "The Messianism of Aggeus and Proto-Zacharias", *CBQ*, 19 (1957), 317f.

Sir 45, 25 and 47, 11.22 also allude to the Davidic Messiah.

As is well known, Messianism was an important theme in the Qumrân literature. The *Damascus Document*, for example, refers four times to the "Messiah of Aaron and Israel".[83] And in the *Manual of Discipline* we find the phrase "until the coming of a/the prophet and the Messiahs of Aaron and Israel."[84] From these and other passages it becomes clear that the men of Qumrân expected three Messianic persons: the Prophet, the Messiah of Aaron, and the Messiah of Israel.[85] Our concern here is with the third one. Milik points out that the Messiah of Israel corresponds to the traditional Messiah of Judah who would come forth from the royal Davidic line, "for in some texts from Cave IV he is called 'Shoot of David' (cf. Jer. 23.5; 33.15; Zech. 3.8; 6.12)."[86]

As to the "sons of Ṣadoq", we know the lofty esteem they enjoyed from Sir 50, 1–21, in which the last great high priest of the Ṣadoqite line, Simon II (died about 200 B.C.),[87] son of Joḥanan, receives generous praise. And in Sir 45, 24, we read (CCD translation):

Therefore on him [Phinees] again God conferred the right,
in a covenant of friendship, to provide for the sanctuary,
So that he and his descendants
should possess the high priesthood forever.

Ironically enough, Simon's line faltered in his sons, Onias III and Jason. Simon's successor to the high priesthood, Onias III, was strongly opposed to the policy of Hellenization imposed by Antiochus Epiphanes (175–163 B.C.). His brother, Jason, however, was not only willing, but did his best to Hellenize Jewry. In the ensuing struggle for power Jason offered Antiochus a sum of money in return for recognition as high priest in place of his brother. Jason succeeded in obtaining the high priesthood, but the precedent of appealing to Antiochus for appointment to that office sounded the

[83] 12, 23–13, 1; 14, 19; 19, 10–11; 20, 1: in Rabin's edition, pp. 63, 65, 71, 31, 37, respectively.

[84] 9, 11. As regards the interpretation of this phrase, see R. E. Brown, "The Messianism of Qumrân", *CBQ*, 19 (1957), 54–66.

[85] Cf. *ibid.*, 66–82.

[86] *Ten Years* ..., 127.

[87] Cross, *op. cit.*, 97.

death knell for the Ṣadoqite line at the Jerusalem temple. In 152 B.C. the Hasmonaean Jonathan was awarded the high priesthood for his support of Alexander Balas, the Syrian king, and in 140 B.C. the *de facto* rights and privileges which Jonathan enjoyed became *de iure* rights for Simon, Jonathan's brother, and his house. Thus the high priesthood was irrevocably transferred from the Ṣadoqites to the Hasmonaeans.[88]

The Qumrân Community which was established at about this time contained a number of the ousted Ṣadoqite priests. These priests held positions of honor and jurisdiction in the sect, as is clear from the *Manual of Discipline*:

> They [the members of the community] are to abide by the decisions of the sons of Zadok, the same being priests that still keep the Covenant, and of the majority of the community that stand firm in it. It is by the vote of such that all matters doctrinal, economic and judicial are to be determined.[89]
>
> He [the man who seeks after inner vision] is to respect the distinctive rank accorded to the sons of Zadok and to the elect of any specific epoch by virtue of their spiritual attitudes, and to appraise them by that criterion, thus adhering to the will of God, as He has commanded.[90]

Now if Ben Sira himself did not compose the psalm between Sir 51, 12 and 13 – a position which we favor, because the psalm is not contained in any of the versions and does not seem to suit the context – then the words, "Give thanks to him who chooses the sons of Ṣadoq to act as priests", could quite plausibly have been written by a member of the Qumrân sect and placed, together with the rest of the psalm, where we find them in the Cairo text.[91]

[88] *Ibid.*, 97–107.

[89] Translation by T. H. Gaster, *The Dead Sea Scriptures* (New York, 1957), 46.

[90] *Ibid.*, 59.

[91] After the writer came to this conclusion, he was gratified to find that R. E. Brown, *art. cit.*, 63, n. 54, also allows this possibility. Pertinent to the discussion at hand are the words of J. Trinquet, "Les liens 'sadocites' de l'Écrit de Damas, des manuscrits de la Mer Morte et de l'Ecclésiastique", *VT*, 1 (1951), 290: "Authentique ou inauthentique, ce psaume, par sa présence dans les fragments hébreux de l'Ecclésiastique parait indiquer qu'au moins ceux-ci furent entre les mains des 'fils de Sadoq'."

For it appears inconceivable that a person far removed from the turbulent events that marked the second century B.C. would write such words extolling the "sons of Ṣadoq" when the Ṣadoqite priesthood in Jerusalem had ceased to function by 152 B.C.

If this hypothesis is correct, the Cairo text of Sir must have been copied from exemplars that were at one time in the (Qumrân) cave near Jericho.

If, however, the psalm is authentic, we must try to account for its omission from the Greek version, which was made some time after 132 B.C., and the Syriac, which was composed before or during the fourth century A.D. We suggest that the psalm may have been expunged from most of the MSS of Sir in order to avoid embarrassing the Hasmonaean high priests.[92] But obviously at least one MS still had to contain the psalm: the MS on which the Cairo text is based. One group of persons who would not hesitate to embarrass the Hasmonaean priesthood would be, of course, the Qumrân sect. Hence, even in the supposition that the psalm is authentic, its preservation could conceivably be attributed to the men of Qumrân. If this is so, then here too the Jericho cave conveniently – and without too much good will – solves the problem as to how the Geniza MS came to include the psalm.

[92] Schechter, *The Wisdom of Ben Sira*, 35, gives a similar explanation: "The reason for [the psalm's] omission by the Greek translator, who in this respect, as in so many others, was followed by his Syrian successor, is not hard to conjecture. Living at a time when the house of Zadok was already superseded by the Maccabean line, the grandson of [Ben Sira] recoiled from giving publicity to a hymn which claimed that the בני צדוק were specially selected for the priesthood." Cf. also Box-Oesterley, *art. cit.*, 277.

IV. RETROVERSIONS FROM SYRIAC IN THE CAIRO HEBREW

As we saw in Chapter I, the chief arguments adduced against the authenticity of the Geniza text of Sirach may be reduced to the following: (1) it is composed in an idiom that is generally hideous; (2) it manifests an affinity to Syriac.

Even though these defects have been grossly exaggerated by the opponents of the Cairo Hebrew, most scholars who have upheld the authenticity of this text have failed to consider or to provide satisfactory answers to these objections. Thus, as we shall see below, Smend, Fuchs, Peters, Box and Oesterley, and Segal, among others, find in the Geniza text evidence for at least two recensions. One recension (close to the *Vorlage* of Greek) embraces those parts of the text which were composed in a more or less classical Hebrew; a second recension (similar to the *Vorlage* of Syriac) is reflected in those passages which are written in late, sometimes even Mishnaic/ Talmudic diction. Consequently, the general rule to be applied to doublets is that the primitive text of Ben Sira is to be seen in those passages which must have been the basis of the grandson's Greek, whereas the popular and modernized form of the text – the doublets themselves – is reflected by Syriac.

The present writer disagrees with both the opponents of the authenticity of the Cairo Hebrew and the proponents of the theory of multiple recensions as summarized in the preceding paragraph.

In this chapter we shall attempt to demonstrate that the "hideous" diction that Torrey, Ginsberg, and others object to results generally from retroversion of a particular Syriac word, phrase, hemistich, or distich(s). But to repudiate the Cairo Hebrew as a whole because of some instances of retroversion is as logical as throwing out the proverbial baby with the dirty wash water. We do not pretend, of course, to solve all the textual problems of the Hebrew text (a complete commentary would be required to do that), but wish merely to prove that whenever we find a verse extant in two forms, of which one closely resembles Greek and the other Syriac, retroversion is in most cases the reason for the second form. From the seven representative samples which are analyzed below in considerable detail, it will become apparent that the partial retroversion hypothesis has weighty text-critical arguments in its support. This is not to affirm, however, that the Cairo text is substantially or in great measure based upon Syriac, as Torrey and Ginsberg state so emphatically (see Chapter I). We wish to affirm only that all the resources of textual criticism must be called upon if one is to make an intelligent use of the Cairo MSS.

The partial retroversion hypothesis is not something new. Sixty years ago, I. Lévi attempted to demonstrate it, but was not successful in winning over the majority of scholars of his time. Since Lévi's time, however, there have come to light many new materials which have enabled the present writer to present the case in a way that makes this hypothesis virtually certain.

A. KNOWLEDGE OF SYRIAC AMONG MEDIEVAL JEWS

That the medieval Jew knew Syriac and could have composed the retroversions which will be defended below, is clear from the following facts:

1. David b. Merwan, a Jewish philosopher and controversialist who flourished in the ninth–tenth century,[1] translated two Christian works from Syriac into Arabic: a commentary on Genesis and one on Ecclesiastes. He was, therefore, well-versed in Syriac literature.[2]

2. The Peshiṭta of Proverbs was incorporated into the Targum of the Hagiographa.[3] This proves that Syriac was known by the Jews up to the rise of Islam and for several centuries afterwards.

[1] Cf. I. Broydé-R. Gottheil, "David (Abu Sulaiman) Ibn Merwan al-Muḳammaṣ (or al-Miḳmaṣ) al-Raḳḳi", *The Jewish Encyclopedia*, 4 (New York-London, 1903), 466.

[2] Cf. Poznanski, *art. cit.*, 29.

[3] Cf. H. Pinkuss, "Die syrische Uebersetzung der Proverbien", *ZAW*, 14 (1894), 109—120.

3. Naḥmanides, a Spanish Talmudist, exegete, and physician who died in Palestine about 1270,[4] employs in his writings the Syriac version of the Book of Wisdom, of Judith, and of Bel and the Dragon.[5]

These facts prove that Syriac was known among the Jews during the period when the Cairo MSS of Sirach were copied, viz. from the ninth to twelfth century.

B. SELECT EXAMPLES OF RETROVERSION

We have made an independent study of the Cairo MSS, and in particular of the 130 verses represented in more than one MS. Upon completing a careful text-critical analysis of the texts, we came to the conclusion that some passages were retranslated from Syriac. Only after we had produced the evidence for the various instances of retroversion did we consult other scholars to learn what they had written about the texts under discussion. Thus, the arguments and conclusions presented below are solely our responsibility.[6]

Sir 5, 4–6

MS C		MS A
אל תאמר חטאתי ומה יהיה לו	4a	אל תאמר חטאתי ומה יעשה לי מאומה
כי ייי ארך אפים הוא	4b	כי אל ארך אפים הוא
	4c	אל תאמר רחום ייי
	4d	וכל עונותי ימחה
אל סליחה אל תבטח	5a	אל סליחה אל תבטת
להוסיף עון על עון	5b	להוסיף עון על עון
ואמרת רבים רחמיו	6a	ואמרת רחמיו רבים
לרוב עוונותי יסלח	6b	לרוב עונותי יסלח
כי רחמים ואף עמו	6c	כי רחמים ואף עמ̆ו
ועל רשעים יניח רגזו	6d	ואל רשעים ינוח רגזו

[4] Cf. I. Broydé, "Moses Ben Naḥman Gerondi", *The Jewish Encyclopedia*, 9 (New York-London, 1905), 87.

[5] Lévi, *The Hebrew Text of the Book of Ecclesiasticus* (Leiden, 1904), x. Cf. also A. Marx, "An Aramaic Fragment of the Wisdom of Solomon", *JBL*, 40 (1921), 58–60.

[6] We do, of course, acknowledge the suggestions of former professors as regards some arguments.

4a μὴ εἴπῃς ἥμαρτον, καὶ τί μοι ἐγένετο (248: + λυπηρόν);
4b ὁ γὰρ κύριός ἐστιν μακρόθυμος. (248: + οὐ μή σε ἀνῇ.)
5a περὶ ἐξιλασμοῦ μὴ ἄφοβος γίνου,
5b (248: ἐν πλεονασμῷ) προσθεῖναι ἁμαρτίαν (248: -τίας) ἐφ' ἁμαρτίαις·
6a καὶ μὴ εἴπῃς ὁ οἰκτειρμὸς αὐτοῦ πολύς,
6b τὸ πλῆθος τῶν ἁμαρτιῶν μου ἐξιλάσεται·
6c ἔλεος γὰρ καὶ ὀργὴ παρ' αὐτοῦ (S, A, C, 248: αὐτῷ), (248: + ταχύνει,)
6d καὶ ἐπὶ (248: τούς) ἁμαρτωλοὺς καταπαύσει ὁ θυμὸς αὐτοῦ.

4a ܠܐ ܬܐܡܪ ܕܚܛܝܬ ܘܠܐ ܗܘܐ ܠܝ ܡܕܡ.
4b ܡܛܠ ܕܐܠܗܐ ܢܓܝܪ ܪܘܚܐ ܗܘ.
4c ܠܐ ܬܐܡܪ ܕܡܪܚܡܢܐ ܗܘ ܡܪܝܐ.
4d ܘܠܣܘܓܐܐ ܕܚܘ̈ܒܝ (ܕܚܘ̈ܒܐ) ܗܘ ܫܒܩ ܠܝ.
5a ܠܐ ܬܬܟܠ ܥܠ ܫܘܒܩܢܐ.
5b ܕܠܐ ܚܛ̈ܗܐ ܥܠ ܚܛ̈ܗܐ ܬܘܣܦ.
6c ܡܛܠ ܕܪ̈ܚܡܐ ܘܪܘܓܙܐ ܥܡܗ.
6d ܘܥܠ ܚ̈ܛܝܐ ܢܬܬܢܝܚ ܪܘܓܙܗ.

Translations:

4a–b

MS A: "Do not say: 'I have sinned, and what will he do to me? (or, if niphal: ... and what will be done to me?) Nothing! For God is slow to anger.' "

MS C: "Do not say: 'I have sinned, and what will happen to him [*sic*]? For Yahweh is slow to anger.' "

Greek: "Do not say: 'I have sinned, and what happened to me? (248: ... and did anything painful happen to me?) For the Lord is long-suffering.' " 248 adds: "He shall not let you go unpunished."

Syriac: "Do not say: 'I have sinned, and nothing happened to me. For God is long-suffering.' "

4c–d

MS A: "Do not say: 'Yahweh is merciful, and he will blot out all of my iniquities.' "

Syriac: "Do not say: 'The Lord is merciful, and a multitude of (Codex Ambrosianus, Lagarde: my) sins he will forgive me.' "

5a–b

MSS A and C: "Do not rely on forgiveness, adding sin upon sin."

Greek: "As regards atonement be not unafraid to add sin upon sins." (248: "... unafraid repeatedly to add sins upon sins.")

Syriac: "Do not rely on forgiveness, lest you add sins upon sins."

6a–b

MSS A and C: "And saying: 'His mercy is great; he will forgive the multitude of my sins.'"

Greek: "And do not say: 'His mercy is great; he will make atonement [*sic*] for the multitude of my sins.'"

6c–d

MS A: "For mercy and anger are with him, and unto [*sic*] the wicked his wrath rests."

MS C: "For mercy and anger are with him, and upon the wicked he causes his wrath to rest."

Greek: "For mercy and anger are from him (S, A, C: with him; 248: ... anger come quickly with him), and upon (248: the) sinners his wrath will rest."

Syriac: "For mercy and anger are with him, and upon the wicked his anger rests."

Commentary:

4a

In MS C לו is a scribal error for לי; as the writer explained in the previous chapter, this is a case of confusion of *yod* and *waw* in the exemplar which the medieval scribe employed. For יהיה of MS C both Greek and Syriac apparently read היה, which, as both Smend[7] and Segal[8] correctly observe, seems to have been the original reading. As regards MS A, we agree with Bacher[9] that ומה יעשה לי

[7] *Op. cit.*, 49. In our references to Smend, Fuchs, Peters, Box and Oesterley, Lévi, and Segal, we are using the works which are cited in note 80 of Chapter III. Thus, in this chapter, unless otherwise indicated, all page references are to those works.

[8] P. 31.

[9] "Notes on the Cambridge Fragments of Ecclesiasticus", *JQR*, 12 (1899—1900), 276.

מאומה is a compound question; as in Ps 13, 2, it is a combination of a question, ומה יעשה לי, and a negative statement, לא יעשה לי מאומה. But unlike Bacher who thinks the wording of MS A is original, we are of the opinion that the Hebrew has been influenced by the Syriac. Clearly enough, מאומה and ܡܕܡ are related. It seems that the Hebrew word was occasioned by the Syriac and not vice versa, because the Hebrew hemistich has too many accents to be original: מאומה makes the half-line unbalanced, and therefore must have been added later. יעשה is harder to account for; it was probably substituted for יהיה by the medieval scribe who thought he would make the meaning more intelligible.

4b

Both Greek and Syriac agree substantially with Hebrew. Whether ייי or אל is original is impossible to say, for we cannot argue from the versions which of these Hebrew words κύριος and ܐܠܗܐ represent. The entries under δυνάστης, θέος, κύριος, and ὕψιστος in Smend's *Griechisch-syrisch-hebräischer Index zur Weisheit des Jesus Sirach*[10] prove conclusively that there is no consistency in the Greek and Syriac translations of the Hebrew divine names. Hence, Segal[11] errs when he states that MS A has אל like Syriac, whereas MS C and Greek agree on ייי. The extra words found in 248 (and in 70 and 106) appear to be a gloss added by the Greek scribes.

4c–d

In our opinion only Lévi[12] suggests the correct explanation of the Hebrew doublet, viz. that it is a retroversion from Syriac. Box and Oesterley[13] do not even state the textual problem accurately, nor do they offer a satisfactory solution by merely describing what one could see for oneself by reading the texts. Peters[14] dismisses these hemistichs as "Dublette". Scarcely any better is Smend's observation:

> Cod. A des Hebr. und Syr. haben 6ab in schlechterer Gestalt vor 5. A wiederholt das Distichon an richtiger Stelle fast

[10] Berlin, 1907.
[11] P. 31.
[12] Part 2, p. 25.
[13] P. 332.
[14] P. 52.

> gleichlautend mit C, Syr. vermeidet die Wiederholung, hat aber für 6b: "und die Menge meiner Sünden vergibt er mir," in Annäherung an A², C und Gr. Übrigens kann 6a ursprünglich nicht auf 4b gefolgt sein.[15]

This statement of the problem does not bring us any closer to a solution of this perplexing text. Even less illuminating is Segal's attempt[16] at explaining this Hebrew distich: [= Greek] בכ״י ג ו י [v. 5] ומקומו אחרי פ״ז; [v. 6a–b] חסר, והוא כפל של פ״ח. We disagree with the last of those three statements, for we believe that 4c–d is a retroversion from Syriac; hence, it does not belong after v. 5. V. 6a–b, found in Greek and in Cairo MSS A and C (with no essential difference between them), is certainly original.

Obviously Syriac and Hebrew MS A are related in 4c–d. It appears extremely improbable, however, that Syriac was translated from a text like that of 4c–d of MS A. For if it were, why does not Syriac also have a v. 6a–b like MS A? But if MS A v. 4c–d was retroverted from the Syriac, then we can very plausibly account for both Syriac and MS A in the following way:

1. Syriac 4c–d was translated from Hebrew 6a–b. The use of ܠܐ ܬܐܡܪ to render the waw-consecutive perfect ואמרת is no serious objection to this hypothesis. For it is possible to construe ואמרת as a continuation of the negative contained in the jussive construction אל תבטח of 5a. Indeed Ben Sira's grandson understood the waw-consecutive in precisely that way when he rendered the phrase by μὴ εἴπῃς. It is, of course, more likely according to the context and normal syntax that ואמרת continues the infinitive construct להוסיף of 5b. Instead of רחמיו רבים in 6a the *Vorlage* of Syriac must have been defective, having only רחמיו; then because the final *waw* was either not clear or was misread as a *yod*, the Syriac translator read רחם יי. This explanation provides a reasonable answer to the question why Syriac 4c is shorter than its Hebrew counterpart, 6a, and why MS A 4c is shorter than 6a, the v. of which it is supposed to be a doublet (*via* the Syriac, in our hypothesis). That Syriac 4d was translated from Hebrew 6b and not from a text like MS A 4d is proved by the fact that (1) ܠܣܘܓܐܐ renders precisely לרוב of

[15] P. 49.
[16] P. 32.

6b, whereas MS A 4d has וכל; and (2) ܢܚܣܐ is the equivalent of יסלח ("he will forgive") of 6b and not of ימחה ("he will blot out") of 4d. To the translation of 6b Syriac added ܠܗ.

2. Syriac finally misplaced the distich corresponding to Hebrew 6a–b after 4a–b.

3. A medieval scribe of the text tradition found in MS A noticed that his Syriac text had a verse 4c–d, whereas his Hebrew exemplar did not. He saw too that Syriac 4c was different enough from Hebrew 6a to make him think that the former was a piece of text that was missing from the latter. Hence, he retroverted Syriac 4c–d into Hebrew. This inner Syriac mistake introduced into MS A by some medieval scribe seems to prove conclusively that retroversion took place. In 4c, Hebrew matches Syriac perfectly. In 4d, the medieval scribe used the loose synonyms וכל and ימחה to retrovert ܘܠܣܘܓܐܐ and ܢܚܣܐ, respectively, probably because he did not want to repeat רוב and יסלח which were already present in 6b; he did not retranslate ܠܗ, for it was unnecessary for the sense.

Further proof of medieval retroversion is offered by the style and arrangement of the hemistichs from vv. 3 to 8, in which we find a series of clauses containing אל plus jussive followed by a כי clause. Thus:

3a אל תאמר ...		3b כי ...
4a אל תאמר ...		4b כי ...

(omit 4c–d because it does not fit into this apparently conscious pattern)

5a ... אל תבטח		6c כי ...
7a אל תאחר ...	7b ואל תתעבר ...	7c כי ...
8a אל תבטח ...		8b כי ...

5a

Syriac agrees essentially with Hebrew. Greek, however, is quite free: ἐξιλασμός means "atonement, propitiation" (for sin), as an act of man, whereas סליחה means "forgiveness" (of sin), as an act of God; and μὴ ἄφοβος γίνου hardly renders accurately the Hebrew thought. Saadia and R. Nissim quote this and the next hemistich. As the first word of 5a Saadia has ואל. The 1519 edition of R. Nissim's *Sēper Maʿăśîyôt* gives ועל הסליחה, while later editions have ובסליחה.[17] Note that R. Nissim flourished in the tenth century;[18] hence, the substantial correctness of his citation may be due either to his seeing a copy of the Sirach fragments from the Jericho (Qumrân) cave or, as Bacher suggests,[19] to his obtaining the quotation from Saadia.

5b

The Uncials agree with Hebrew; the Cursives have a gloss. The Syriac construction, different from Hebrew and Greek, changes the sense but not substantially.

6a–b

Syriac, as noted above, misplaced this distich after 4a–b. The clause introduced by the waw-consecutive perfect ואמרת (Saadia who quotes this entire v. has ואמרתה) is, as we saw above, most likely a continuation of להוסיף and makes perfectly good sense. Hence ואמרת need not be emended to (ו)אל תאמר, which Segal[20] thinks was the original reading. The orthography עוונותי in MS C is normal in the Qumrân literature; for citations see K. G. Kuhn, *Konkordanz zu den Qumrantexten.*[21] Greek mistranslated יסלח, just as it did in the analogous situation in 5a. R. Nissim, who also quotes this entire verse, has ... עונותינו ... ותאמר.

6c–d

MS C contains an inferior reading in d: יניח for ינוח which is reflected by Greek and Syriac; hence, the latter reading is to be preferred. 6d appears again in 16, 11d where יגיח is given in place of יניח/ינוח. As noted in the previous chapter, יניח is another instance of confusion of *yod* and *waw*. But ועל in 6d of MS C is certainly correct; ואל of MS A is clearly a mistake. Saadia and R. Nissim

[17] Cf. *The Wisdom of Ben Sira: Portions of the Book Ecclesiasticus from Hebrew Manuscripts in the Cairo Genizah Collection Presented to the University of Cambridge by the Editors*, ed. by S. Schechter-C. Taylor (Cambridge, 1899), 43.

[18] Lévi, Part 2, p. 25, n. 5.

[19] *Art. cit.*, 284.

[20] P. 32.

[21] Göttingen, 1960, 158, under the entry עוון/עון.

testify to the correctness of MS C. For רגזו of both MSS A and C, Saadia and R. Nissim offer עזו, which has no backing either in the versions nor in the Cairo Hebrew. Strangely enough, some MSS of the Old Latin in 6c reflect both B and 248: "... ab illo (B: παρ' αὐτοῦ; but S, A, C, 248: παρ' αὐτῷ) cito proximant (only 248: ταχύνει)."

In concluding the text-critical commentary on these verses we call attention to the authenticity and the evident superiority of the Cairo Hebrew over both Greek (see 5a–b and 6b) and Syriac (see 4a and 5a–b), despite the obvious corruption in MS A, 4c–d.

Sir 10, 31

MS B		MS A
הנכבד בעיניו בעשרו איככה	31a	נכבד בעשרו איככה
ונקלה בעשרו בעיניו איככה	31b	ונקלה בעיניו איככה
המתכבד בדלותו בעשרו מתכבד יתר	31c	[המת]כבד בדלותו בעשרו מתכבד יתר
והנקלה בעשרו בדלותו נקלה יתר	31d	והנקלה בעשרו בדלותו נקלה יותר

31a ὁ δὲ δοξαζόμενος (248: ὁ δεδοξασμένος) ἐν πτωχείᾳ, καὶ ἐν πλούτῳ ποσαχῶς;

31b καὶ ὁ ἄδοξος ἐν πλούτῳ, ἐν πτωχείᾳ ποσαχῶς;

31a ܕܡܝܩܪ ܒܡܣܟܢܘܬܐ (ܒܡܣܟܢܘܬܗ) ܒܥܘܬܪܗ ܚܕ ܟܡܐ.

31b ܘܕܙܠܝܠ ܒܡܣܟܢܘܬܗ ܒܥܘܬܪܗ ܚܕ ܟܡܐ.

Codex Ambrosianus, Lagarde: ܘܕܙܠܝܠ ܒܥܘܬܪܗ ܒܡܣܟܢܘܬܗ ܚܕ ܟܡܐ.

Translations:

31a–b

MS A: "He who is honored in his wealth, how much more? and he who is lightly esteemed in his eyes, how much more?"

MS B: "He who is honored in his eyes, in his wealth how much more? and he who is lightly esteemed in his wealth, in his eyes how much more?"

Greek: "He who is honored in poverty, and [*sic*] in wealth how much more? and he who is without honor in wealth, in poverty how much more?"

A, C, 248, and other Cursives: "He who has been honored ..."

Syriac (Walton): "He who is honored in (Codex Ambrosianus, Lagarde, Mosul: his) poverty, in his wealth (this phrase accidentally given twice in Codex Ambrosianus) how much more? (Walton, Mosul) and he who is despised in his poverty, in his wealth how much more?"

Codex Ambrosianus, Lagarde: "... and he who is despised in his wealth, in his poverty how much more?"

31c–d

MSS A and B: "He who is honored in his poverty is honored more in his wealth, and he who is lightly esteemed in his wealth is more lightly esteemed in his poverty."

Commentary:

31a–b

In MS A, a word has been left out of each hemistich; hence, the line makes no sense at all. MS B – the leaf containing this line is one of the two most recent leaves to become known to the scholarly world[22] – has an extra word in each hemistich, but because of a scribal error the line makes little sense. But if we drop the first *yod* in בעיניו, found in both hemistichs, we get בעניו, *b^eʿonyô* ("in his poverty"), which must have been the original reading since it makes excellent sense in the context and enables us to see the basis of Greek and Syriac. The corrupt reading בעיניו could have been achieved by either one of two processes: (1) the medieval scribe saw in his exemplar בעניו, but since he thought that this orthography was an Aramaism[23] for בעיניו, he added a *yod* after the *ʿayin*; or (2) there was a *mater lectionis* after the *ʿayin* in the medieval scribe's exemplar, but it was read as a *yod* rather than as a *waw* (in which case, we would have another instance of confusion of *waw*

[22] The leaf was first published by J. Schirmann, "*Dappîm nôs^epîm mittôk sēper 'ben-Sîrā'*", *Tarbiẕ*, 29 (1959–1960), 129ff.; facsimiles are between pp. 130 and 131. I re-edited this leaf in "The Recently Identified Leaves of Sirach in Hebrew", *Bib*, 45 (1964), 156; facsimiles on TAB. I and II.

[23] The Aramaism עני, *ʿênê*, occurs at least twice in the non-biblical texts from Qumrân: *The Damascus Document*, 2, 16, and *The Habakkuk Commentary*, 5, 1 (first hand).

and *yod*) – thus the original would have been בעוניו, an orthography which is also found in 13, 24b, ורע העוני על פי זדון.[24] Greek is essentially correct, although the addition of the first καί ruins the balance of the line, and πτωχείᾳ and πλούτῳ, found in both hemistichs, are not modified by the third person personal pronoun, like their counterparts in Hebrew. Syriac in Codex Ambrosianus and in Lagarde's edition is correct, but in Walton's polyglot and in the Mosul edition there is an obvious mistake: the second and third words of the second hemistich have been accidentally reversed. It is perfectly clear that Syriac was translated from Hebrew 31a–b, the original of which we now have thanks to the recently identified fragment of MS B.

31c–d

This line is peculiar to both MSS A and B, not being found in either Greek or Syriac. Most scholars agree that the line is not original.[25] However, we find unsatisfactory all attempts at explaining this doublet that have come to our attention – Box and Oesterley[26]: "(Hebrew) adds an explanatory doublet"; Smend[27]: "Hebr. hat den Vers in verstümmelter Gestalt, dann noch einmal in Form einer Erklärung, die sich auch durch den passivischen Gebrauch von מתכבד als jünger verrät"; Fuchs[28]: "Das zweite Distichon ... wurde zur Erklärung der verstümmelten Zeile gebildet"; Peters[29]: "Die zweite Hälfte [31c–d] mit ihren überlangen Stichen ist erläuternde Rektifizierung des verderbten Textes der ersten Hälfte [31a–b]"; Segal[30]: תוספת של ביאור לפסוק הקודם; E. Vogt[31]: "Haec varians explicativa [31c–d] deest in LXX Syr."

[24] The use of *waw* as *mater lectionis* for short "o" is permissible at Qumrân.

[25] Lévi, part 2, p. 70, was baffled by 31a–d. He seemed to consider 31c–d as original, for he thought 31a–b, "qui n'est ni en G. ni en S., est étrange." Since Lévi did not have at his disposal MS B's form of 31a–b, his observation is understandable.

[26] P. 352.

[27] P. 101.

[28] P. 20.

[29] P. 94.

[30] P. 67.

[31] "Novi textus hebraici libri Sira", *Bib*, 41 (1960), 186.

We submit that 31 c–d is a medieval retroversion from Syriac, and that the retroversion was effected by some scribe of the text tradition represented by MS A from which the scribe of MS B, the younger of the MSS (as was indicated in the previous chapter[32]), copied it.

First of all we should note the Mishnaic/Talmudic diction and syntax of the doublet: (1) דלות, a late Hebrew word, occurs nowhere in the Old Testament or Qumrân literature published up to 1960 (Kuhn's concordance does not list the word); (2) instead of נכבד (present in 31 a), the normal passive of כבד, 31 c has מתכבד, the hithpael (nithpael), a favorite conjugation for expressing the passive with Mishnaic[33] and medieval authors. Note also that the hithpael of כבד occurs only three times – Prv 12, 9; Na 3, 15 (twice) – in the Hebrew canon, and, as far as we could discover, three other times in Hebrew Sir – 3, 10; 10, 26f.; in all six places the meaning is *reflexive, not passive*. The normal *passive* of כבד in the Hebrew canon is the niphal. The same is true of Sir in Hebrew. We found eight occurrences of the niphal of כבד in Sir – 10, 19.20. 24.30 (twice).31 a; 44, 7; 48, 6; in each instance the meaning is passive.

Secondly, we should note that 31 c–d is a declarative sentence. The Hebrew original, which is contained in MS B once we emend בעיניו in each hemistich, is in the form of a question; Greek also has a question. Syriac, however, can be either a question or a declarative sentence: "He who is honored in his poverty, in his wealth (will be honored) much more ..."

From these facts it seems reasonable to conclude that 31 c–d could not be original, but must have been added to the text. But we disagree that the line is an explanatory addition or correction or variant (see the opinions quoted above). For if that were the case, we would be forced to assume that the medieval copyist knew what 31 a–b meant. On the contrary, it appears that 31 a–b, if understood at all, was not understood in the sense of 31 c–d. For if it were, why did not the medieval scribe merely correct the defective reading in 31 a–b?

[32] See n. 79 of Chapter III.

[33] Cf. M. H. Segal, *A Grammar of Mishnaic Hebrew* (Oxford, 1958), 67, par. 140.

Moreover, the Mishnaic/Talmudic diction and syntax of 31c–d prove that these hemistichs must have been added at a comparatively late date. Now, as was demonstrated in the last chapter, what is authentic in the Cairo fragments of Sir more than likely was recovered from the Jericho (Qumrân) Cave in about the year 800 A.D. Consequently, any substantial addition to the text must have been made after that date. If such is the case, then 31c–d was added after Syriac 31a–b had been in existence for centuries. Hence, Syriac 31a–b could not have been translated from Hebrew 31c–d, as Lévi suggests;[34] but the reverse could indeed have taken place.

From the foregoing we can argue that 31c–d came into existence in somewhat the following manner:

1. Some medieval scribe could make no sense out of 31a–b, but out of respect for the text he wrote out the line anyhow. Then he checked his Syriac version to see what that read. It was clearly different from Hebrew.

2. Since Syriac made excellent sense, he decided to retranslate it into Hebrew. In so doing, he understood Syriac as a positive statement; this is, as we indicated above, a possible way to render the Syriac.

That the retroversion was made from Syriac, not from Greek, is proved by two facts: (1) Syriac has the third person singular suffix on the words for "poverty" and "wealth", whereas in Greek these words are not qualified at all; (2) the Greek line can be only a question, but the Syriac can be understood either as a statement, as in Hebrew 31c–d, or as a question.

Sir 15, 14

MS B		MS A
[א]ל[הי]ם מבראשית הוא מראש ברא אדם	14a	אלהים מבראשית א ברא אדם
וישיתהו ביד [חותפו]	14b	וישתיהו ביד חותפו
ויתנהו ביד יצרו	14c	ויתנהו ביד יצרו

14a αὐτὸς ἐξ ἀρχῆς ἐποίησεν ἄνθρωπον,

14b καὶ ἀφῆκεν αὐτὸν ἐν χειρὶ διαβουλίου αὐτοῦ.

[34] Part 2, p. 71.

ܗܘ (ܐܠܗܐ) ܡܢ ܒܪܫܝܬ ܒܪܐ ܒܢܝ̈ ܐܢܫܐ. 14a
ܘܐܫܠܡ ܐܢܘܢ ܒܝܕ ܝܨܪܗܘܢ. 14b

Translations:

14a

MS A: "From in [*sic*] the beginning when God created man,"

MS B: "From the beginning when He created man,"

Greek: "He Himself from the beginning created man,"

Syriac: He (Codex Ambrosianus, Lagarde: God) from the beginning created man,"

14b

MS A: "He put him at the disposal of [literally: in the hand of] his despoiler."

MS B: "He put him at the disposal of [his despoiler]."

14c

MS A: "And He made him subject to [literally: gave him into the hand of] his natural inclination."

MS B: "And He made him subject to his natural inclination."

Greek (14b): "And He left him subject to [literally: in the hand of] his own decision."

Syriac (14b): "And He put them at the disposal of [literally: in the hand of] their natural inclination."

Commentary:

14a

We have translated ברא as an infinitive construct, and we have taken the first *waw* of 14b as *waw* of apodosis. It is possible, of course, to translate ברא as a qal perfect, but our translation seems preferable.[35] In our opinion MS B contains the original text of Ben Sira. We offer as proof the following: (1) הוא of MS B is reflected by αὐτός (although Old Latin has "Deus"!) and by ܗܘ in part of the Syriac tradition (Walton, Mosul); (2) מראש of MS B seems

[35] Likewise in Gn 1, 1, ברא most likely should be read as an infinitive construct; cf. J. B. Bauer, "Sir. 15, 14 et Gen. 1, 1", *VD*, 41 (1963), 243f.; *idem*, "Der priesterliche Schöpfungshymnus in Gen. 1", *TZ*, 20 (1964), 1–9; F. Vattioni, "Genesi 1, 1 ed Eccli. 15, 14", *Augustinianum*, 4 (1964), 105–108.

preferable to the reading מבראשית of MS A. The use of the preposition מן with בראשית may, of course, be legitimate Hebrew, for the phrase בראשית (Gn 1, 1) may have become by this time such a stock phrase that it is taken as a single noun. The reading ܠܩܕܡܝܢ is found in Codex Ambrosianus and in Lagarde's edition. Now, clearly enough, Syriac (with ܠܩܕܡܝܢ, not ܗܘܐ) and the reading of MS A are related to one another. It seems probable that at least the first two words of MS A appear to have been retroverted from a type of Syriac text that we find in Codex Ambrosianus and in Lagarde. But this probability is not insisted upon, for it is not the main point at issue in the discussion of this verse.

As far as we could discover, no one has provided a satisfactory explanation of the ט written over the ש in מבראשית and the ח over the ד in אדם (MS A); a similar ט occurs in 11, 25a.[36] The א which follows מבראשית has over it a dot which cancels the letter.

Syriac's ܒܢܝ ܐܢܫܐ is one of the usual ways to translate אדם (cf. 5, 13; 10, 12; 15, 17; 39, 26); the singular ܒܪ ܐܢܫܐ is also used (cf. 10, 11; 11, 2.4.27; 13, 15).

14b

This hemistich is found only in Hebrew. The reading וישתיהו of MS A is obviously a mistake for וישיתהו which we find in MS B. The lacuna in MS B most probably contained the same text as MS A. There is general agreement among scholars that this half-line is a gloss. We have, however, found no plausible or convincing explanation for the existence of this doublet.

Lévi writes:

> Le deuxième et le troisième stiches sont des doublets; le dernier est conforme aux versions; le premier, qui affecte une certaine élégance, peut se ramener à la même leçon originale: חותפו (mot employé encore 35, 21 [= 32, 21] et 50, 4) est ici

[36] A. Cowley's explanation, "Notes on the Cambridge Texts of Ben Sira", *JQR*, 12 (1899–1900), 110, that ח and ט are numerals indicating that " אדם is to be read eighth and מבראשית ninth word in the line", is not convincing, for as Taylor rightly observes, "The Wisdom of Ben Sira", *JQR*, 15 (1902–1903), 624, the order of words suggested by Cowley would not be natural.

synonyme de "ennemi" (Schechter) = צר: l'original portait יצר comme en *c*, qui a été lu par quelque copiste צר.[37]

Lévi's diagnosis appears farfetched and highly improbable. Smend's analysis[38] is misleading: "In b [= our b–c] hat Hebr. zwei Varianten, Syr. übersetzt anscheinend die zweiter.... Gr. gibt z. T. die erste Variante wieder." This second statement is simply not true; Greek is a translation of Hebrew 14c, and as we shall see below, the doublet in question was added hundreds of years after the Greek version was composed. Smend, however, does admit that 14b is reminiscent of Syriac 4, 19. Fuchs[39] has little to offer toward a solution of this textual problem: "St. II [= 14b] in H, den G und S nicht kennen, ist Dublette zu St. III und bietet sicher eine sekundäre Lesart. Das auffallende חותפו läßt sich übrigens auf יצרו zurückführen." Peters[40] does not even attempt an explanation, but merely writes that 14b "ist Dublette zu St. III [= 14c], om Gr Syr." Box and Oesterley[41] state that 14b is a gloss that was "added for doctrinal purposes"; then they explain:

> A later scribe, realizing the difficulty which could be urged, that as the Creator of all things God must have created the *Yeṣer* with its tendency to evil as well as to good, added the gloss that God delivered man from his spoiler (i.e. Satan ...); cp. iv, 19. This later scribe, in his turn, however, did not realize that the difficulty still remained.

The difficulty still indeed remained, for Box and Oesterley misunderstood the gloss; ישיתהו ביד חותפו could hardly suggest that God "delivered man from his spoiler." In fact, as R. E. Murphy[42] correctly points out, "the Hebrew has just the opposite: *byd* (not *myd*)." After stating that 14b is found neither in Greek nor in Syriac, Segal[43] notes that this half-line "[= variant] הוא כפל או ג״א של טור ג." Referring to the occurrence of חתף in 1QH 5, 10, Murphy thinks that the person responsible for 14b is interpreting the v. in

[37] Part 2, p. 110.
[38] P. 142.
[39] P. 37.
[40] P. 130.
[41] P. 371.
[42] "*Yēṣer* in the Qumran Literature", *Bib*, 39 (1958), 335.
[43] P. 97.

question "in a manner related to the doctrine of Qumran." Thus, 14b "is a 'dualistic' gloss à la Qumran, which explains *yṣr* in terms of a principle of evil which dominates a man." But in a note, Murphy adds: "It has been pointed out to me that the gloss is a retroversion of the Syriac of 4: 19. Even if it is merely that, it may have been motivated as explained above, but without any reference to Qumran ideas."[44] We maintain that 14b is best explained as a medieval retroversion from Syriac 4, 19b. We agree with Murphy that the gloss "explains *yṣr* in terms of a principle of evil which dominates a man." But we should like to date the gloss to some time after the discovery of the Sir text in about 800 A.D. in the Jericho (Qumrân) Cave, whereas Murphy seems to allow either a Qumrân or a medieval origin of the gloss.

Syriac 4, 19b reads: ܘܐܫܠܡܝܘܗܝ ܒܝܕ ܚܛܘ̈ܦܐ, "And I [i.e. Wisdom] shall surrender him into the power of [literally, into the hand of] the plunderers/despoilers." The Cairo Hebrew half-line is: ואסגירנו לשדדים, "And I shall deliver him up to despoilers." Although the construction with "לְ" is idiomatic (cf. Am 1, 6.9; Ps 78, 48.50.62), the original of Ben Sira most likely had ביד,[45] a reading reflected by Syriac and by Greek: καὶ παραδώσει αὐτὸν εἰς χεῖρας πτώσεως αὐτοῦ, "And she [i.e. Wisdom] will deliver him into the hands of his downfall/calamity."[46]

Now we should note the following points:

1. Hebrew 15, 14b corresponds very well to Syriac 4, 19b; a change of subject took place, of course, because the verbs in 15, 14 have third person singular subjects; the third person masculine singular suffix (חותפו) was added most probably because יצרו of 14c also has that suffix. The word ܚܛܘܦܐ in 4, 19b has the plural dots in the MSS and editions consulted, but those consonants could be read also as a singular noun.

[44] *Art. cit.*, 335.

[45] The phrase ביד is also idiomatic with the hiphil of סגר; cf. Jos 20, 5; 1 Sm 23, 11f. 20; 30, 15; Ps 31, 9; Lam 2, 7.

[46] What seems to be behind πτώσεως αὐτοῦ is, as H. Herkenne, *De veteris latinae Ecclesiastici capitibus I–XLIII* (Leipzig, 1899), 78, observes, שֹׁדוֹ. But oddly enough, Old Latin has: "et tradet eum (illum) in manus inimici sui", a reading which is close to Hebrew. Here Old Latin most likely was based upon a Greek Text that was different from the one we now possess, in which there is no variant for πτώσεως in either the Uncials or the Cursives.

2. The words חתף (15, 14b) and ܚܛܘܦܐ (4, 19b) have basically the same root and meaning. In fact, Hebrew and Syriac have the root with either a ת or a ט as the second consonant. In Syriac ܚܛܦ is more common than ܚܬܦ; in Hebrew it is difficult to determine which form is more usual, since both חתף and חטף rarely occur in Biblical Hebrew.[47] This root is not the only one in which such an interchange takes place between the middle order (ת) and the emphatic (ט) in the dental class of consonants. For example, the root קטל in Hebrew and Aramaic becomes *qtl* in Old South Arabic, Arabic, and Ethiopic;[48] other examples are: קטן (Hebrew and Aramaic) – *qatānu* (Akkadian); קטף (Hebrew and Aramaic) – *qatāpu* (Akkadian); קטר (Hebrew, Ugaritic, and Aramaic) – قتّر (Arabic).[49]

3. Since there is only one occurrence of חתף as a verb form (an imperfect) in the Hebrew Bible (Job 9, 12), it is virtually impossible that a biblical phrase inspired the glossator to add 14b. And the use of חתף only once also in the non-biblical Qumrân literature (1QH 5, 10) – חמת תנינים כול מזמותם לחתף – hardly provides sufficient grounds for a nexus between the Qumrân line and Sir 14b. True, חתף occurs also in Sir 32, 21 and 50, 4, but the context of these passages is so different from 15, 14b that their possible relationship to the gloss in question is extremely improbable.

4. It is most improbable that the great similarity between Syriac 4, 19b and Hebrew 15, 14b resulted from coincidence, especially in view of the fact that, as noted above, חתף is such a rare verb.

5. The reason why the medieval Jewish scribe was reminded of Syriac 4, 19b is that both in 15, 14b and in 4, 19b Syriac employs the identical expression, viz. the causative of ܫܠܡ plus the phrase ܩܕܡ. Neither the Hebrew text itself nor the Greek make use of the

[47] חתף as a verb occurs only once (Job 9, 12); as a noun, חֶתֶף, once also (Prv 23, 28). חטף occurs only as a verb: Jgs 21, 21; Ps 10, 9.

[48] The proto-Semitic root of this verb most probably is *qtl*.

[49] The reason for the switch from ת to ט in Hebrew and Aramaic in those stems is that these languages prefer an emphatic consonant (ט) after another emphatic (ק). Akkadian phonology, on the contrary, does not like different emphatics in the same word; cf. E. E. Knudsen, "Cases of Free Variants in the Akkadian *q* Phoneme", *JCS*, 15 (1961), 84, and F. W. Geers, "The Treatment of Emphatics in Akkadian", *JNES*, 4 (1945), 65–67.

same idiom in these two passages. Hence, the dependence of Hebrew 15, 14b upon Syriac 4, 19b appears certain.

Therefore, retroversion from Syriac 4, 19b supplies the most plausible explanation of the Hebrew gloss in question.

14c

Both Greek and Syriac (14b) render Hebrew faithfully (although Syriac stays with the plural it started out with in ܒܢܝ ܐܢܫܐ of 14a); hence, there is no justification for postulating, as Smend does, any dependence of Greek 14b on Hebrew 14b.

Sir 15, 15

MS B		MS A
אם תחפץ תשמר מצוה	15a	אם תחפץ תשמר מצוה
(ותבונה / לע רצונו) ואמ֯ונה לעשות רצו֯ן אל	15b	ותבונה לעשות רצונו
[ואם] ת֯[א]מין ב֯ו ג֯ם את֯ה ת֯ח֯יה:	15c	אם תאמין בו גם אתה תחיה

15a ἐὰν θέλῃς συντηρήσεις ἐντολάς
15b καὶ πίστιν ποιῆσαι εὐδοκίας.

ܘܐܢ (ܐܢ) ܬܨܒܐ ܬܛܪ ܦܘܩܕܢܘܗܝ. 15a
ܘܐܢ ܬܗܝܡܢ ܒܗ ܐܦ ܐܢܬ ܬܚܐ. 15b

Translations:

15a

MSS A and B: "If you wish, you can keep the law [literally: the commandment]."

Greek: "If you wish, you will keep the commandments."

Syriac: "(Codex Ambrosianus: And if) If you wish, you can keep his commandments."

15b

MS A: "For [literally: and] (it is) understanding/good sense to do his will."

MS B: "For (it is) faithfulness/loyalty to do the will of God."

Greek: "And the faith so as to do (things) of (his) good pleasure" (?)/"And to exercise faithfulness [literally: to do the faith] is (a sign of/a matter of) good will" (?).

Syriac: "And if you believe in him, you too will live."

15c

MS A: "If you believe in him, you too will live."
MS B: "[And if] you belie[ve] in him, you too will live."

Commentary:

15a

Hebrew is certainly genuine, showing no dependence whatever on either Syriac or Greek. In fact, only Hebrew can serve as the common basis of Greek and Syriac. The fact that Greek and Syriac have ἐντολάς and ܦܘܩܕܢܘܗܝ, respectively, does not argue against the originality of מצוה, for in other parts of Sir (10, 19; 32, 23; 37, 12; 45, 5) as well as in Prv 19, 16 and Eccl 8, 5, מצוה is employed in the same sense as here, viz. as a collective noun, "the commandment/the law" which embraces the totality of the commandments. The grandson translates מצוה in all the above passages by ἐντολαί. Syriac, however, is inconsistent, employing the plural (ܦܘܩܕܢܐ) again in 10, 19, but the singular in 32, 23. Syriac adds the third person singular masculine suffix to ܦܘܩܕܢܐ.

15b

As is frequently the case, MS B contains in its margin the reading of MS A. Note that לע in MS B margin is an abbreviation for לעשות. Before Schirmann's discovery of the leaf of MS B containing this v.,[50] Smend,[51] Fuchs,[52] Peters,[53] and CCD[54] correctly emended MS A to read אמונה, a word for which we now possess MS evidence. This word is most likely the original of Ben Sira, for it is reflected by πίστιν and seems to be the basis for Syriac's ܬܗܝܡܢ. Whether רצון אל (MS B) is to be preferred to רצונו (MS A, MS B margin) is difficult to determine, for in Greek the corresponding word (εὐδοκίας) is not qualified at all. If, as seems probable, Ben Sira, when

[50] "*Dap ḥādāš mittôk sēper ben-Sîrā' hā-'ibrî*", *Tarbiz*, 27 (1957–1958), 440–443. See my edition of this leaf in *Bib*, 45 (1964), 160, 162; facsimiles on TAB. III and IV.

[51] P. 143.

[52] P. 38.

[53] P. 131.

[54] Cf. CCD's critical note on this v.

writing this hemistich, had in mind Prv 12, 22 – וְעֹשֵׂי אֱמוּנָה רְצוֹנוֹ – then we have an argument in favor of רצונו.

Greek is very enigmatic and almost defies translation. Old Latin offers little help toward a solution of the unusual grammar and syntax the grandson gives us in this half-line: "(a) Si volueris mandata (some editions add: *servare*) conservabunt te, (b) et in perpetuum fidem placitam facere."[55] Presumably, εὐδοκίας is a genitive singular, not an accusative plural.[56]

The Syriac translation of this hemistich will be discussed below.

15c

The size of the lacunae in MS B makes our reconstruction of the text practically certain. In the first lacuna there is space for three letters; Schirmann, however, suggests only two: [אם]. Scholars generally agree that this Hebrew half-line is an addition to the text of Ben Sira.

Smend thinks that "Syr. drückt statt b die schlechte Glosse des Hebr. aus."[57] Fuchs writes:

> St. III [= 15c] des H, den G nicht kennt, ist Zusatz und hat in S den ursprünglichen zweiten Stichos verdrängt. Nach G hat H früher אמונה statt תבונה gehabt, aber auch jenes ist, wie πίστιν des G, hier befremdend. Nach dem vorhergehenden Verse, wie den nachfolgenden, ist hier von der Willensfreiheit die Rede, und man erwartet, nachdem in St. I die Freiheit, Gutes zu tun, erwähnt ist, in St. II die andere Seite der Freiheit erwähnt zu finden, die Freiheit zum Bösen. Mir scheint, daß

[55] Cf. H. Herkenne, *op. cit.*, 148f.

[56] Some translations of this Greek half-line: E. J. Goodspeed, *The Apocrypha*, in *The Complete Bible, An American Translation* (Chicago, 1951), 102: "And acting faithfully rests on your own good pleasure." H. Duesberg-P. Auvray, *Le livre de l'Ecclésiastique [La Sainte Bible de Jérusalem]*, 2d ed. (Paris, 1958), 75: "Rester fidèle est en ton pouvoir." C. Spicq, "L'Ecclésiastique", in *La Sainte Bible*, ed. L. Pirot-A. Clamer, 6 (Paris, 1951), 645: "Et la fidélité sera le fait de [ta] bonne volonté." J. Hadot, "L'Ecclésiastique ou le Siracide", in *La Bible, L'Ancien Testament*, 2 (Paris, 1959), 1757: "Assurer la fidélité dépend du bon plaisir." V. Rysell, "Die Sprüche Jesus', des Sohnes Sirachs", in *Die Apokryphen und Pseudepigraphen des alten Testaments*, ed. E. Kautzsch, 1 (Tübingen, 1921), 306: "Und Treue zu üben (ποιῆσαι als Subjekt) ist [Sache des] Wohlgefallens."

[57] P. 142.

> das תאמין des Zusatzes auf die ursprüngliche Gestalt des Verses schließen läßt. St. II dürfte gelautet haben: ואם תמאן לא תעשה רצונו .... Der Anstoß, den man an dem Stichos nahm, war wohl Anlaß für das Eindringen von אמונה und die Zusammenziehung des לאתעשה in לעשות, während in einer andern Rezension, der Vorlage des S nämlich, St. II wegen des Anstoßes die Form des Zusatzes in H in Anlehnung an Hab 2, 4 erhielt. In H wurden beide Lesarten nebeneinander gestellt.[58]

Fuchs' conjecture has no foundation in either Greek or Syriac; hence, it should not be taken seriously. Peters[59] refers to Hebrew 15c as a "Zusatz" which was occasioned by Hb 2, 4; Box and Oesterley[60] are of the same opinion. Regarding 15b Segal writes: ואולי ״ואמונה״ של י[= Greek] הוא שיבוש מן: וְתֵאָמֵן, ומזה ״תאמין״ שבכפל הבא, כלומר אם תחפוץ תהיה נאמן, חזק ונכון, לעשות רצון יי (יש׳ ז ט, דה״ב כ כ)· ס [= Syriac] משמיט כל הטור[61]. And concerning 15c Segal writes: חסר ב י. והוא תוספת והרחבה על פי חב׳ב ד אגב ״ואמונה״ (י)· או ״ותאמן״ (לפי הגהתנו)[62]. Segal's rewriting of the first word in 15b appears unwarranted; and his assumption that 15c is an inner Hebrew addition occasioned by Hb 2, 4 is, as we shall see below, open to question. With reference to 15b Lévi says:

> Au lieu de ce nom [תבונה], G. a lu אמונה "foi" et a traduit littéralement, ce qui rend la phrase peu intelligible. Ce qui est déconcertant, c'est que S. parle également ici de "foi": "Si tu as foi en lui, toi aussi tu vivras." On ne peut se rendre compte de cette rencontre qu'en supposant une adaptation, non de l'hébreu, mais du grec ...[63]

Lévi's comment on 15c is: "C'est l'exacte reproduction de S.; si les conjectures que nous venons d'exposer sont fondées, ce doublet est un des exemples les plus probants de l'influence de S. sur notre hébreu."[64] We disagree with Lévi as to the original reading of 15b. As was shown above, the word אמונה has the backing of MS

58 P. 38.
59 P. 131.
60 P. 371.
61 P. 97.
62 *Ibid.*
63 Part 2, pp. 110f.
64 *Ibid.*, 111.

B as well as Greek and Syriac. Hence, it seems very unlikely that Syriac 15b is an adaptation of Greek. Because of his faulty analysis Lévi presents a weak case for the retroversion hypothesis.

Quite obviously, Hebrew 15c and Syriac 15b are related to one another. We agree that Hebrew 15c is retroverted from Syriac, but not for the reasons Lévi alleges. It is, of course, possible that Syriac is based upon Hebrew 15c (as Smend and others would have it), but this theory does not appear probable, since it is extremely unlikely that 15c, as an inner Hebrew gloss based upon Hb 2, 4 (Smend, Peters, Segal), was added to the text before 68 A.D., as indeed it would have to be, if our hypothesis is correct concerning the discovery of the Hebrew text of Sirach in the Jericho (Qumrân) Cave. It seems far more reasonable to assume that the history of this v. went something like this:

1. From ואמונה the Syriac translator took two ideas: perseverance (in the commandments), and permanence which is also contained in the root אמן, as in Is 7, 9c (אִם לֹא תַאֲמִינוּ כִּי לֹא תֵאָמֵנוּ; Peshiṭta: ܘܐܢ ܠܐ ܬܗܝܡܢܘܢ ܐܦ ܠܐ ܬܬܩܝܡܘܢ) and 2 Par 20, 20c (הַאֲמִינוּ בַּיהוָה אֱלֹהֵיכֶם וְתֵאָמֵנוּ; Peshiṭta: ܘܗܝܡܢܘ ܒܡܪܝܐ ܠܐܠܗܟܘܢ ܘܬܬܗܝܡܢܘܢ). Rather than translate Hebrew 15b, therefore, he made up a paraphrase. But to avoid repeating the verb אמן, he decided to write his half-line in terms of Hb 2, 4b (וְצַדִּיק בֶּאֱמוּנָתוֹ יִחְיֶה; Peshiṭta: ܘܙܕܝܩܐ ܒܗܝܡܢܘܬܗ ܢܚܐ), a text clearly related to the one in question. Thus, he ignored the rest of Hebrew 15b as being parallel to תשמר מצוה of 15a and, consequently, already translated.

2. After the medieval scribe copied out v. 15 which originally had only hemistichs a and b, he noticed that Syriac had something different in place of b. Hence, he decided to retranslate the Syriac half-line into Hebrew.

This hypothesis plausibly accounts for: (1) the omission of 15c in Greek; (2) the difference between Hebrew 15b and Syriac 15b; (3) the identity between Syriac 15b and Hebrew 15c.

Sir 15, 20

MS B		MS A
[לא צוה אנוש] לחטא	20a	לא צוה אנוש לחטא

ולא למד שקרים לאנשי כזב [ולא החלים אנשי] כזב	20b	ולא החלים אנשי כזב
ולא מרחם על עושה שוא ועל מגלה סוד	20c	ולא מרחם על עושה שוא ועל מגלה סוד

20a καὶ (omitted by S, A, C, 248) οὐκ ἐνετείλατο οὐδενὶ ἀσεβεῖν,
20b καὶ οὐκ ἔδωκεν ἄνεσιν οὐδενὶ ἁμαρτάνειν.

20a ܠܐ ܦܩܕ ܠܒܢܝ̈ ܐܢܫܐ ܕܢܚܛܘܢ.
20b ܘܠܐ ܐܡܪ ܠܒܢܝ̈ ܒܣܪܐ ܕܢܒܐܫܘܢ.
20c ܘܠܐ ܡܪܚܡ ܥܠ ܥܒ̈ܕܝ ܫܘܩܪܐ.

Translations:

20a–b

MS A: "He did not order man to sin, and he did not give strength to deceitful men."

MS B: "[He did not order man] to sin, and he did not teach lies to deceitful men, [and he did not give strength to] deceit[ful men]."

Greek: "And [omitted by S, A, C, 248] he did not order anyone to be ungodly, and he did not give license to anyone to sin."

Syriac: "He did not order men to sin, and he did not tell the sons of flesh to do evil."

20c

MSS A and B: "And he does not have mercy on him who does vanity or on him who reveals a secret."

Syriac: "And he does not have mercy on those who make falsehood."

Commentary:

20a

MS A appears original. The size of the lacuna in MS B,[65] of which only four letters are legible in this half-line, seems to indicate that this MS read the same as MS A. Greek is slightly different. Syriac agrees substantially with Hebrew.

Syriac 20b, however, does not seem to be a translation of Hebrew 20b (as represented in MS A), but rather a second attempt at rendering Hebrew 20a, or perhaps an inner Syriac doublet of the

[65] See the facsimile (TAB. IV) referred to in n. 50.

first hemistich. The reason is that Syriac 20b, except possibly for ܠܐ ܐܡܪ, employs fairly exact synonyms to state the very thought contained in 20a of both MS A and Syriac itself, whereas if Syriac 20b were a translation of Hebrew 20b, as Smend,[66] Peters,[67] Fuchs,[68] and Segal[69] would have it, then it appears extremely difficult to account for the Syriac. Even ܠܐ ܐܡܪ could plausibly be an exact rendering of לא צוה or an equivalent of ܦܩܕ.[70]

20b

MS B gives two hemistichs instead of one as in MS A. In the second hemistich in which only the last word כזב is preserved, the lacuna in MS B is just large enough[71] to contain the reading of MS A. The first hemistich of MS B, however, reads differently: ולא למד שקרים לאנשי כזב. Concerning this half-line Segal[72] merely notes: כל הטור הוא תוספת החסרה בכ״י א. It is not easy to determine precisely the origin of this hemistich; but without too much insistence we suggest that this extra half-line may be a partial retroversion based upon Syriac 20b–c. If that is the case, the medieval retroverter read ܐܡܪ of 20b as ܠܡܪ. Even though ܠܡܪ (either a pᵉal or pael) does not mean "to teach", it is not difficult to see why the retroverter would so understand the Syriac verb, for the intensive conjugation of this root in Jewish Aramaic[73] and in Hebrew does indeed mean "to teach". The word שקרים presumably was occasioned by ܫܘܩܪܐ of 20c, and לאנשי כזב was merely repeated from MS B's next hemistich, which, as we indicated above, most likely read the same as MS A.

As regards ולא החלים אנשי כזב contained in MS A and most probably to be read also in the lacuna of MS B, many authors consider this hemistich original, although there is some disagreement as to

[66] P. 144.
[67] P. 131.
[68] P. 40.
[69] P. 98.

[70] Classical Arabic أَمَرَ means "to command". Such a nuance for this root in the other Semitic languages is not unknown.

[71] See the facsimile referred to in n. 65.

[72] P. 368.

[73] J. Levy-H. L. Fleischer, *Neuhebräisches und Chaldäisches Wörterbuch über die Talmudim und Midraschim*, 2 (Leipzig, 1879), 510f.

the meaning of החלים. Peters[74] and Vogt[75] render this verb "to give dreams/to cause to dream", while Smend,[76] Box and Oesterley,[77] and CCD translate by "to give strength/to make strong". But in view of the manner in which the ancient versions translate the verb, there is good reason to doubt that החלים, though a *lectio difficilior*, is original. Ben Sira's grandson translates the verb in this hemistich by ἔδωκεν ἄνεσιν, which is not even close to the thought of החלים. But if instead of לא החלים we read לא חמל (על) ("he did not have compassion on/spare"), then the grandson's Greek has an intelligible basis in Hebrew. That is to say, the grandson took the meaning of "spare"[78] out of לא חמל; hence, οὐκ ἔδωκεν ἄνεσιν, "he did not give relaxation/indulgence/license". To obtain the reading חמל we have merely to rearrange the consonants of החלים and drop י and ה. Such a procedure is not unknown in correcting other parts of the Hebrew Bible. This reading receives further support from the fact that the grandson in 49, 10 translates החלימו by παρεκάλεσεν ("to summon/to cheer on, encourage, excite"), a good enough rendering of the Hebrew. It is noteworthy that the LXX also uses παρακαλέω to translate תַּחֲלִימֵנִי in Is 38, 16, and חֹלְמִים in Ps 126, 1. Hence, in view of the fact that the grandson did not render the verb in 20b by παρακαλέω or by some other Greek verb of similar meaning but instead used the expression ἔδωκεν ἄνεσιν, it seems certain that he did not read החלים. Now Syriac 20c, which will be discussed below, also bears witness to the reading חמל as the original Hebrew verb in this hemistich. The Syriac rendering of this verb is ܡܪܚܡ, which takes from חמל the derived, but usual, meaning "to have compassion upon/to have mercy on"; cf. Hebrew and Syriac in 16, 9. Thus, Greek and Syriac can have as a common basis in Hebrew only the verb חמל, whereas החלים explains neither Greek nor Syriac. From the text-critical point of view, therefore, חמל appears to be original.

Now it may be argued that an object after the verb חמל must be preceded by על or אל. Fortunately, MS A takes care of this diffi-

[74] P. 130f.

[75] "Novum folium hebr. Sir 15, 1–16, 7 MS B", *Bib*, 40 (1959), 1062.

[76] P. 144.

[77] P. 371.

[78] Cf. Jer 50, 14 and Job 20, 13.

culty: in 15, 19b, which in the MS is contained in the line above 15, 20b, the scribe inserted על after the verb יכיר, then canceled it by putting dots above and below the על (see p. 63). This על does not, of course, belong in 15, 19b; hence, the cancellation. We submit that this על originally followed לא חמל.

Segal[79] also has some misgivings about Hebrew 20b (MS A). After discussing the hemistich as contained in the Cairo fragment, he writes: יש לשער שהגרסה המקורית היתה: וְלֹא אִשֵּׁר אִישׁ לְכַזֵּב, ומזה ב ע[= Hebrew text]: אשר-חזק-החלים, איש לכזב-אנשי כזב; ב י[= Greek]: אשר-הרשה-נתן רשות, לכזב-לחטא; וב ס[= Syriac]: אשר-אמרלכזב-להרשיע. Segal's conjecture is a bit too fanciful and requires too much rewriting to merit serious consideration. On the other hand, the reading we have offered above in addition to providing the only intelligible common basis for both Greek and Syriac, requires merely the rearranging of the consonants of one word, החלים, and the dropping of י and ה.

The Syriac translation of Hebrew 20b will be discussed in the next section.

20c

This lengthy half-line is, as all authors consulted agree, an addition, not represented at all in Greek and only partially reflected in Syriac. One of the reasons for questioning the authenticity of this hemistich is that the participle continuing the two finite verbs of the previous half-lines, is a serious violation of second century B.C. Hebrew syntax. In Syriac, however, such a construction may be tolerated.[80] Thus Syriac 20c could hardly be based upon Hebrew 20c, which appears decidedly medieval in syntax; but the Hebrew hemistich up to the word שוא could quite conceivably be based upon Syriac, as we shall see forthwith.

If, as seems very probable, Syriac 20b is based upon Hebrew 20a, it is more than likely that Syriac 20c is a translation of Hebrew 20b. Indeed it appears critically certain that the Syriac translator, like Ben Sira's grandson before him, read in his *Vorlage* not החלים but

[79] P. 98.

[80] Cf. T. Nöldeke, *Kurzgefaßte syrische Grammatik*, 2d and improved ed. (Leipzig, 1898), 206f., pars. 272 and 275; English translation by J. A. Crichton (London, 1904), 215f.

חמל על (hence, ܡܪܚܡ ܥܠ); then he rendered אנשי כזב by ܒܒ̈ܢܝ ܫܘܩܪܐ, which is accurate enough. In this hypothesis we can reasonably account for Syriac 20c. The use of the first participle in 20c is permissible Syriac syntax, as we noted above. Therefore, we suggest that the most plausible explanation of the typically medieval Hebrew of ולא מרחם על עושה שוא, is that it is a retroversion from Syriac; only Lévi[81] admits this hypothesis. In retranslating into Hebrew the medieval Jew did not bother to employ the usual syntax found in the rest of Sir, but used the Syriac construction. In any case, the medieval Jew without much strain could tolerate a participle continuing two finite verbs.

The phrase ועל מגלה סוד is an extra flourish added by the retroverter or perhaps by a scribe, who most likely had in mind Prv 11, 13, הוֹלֵךְ רָכִיל מְגַלֶּה־סוֹד, or Prv 20, 19, גּוֹלֶה־סוֹד הוֹלֵךְ רָכִיל. Those three words in Sir 15, 20c may have been supplied, as Lévi suggests,[82] in order to fill out the distich.

Sir 16, 3

MS B		MS A
אל תאמין ב]חֿיֿיֿהם]	3a	אל תאמין בחייהם
ואל תבטח בחיליהם	3b	ואל תבטח בעקבותם
ואל תבטח ב]עֿקבותם]		
כֿי לא תהיה להם אחרית טובה	3c	כי לא תהיה להם אחרית טובה
כי טוב] אחד עושה רצון אל מאלף]	3d	כי טוב אחד עושה רצון מאלף
ומות ערירי מאחרית זדון	3e	ומות ערירי ממי שהיו לו בנים
טו]ב מות ערירי ממי שיהיו לו בנים]		רבים עֿוֿלה ומאחרית זדון
רבים בני עולה ומאחרית זדין		

3a μὴ ἐνπιστεύσῃς τῇ ζωῇ αὐτῶν,

3b καὶ μὴ ἔπεχε ἐπὶ τὸν τόπον [S, A, 248: τὸ πλῆθος] αὐτῶν·
S^c.a: + στενάξεις γὰρ πένθει ἀώρῳ καὶ ἐξαίφνης αὐτῶν συντέλειαν γνώσεται.

3c κρείσσων γὰρ εἷς (248: + δίκαιος) ἢ χίλιοι,
(S^c.a: κρείσσων γὰρ εἷς δίκαιος ποιῶν θέλημα κυρίου ἢ μύριοι παράνομοι)

3d καὶ ἀποθανεῖν ἄτεκνον ἢ ἔχειν τέκνα ἀσεβῆ.

[81] Part 2, pp. xxxi, 113.
[82] *Ibid.*, 113.

ܠܐ ܬܬܟܠ ܥܠ ܚܝܝܗܘܢ. 3a
ܘܠܐ ܬܗܝܡܢ ܕܗܘܐ ܠܗܘܢ ܚܪܬܐ ܛܒܬܐ. 3b
ܡܛܠ ܕܛܒ ܗܘ ܚܕ ܕܥܒܕ ܨܒܝܢܐ ܡܢ ܐܠܦܐ (ܐܠܦ). 3c
ܘܗܘ ܕܡܝܬ ܕܠܐ ܒܢܝܐ ܡܢ ܗܘ ܕܗܘܘ ܠܗ ܒܢܝܐ ܣܓܝܐܐ ܕܥܘܠܐ. 3d

Translations:

3a

MS A: "Do not be sure of their lives."

MS B: "[Do not be sure of] their lives."

Greek: "Do not put your trust in their lives."

Syriac: "Do not trust in their lives."

3b

MS A: "And do not trust in their end/future."

MS B: "And do not trust in their powers, [and do not trust in] their end."

Greek: "And do not rely on their place (S, A, 248: their multitude/number)." S[c.a]: "For you shall groan [read perhaps: he ...] from an ultimely grief and of a sudden he shall know their outcome."

Syriac: "And do not believe that they will have a good end."

3c

MSS A and B: "For they will not have a good end."

3d

MS A: "For one person who does the will [sc. of God] is better than a thousand."

MS B: "[For] one person who does the will of God is [better] than a thousand."

Greek (c): "For one person (248: one just person) is better than a thousand." (S[c.a]: "For one just person doing the will of the Lord is better than ten thousand lawless persons.")

Syriac (c): "For one person who does the will [sc. of God] is better than a thousand."

3e

MS A: "And to die childless (is better) than the one who has many children, wickedness [*sic*], or an insolent posterity."

MS B: "And to die childless (is better) than an insolent posterity; to die childless is bet[ter] than the one who has many children, wicked children, or an insolent posterity."

Greek (d): "And to die childless (is better) than to have godless children."

Syriac (d): "And he who dies without children (is better) than the one who has many wicked children."

Commentary:

3a

The lacuna in MS B is large enough to contain the reading of MS A; hence, our conjecture is quite probable.[83] Hebrew is genuine, having been suggested perhaps by Dt 28, 66 and Job 24, 22. Greek renders Hebrew accurately. Syriac reverses the verbs in a and b, but, except for that, it too is a faithful translation of our Hebrew text.

3b

The lacuna in MS B almost certainly read the same as MS A. MS B, however, gives two hemistichs instead of one; the first seems to be a gloss prompted by Ps 49, 7, which refers to "my wicked ensnarers" as הַבֹּטְחִים עַל־חֵילָם. Hebrew as represented in MS A is original, being reflected directly by Syriac and obliquely by Greek. The word עקבותם is the plural of עָקֵב, "heel; footprint; rear (of a troop of men)". From the meaning of "rear" we could obtain the idea of "end". This is not stretching the word too far, for in Gn 3, 15 the Jerusalem Targum explains עָקֵב in this way: בְּעִקְבָא בְּסוֹף עָקֵב יוֹמַיָּא.[84] Syriac (ܚܪܬܐ) also understands עקבות as "end". The phrase τὸν τόπον αὐτῶν, found in Codices B and 308, also seems to go back to עקבותם; that is to say, this Greek takes from the Hebrew word the idea of "footprint/*place* where the foot has touched". In any case, difficult as this Greek may be, it is preferable to the easier reading contained in Codices A, S, 248, and many

[83] See the facsimile referred to in n. 65.

[84] We cite this text as found in the Walton Polyglot, 4, Appendix (London, 1657), 6.

other Cursives: τὸ πλῆθος αὐτῶν. For Old Latin, "et ne respexeris in labores illorum (2 MSS and the editions: *eorum*)" (a reading which suggests as its *Vorlage* ἐπὶ τὸν κόπον or τοὺς κόπους),[85] seems to favor τόπον over πλῆθος.

The verb ἔπεχε (an imperative, which is a rather poor way of continuing the negative subjunctive, used as a prohibition, in the previous half-line)[86] is not altogether unusual as a translation of תבטח, for the grandson employs ἐπέχειν to render בטח in 5,8; 13, 11; 15, 4; 32, 15. In Classical, LXX (excepting Sir), and New Testament Greek, however, ἐπέχειν never has the meaning "to rely upon/to trust".[87] The addition found in $S^{c.a}$ was probably occasioned by texts like the LXX of Prv 10, 6; 11, 30; 13, 2; Ws 14, 15.

As we noted above, Syriac's ܬܗܝܡܢ renders תאמין of the previous hemistich. Although Syriac gives a paraphrase rather than a translation, it nevertheless reflects the Hebrew original.

3c

This half-line exists only in Hebrew and is obviously an addition, as all scholars agree. Smend[88] thinks that Syriac combines Hebrew 3b and 3c; Fuchs[89] also admits this possibility, but favors the idea that Syriac had as its *Vorlage* a text like Hebrew 3c. The hemistich under discussion is, in Segal's opinion,[90] תוספת של ביאור

[85] This is the suggestion of Herkenne, *op. cit.*, 149.

[86] The aorist subjunctive (usually in the second person) is often used to express prohibitions; in place of the aorist subjunctive the present imperative may be used. Cf. H. W. Smyth, *Greek Grammar*, rev. by G. M. Messing (Cambridge, Mass., 1956), 404, par. 1800.

[87] In Classical Greek, ἐπέχειν signifies "to hold/hold upon; to present/offer; to hold or direct towards; to keep in check; to reach or extend over a space; to have power over"; so H. G. Liddell-R. Scott-H. S. Jones-R. McKenzie, *A Greek-English Lexicon* (Oxford, 1953), 619f. In the LXX, ἐπέχειν is used to render בין, בצע, חדל, חול, יחל, לאה, מנע, עצר, and קוה; cf. Hatch-Redpath, *A Concordance to the Septuagint*, 511. In the NT, ἐπέχειν means "to hold fast; hold toward/aim at; to stop/stay"; so W. F. Arndt-F. W. Gingrich, *A Greek-English Lexicon of the New Testament and Other Early Christian Literature* (A translation and adaptation of W. Bauer's *Griechisch-Deutsches Wörterbuch zu den Schriften des Neuen Testaments und der übrigen urchristlichen Literatur*, 4th rev. and augmented ed., 1952) (Chicago-Cambridge, 1957), 285.

[88] P. 145.

[89] P. 41.

[90] P. 99.

ל'בעקבותם'. This "explanatory addition" must antedate Syriac, since Segal, like Smend before him, assumes that Syriac, except for בעקבותם, is based upon Hebrew b–c.

We, however, disagree with these views, for we do not think it likely that the Hebrew gloss was inserted into the text before the Syriac version was composed. For if the gloss were added that early, we would be forced to go back one more step; that is to say, we must assume that the gloss, by its presence in the Cairo fragments, antedates 68 A.D., since these fragments represent substantially a text that was recovered from the Jericho (Qumrân) Cave. This assumption does not at all seem reasonable. But it is indeed probable that Syriac 3b is a translation (admittedly somewhat free) of Hebrew 3b (MS A). If that is the case, the most reasonable account of Hebrew 3c is that it is a retroversion of Syriac 3b.

3d

The reconstruction of the first five consonants in MS B is virtually certain. MS B adds אל after רצון in an attempt to make intelligible the reading which is represented in MS A. But the words עושה רצון אל do not seem to be authentic for three reasons: (1) since the number אלף has no noun after it, the words after אחד are uncalled for; (2) these words give the half-line too many accents (at least five) to fit into the normal two to four beat rhythm that is found in the rest of Ben Sira's work; (3) these words have no counterpart in the best witnesses of the Greek MSS tradition. Hence, this half-line most probably read: כי טוב אחד מאלף. Smend,[91] Box and Oesterley,[92] Segal,[93] and CCD[94] also prefer this reading.

The Uncials reflect our proposed reading. Codex 248 adds δίκαιος after εἷς, but this is most likely an inner Greek expansion. The extra words found after εἷς in S[c.a] – δίκαιος ποιῶν θέλημα κυρίου ἢ μύριοι παράνομοι[95] – are also best explained as an inner Greek gloss with

[91] P. 145.

[92] P. 372.

[93] P. 99.

[94] Cf. the critical note and translation.

[95] A similar reading is also found in Chrysostom (*PG*, 53, 186. 363; *PG*, 63, 169): κρείσσων εἷς ποιῶν τὸ θέλημα Κυρίου ἢ μυρίοι παράνομοι. But not much

no basis in a Hebrew *Vorlage*, for a half-line such as this in Hebrew would be simply overloaded. The Greek gloss may have been occasioned by Ps 103, 21, which in $S^{c.a}$ reads: εὐλογεῖτε τὸν κύριον, ... ποιοῦντες τὸ θέλημα αὐτοῦ. Old Latin does not help in establishing the original Greek reading: "Melior est enim unus timens Deum, quam mille filii impii." Old Latin adds glosses after both numerals! And the gloss after "unus" is different from the glosses of 248 and $S^{c.a}$ after εἷς.

Syriac is definitely related to the reading found in MS A or vice versa. Now if our contention is correct that עושה רצון is inauthentic, it seems reasonable to conclude: (1) that the Hebrew/Syriac gloss, "(one) who does the will [sc. of God]", originated with the Syriac translator, under the influence of a Greek text like that of $S^{c.a}$; and (2) that a medieval Jewish scribe in the text tradition represented by MS A retroverted the Syriac gloss into Hebrew. Later when the scribe of MS B was writing his text, he noticed that one of his exemplars (he had several, as we indicated in the last chapter) contained the extra words עושה רצון; since this gloss did not make much sense, he added the word אל.

3e

Before Schirmann's discovery of the leaf of MS B containing this fascinating v., scholars generally agreed that the words ... ממי עולה ... in MS A are not authentic. As regards the reconstruction of עולה, we should note that in the MS there are slight traces of the *'ayin* and *waw*; but at any rate there is space for only two letters. Hence, the reading עולה seems to be the only one possible. Thanks to Schirmann's discovery we now possess MS evidence (in the first four words of 3e in MS B) for the original text of Ben Sira. Although Greek adds ἔχειν (a verb of similar meaning is to be understood in the elliptical Hebrew half-line), it nevertheless clearly reflects the original reading as found in MS B.

---

critical value is to be put upon this witness, for in another place (*PG*, 55, 312) he gives the text in two forms: κρεῖσσον [*sic*] γὰρ εἷς ἢ χίλιοι καὶ ἀποθανεῖν ἄτεκνον ἢ ἔχειν τέκνα ἀσεβῆ [= the Uncials] καὶ κρείσσων εἷς ποιῶν τὸ θέλημα Κυρίου ἢ μυρίοι παράνομοι [= $S^{c.a}$].

The Syriac translator would have nothing to do with the poetic conciseness which is so typical of Hebrew poetry. Consequently, he spells out in dull, cumbersome prose the nuances so beautifully suggested in the Hebrew half-line. Syriac does nevertheless reflect the original Hebrew.

The Mishnaic/Talmudic flavor of ממי שהיו לו בנים רבים עׄוׄלה certainly points to a late date for the composition of this gloss found in MS A. The last three words are, of course, impossible as Hebrew, indicating undoubtedly that the addition as a whole did not originate as an inner Hebrew gloss. Yet despite this clear indication, Smend,[96] Fuchs,[97] Peters,[98] and Segal[99] suggest that the gloss originated as a Hebrew doublet to explain מאחרית זדון. Fuchs even attempts to account for the ungrammatical form of the gloss's last three words: "Der Text in H geht wohl auf בני עולה zurück, eine Randglosse רבים drang dann vor עולה ein und wurde Anlaß בני in בנים zu verwandeln."[100] We emphatically disagree with the opinions of these scholars. We think that this doublet is one of the best instances of retroversion from Syriac. In fact, the manner in which the gloss appears in the recently discovered leaf of MS B makes retroversion virtually undeniable, as we shall see forthwith.

After offering the genuine text of Ben Sira (ומות עריריי מאחרית זדון), MS B presents us with an expanded form of the doublet contained in MS A. The reconstruction of the first two consonants, [טו]ב, is reasonably certain. Instead of the anomalous last three words of the doublet in MS A, MS B provides us with a grammatically correct phrase: בנים רבים בני עולה. But it seems hardly probable that a Jewish scribe would write such a Hebrew phrase, *unless he were making a slavish translation from another language.* For if the scribe were composing on his own initiative a Hebrew paraphrase or variant of Ben Sira's original text, he would have written בני עולה רבים or added after בנים רבים one of the many adjectives meaning "evil, wicked, godless" (נבלים, זדים, רשעים, רעים). Since, therefore, he wrote the extremely clumsy but nevertheless

[96] P. 145.
[97] P. 42.
[98] P. 134.
[99] P. 99.
[100] P. 42.

grammatically correct phrase בנים רבים בני עולה, he must have made a word for word translation of the perfectly normal (grammatically and syntactically) Syriac phrase ܒܢ̈ܝܐ ܣܓܝ̈ܐܐ ܕܥܘܠܐ. Thus, retroversion appears to be the only reasonable explanation of the origin of this doublet.[101]

Segal, however, who had only the evidence of MS A available at the time he wrote his article and commentary, saw in 3e another illustration for his theory that the Cairo Hebrew represents more than one recension.[102] He states that the words which we consider to be retroverted from Syriac, derive from a "simplified colloquial Hebrew" recension (the *Vorlage* of Syriac), whereas the phrase מאחרית זדון comes from "a more or less severe classical Hebrew" recension (the *Vorlage* of Greek).[103] The Cairo Hebrew (a third recension, "not derived from any of the other recensions [as] is proved by the fact that it often preserved the original reading in passages which have become corrupted in the other recensions")[104] "has a rule preserved the two forms [the *Vorlagen* of Greek and Syriac] side by side."[105] One of the cardinal assumptions in Segal's elaborate theory is that "the Hebrew text continued to be read and copied freely for some twelve centuries after Ben Sira's grandson."[106] But this assumption is extremely improbable, for, as we have shown in the last chapter, the generally inexact quotations of Sirach by the rabbis before Saadia prove that these authors did not have at their disposal a text of Sirach like the one preserved in the Cairo MSS. Moreover, it is more than likely that the basic text embodied in the Geniza fragments goes back ultimately to the caves of Qumrân. Consequently, any additions to the text prior to 800 A.D., when

[101] Lévi (part 2, p. 114) also argues for retroversion, but his argument rests upon a faulty reconstruction of the word following רבים; he thinks the word should be [מעו]לה. Since, as we pointed out above, the lacuna is large enough for only two consonants, Lévi's reconstruction is out of the question, and his case becomes unconvincing.

[102] "The Evolution of the Hebrew Text of Ben Sira", *JQR*, n. s., 25 (1934 to 1935), 91–149; 16, 3e is discussed on p. 119. See also his *Sēper ben-Sîrā' hašālēm*, 99. Cf. Chapter I, above, pp. 21–22.

[103] *Art. cit.*, 118.

[104] *Ibid.*, 132.

[105] *Ibid.*, 118.

[106] *Ibid.*, 133. Cf. also Segal's "*Sēper ben-Sîrā' b^{e}qûmrân*", *Tarbiẓ*, 33 (1963 to 1964), 245f.

the text was recovered from the Jericho (Qumrân) Cave, must antedate 68 A.D. But, as Segal himself admits,[107] 16, 3e is written in a late diction and style. This hemistich, in our opinion, must have been added after 800 A.D., and after the Syriac translation had been in existence for some centuries. The Syriac half-line, consequently, could not have been based upon the Hebrew doublet, but the reverse could and indeed did take place.

Sir 32, 16

MS E		MS B
[ירא ייי י]בין משפט	16a	ירא ייי יבין משפט
ותתבולות מנשף יוציא	16b	ותחבולות מנשף יוציא
[יראי ייי יבי]נו משפטו	16c	יראי ייי יבינו משפטו
ותכמות יוצי[או] מלבם	16b	וחכמות וכחֿמות [*sic*] רבות יוציאו מלבם

35, 16a οἱ φοβούμενοι κύριον εὑρήσουσιν κρίμα,
16b καὶ δικαιώματα ὡς φῶς ἐξάψουσιν.

16a ܕܕܚܠܝܢ ܠܐܠܗܐ ܡܬܚܟܡܝܢ ܒܕܝܢܘܗܝ.
16b ܘܚܟܡܬܐ ܣܓܝܐܬܐ ܡܢ ܠܒܗܘܢ ܢܦܩܘܢ.

Translations:

16a–b

MS B: "He who fears Yahweh understands judgment and draws forth skillful direction out of the darkness."

MS E: "[He who fears Yahweh un]derstands judgment and draws forth skillful direction out of the darkness."

Greek (35, 16): "They who fear the Lord will discover judgment and will kindle acts of justice like a light."

Syriac: "They who fear God become wise in his judgments and bring forth great wisdom/skill from their hearts."

16c–d

MS B: "They who fear Yahweh understand His judgment and draw forth great wisdoms [*sic*] (great wisdom [?]) from their hearts."

[107] *Sēper* . . ., 99.

MS E: "[They who fear Yahweh underst]and His judgment and [draw] forth wisdom from their hearts."

Commentary:

16a

The restoration of the first seven consonants of MS E is practically certain. This hemistich seems to be based upon Prv 28, 5: אַנְשֵׁי־רָע לֹא יָבִינוּ מִשְׁפָּט וּמְבַקְשֵׁי יְהוָה יָבִינוּ כֹל. In 16a–b Greek and Syriac have the subject and the two verb predicates in the plural, whereas Hebrew has them in the singular; hence, we should perhaps emend the Cairo Hebrew as follows: יראי ייי יבינו משפט ותחבולות מנשף יוציאו. Such an emendation receives some support from the passage in Prv. The verb εὑρήσουσιν is somewhat free as a rendering of יבינ(ו). Nowhere else either in Sirach or in the rest of the LXX is εὑρίσκειν employed to translate בין. The Syriac expression ܕܢܬܒܩܘܢ (ethpaal), though not an exact translation of יבינ(ו), is, however, considerably more faithful to Hebrew than is Greek. On his own initiative the Syriac translator added the third singular masculine suffix to the word for "judgments"; neither Hebrew nor Greek qualify the word at all.

16b

The rare word תחבולות occurs only six times in the Hebrew canon (Prv 1, 5; 11, 14; 12, 5; 20, 18; 24, 6; and Job 37, 12), and twice certainly, once doubtfully in the Cairo fragments of Sirach (6, 25?; 32, 16; and 37, 17). The LXX renders the word by κυβέρνησις in Prv 1, 5; 11, 14; 24, 6; and by κυβερνᾶν in Prv 12, 5. Both translations are accurate enough. In Hatch and Redpath, Theodotion is listed as having κυβέρνησις in Prv 20, 18, a verse not extant in the LXX. Symmachus employs the same translation for Job 37, 12. But in the verse from Job, the Theodotionic insert within the LXX tradition merely transliterates the Hebrew: ἐν θεεβουλαθώθ! Ben Sira's grandson also had his problems with תחבולות. In 6, 25 he translates בתחבולתיה, by τοῖς δεσμοῖς αὐτῆς, but Smend[108] doubts that the word is original, preferring the reading בחבלותיה. In 37, 17 the

[108] P. 59.

grandson translates עקר תחבולות[109] by ἴχνος ἀλλοιώσεως. In the hemistich under discussion he renders תחבולות, which is certainly original, by δικαιώματα, another poor guess. It seems fair to conclude, therefore, that the grandson did not know the meaning of תחבולות, nor was he aware of the LXX's good translations, κυβέρνησις/κυβερνᾶν, for the word in the passages indicated above.

The use of ὡς φῶς as a translation of מנשף is also weak; it may be as Smend,[110] Peters,[111] and Segal[112] suggest, that Greek read כרשף ("like a flame"). The translation ἐξάψουσιν for יוציא(ו) is open to question too, for ἐξάπτειν means either "to fasten to/place upon", or "to set fire to/kindle/inflame". In view of the Greek context it is clear that the meaning "to kindle" was intended. Again as Smend, Peters, and Segal suggest, perhaps Greek read יציתו (hiphil: "to set fire to/kindle") for יוציא(ו). Against these conjectures, however, J. Marcus[113] submits: "... ὡς φῶς ἐξάψουσιν may have been influenced by the LXX translation of Ps. 37, 6: והוציא כאור צדקך καὶ ἐξοίσει ὡς φῶς τὴν δικαιοσύνην σου."

In 16b Syriac used a paraphrase – ܢܩܘܫܬܐ ܕܡܕܒܪܢܘܬܐ (good Syriac diction) – to render תחבולות, probably because there is no Syriac noun having the same root as the Hebrew word. In 6, 25 where the Cairo Hebrew has בתחבולתיה, Syriac translates by ܒܡܘܒܠܗ̇ ("by her burden"), but as mentioned earlier, Hebrew is doubtful here. Syriac omits 37, 17, a verse in which Hebrew again has תחבולות.

Syriac made the not unusual slip of reading מנפש instead of מנשף. Such an explanation of ܡܢ ܢܦܫܗ, appears much more convincing than the one supposed by Smend,[114] Fuchs,[115] Peters,[116] and Segal,[117]

[109] This is the reading of MS D. MS E has עקרת תחבולות, but in the margin it gives עקר.

[110] P. 292.

[111] P. 268.

[112] P. 208.

[113] *The Newly Discovered Original Hebrew of Ben Sira (Ecclesiasticus xxxii, 16–xxxiv, 1): The Fifth Manuscript and a Prosodic Version of Ben Sira (Ecclesiasticus xxii, 22–xxiii, 9)* (Philadelphia, 1931), 12. This work appeared originally in the *JQR*, n. s., 21 (1930–1931), 223–240.

[114] P. 292.

[115] Pp. 73f.

[116] P. 268.

[117] Pp. 207f.

viz. that the Syriac phrase is a translation of מלבם (16d), which in turn is a simple doublet of Hebrew 16b.

16c–d

The first word of 16d in MS B is an obvious mistake which the scribe dutifully corrected by his marginal note. Hebrew 16c–d and Syriac 16a–b quite obviously are related to one another. As already indicated, Smend *et al.* would have the Syriac line depend upon the Hebrew, whereas we maintain that the reverse is true.[118] Merely stating that 16c–d is a doublet or even a second recension of 16a–b is, of course, the simplest way of accounting for the extra distich. But the question remains: how or why did the presumed doublet or second recension come about? How, for example, can we reasonably explain the unusual (to indulge in understatement) expression חכמות רבות? The normal plural of חָכְמָה, which would be חֲכָמוֹת, does not occur in biblical Hebrew nor in the non-canonical writings from Qumrân published up to 1960.[119] And if we read חכמות as חָכְמוֹת, the rather rare word for "wisdom (personified)" as in Ps 49, 4; Prv 1, 20; 9, 1; 24, 7; and, as many conjecture, Prv 14, 1, then we must decide whether this noun is singular or plural. If it is a real singular, as J. Barth,[120] Gesenius-Kautzsch,[121] and Bauer-Leander[122] maintain, then we should expect a singular adjective to modify it, viz. רבה.[123] If, however, it is a plural, as Brockelmann,[124]

[118] Lévi, part 2, p. 159, also maintains this position, but, as indicated in the introduction to this chapter, our conclusion was arrived at independently.

[119] Cf. Kuhn, *Konkordanz* ..., 72.

[120] *Die Nominalbildung in den semitischen Sprachen,* 2d ed. (Leipzig, 1894), 411, par. 259c.

[121] *Hebrew Grammar,* trans. by A. E. Cowley 2d ed. (Oxford, 1910), 398, par. 124*e*; cf. also p. 241, par. 68 *l*.

[122] *Historische Grammatik der hebräischen Sprache des alten Testaments,* 1 (Halle a.S., 1922), 506, par. 61tι.

[123] We should recall here that in Prv 1, 20 and 9, 1 where חָכְמוֹת is subject of the sentence, the verb predicates are singular. Three of these verbs have direct objects with the third feminine suffix attached; the suffix in all cases is singular.

[124] *Grundriß der vergleichenden Grammatik der semitischen Sprachen,* 2 (Berlin, 1913), 59, par. 29b.

Joüon,[125] and Brønno[126] think, then it could be modified by a plural adjective. Using Mandelkern's and Kuhn's concordances, we checked every occurrence of חָכְמָה and חָכְמוֹת in biblical Hebrew and in the Qumrân literature: never is either word qualified by an adjective. Hence, to say the least, it is extremely improbable that חכמות רבות originated as an inner Hebrew doublet or represents a second recension of the original תחבולות. In addition to the arguments adduced thus far, we should recall that in the theory of Smend *et al.* the doublet or recension must antedate the Syriac version, which was composed by the end of the fourth century A.D., at the latest. But as we took great pains to establish in the last chapter, it is more than likely that the text represented by the Cairo Hebrew fragments of Sirach came from the Jericho (Qumrân) cave that was discovered about the year 800 A.D. Thus if the theory of Smend *et al.* were correct, we would be forced to date the doublet or recension at least as far back as 68 A.D.!

If, however, Hebrew 16c–d was retroverted from Syriac which in turn had been translated from Hebrew 16a–b, then we can very reasonably account for the abnormal phrase, וחכמות רבות; it is simply a slavish translation of the perfectly normal Syriac ܘܚܟܡܬܐ ܣܓܝܐܬܐ.[127] The medieval Jewish retranslator read the Syriac words as plurals and the orthography[128] allows such an interpretation, but the Syriac MSS and editions that we consulted do not have the two dots which indicate the plural over either of these two words. The scribe of MS E omitted רבות from the retroversion found in his exemplar, thus making the hemistich read at least like normal Hebrew.

[125] *Grammaire de l'hébreu biblique*, 2d ed. (Rome, 1947), 211, par. 88 M*k*.

[126] *Studien über hebräische Morphologie und Vokalismus auf Grundlage der Mercatischen Fragmente der zweiten Kolumne der Hexapla des Origenes* (Leipzig, 1943), 187.

[127] We should note here that the Syriac title of the Book of Wisdom is ܚܟܡܬܐ ܪܒܬܐ ܕܫܠܝܡܘܢ, which literally translated means "The Great Wisdom of Solomon". In Sir 9, 1 of Syriac we also find ܚܟܡܬܐ ܒܝܫܬܐ, which means "a base scheme/plan".

[128] The plural ܚܶܟ̈ܡܳܬܳܐ does indeed occur; cf. R. Payne Smith *et al.* (eds.), *Thesaurus syriacus*, 1 (Oxford, 1879), 1267f. for references to the literature where this plural is found.

Before taking our leave of this textually interesting verse, we should note that 16a–b is one of the many distichs that prove beyond a doubt that the Cairo Hebrew on the whole could not possibly be based upon either Syriac or Greek, *pace* Ginsberg, Torrey, Goodspeed, Hadas (see Chapter I). No one retranslating from Syriac or Greek would use the rare word תחבולות to render ܢܡܘ̈ܣܐ ܦܘܩܕ̈ܢܐ or δικαιώματα, respectively.

V. SOME CONCLUSIONS

Now that we have completed our study of the five Hebrew MSS of Sirach that were recovered from the Qaraite Synagogue in Old Cairo, we should like to suggest a few conclusions. These we shall divide into two groups: (1) conclusions resulting from our text-critical analysis of the Cairo MSS; and (2) conclusions resulting from our historical study.

A. CONCLUSIONS FROM THE TEXT-CRITICAL ANALYSIS

1. Since there are so many vv. whose authenticity is incontestable, we must conclude that unless the contrary is demonstrated the Geniza MSS contain the original text or something very near to the original text of Ben Sira. Indeed, the Cairo MSS must be presumed genuine unless serious and weighty evidence can be adduced against the originality of a particular passage. In Chapter IV, for example, we have proved that certain parts of the Geniza Hebrew are quite spurious, being retranslated from the Syriac Peshiṭta. But only after all the resources of textual criticism have been fully exploited and no other plausible explanation seemed possible, did we conclude that a particular text was the product of a medieval retranslator's pen rather than Ben Sira's.

2. Even in those places where retranslation seems undeniable, we find genuine Ben Sira material in the surrounding context. In our discussion of Sir 5, 4–6 (see Chapter IV) we saw, for example, that the Geniza text of 5, 4a–b. 5a–b. 6a–d was generally superior to both Greek and Syriac, despite the retroversion that was proved to exist in 5, 4c–d (MS A). A similar situation prevails in the six other samples of retranslation that have been analyzed.

3. No serious translation of Sir can be attempted unless the Cairo MSS are critically and carefully utilized, for often the grandson's Greek and the Syriac translation, not to mention the Old Latin, are so corrupt that only the Geniza Hebrew provides us with the inspired message of Ben Sira.

4. Though generally authentic, the Cairo fragments must be employed with a great deal of caution, constant reference being made to Greek and Syriac, and to Old Latin, when necessary. For in addition to partial retroversion, the Geniza MSS contain more than the normal share of scribal errors, glosses, and other corruptions.

5. The skepticism of D. S. Margoliouth, G. Bickell, E. J. Goodspeed, C. H. Gordon, A. Büchler, R. Storr, M. Hadas, C. C. Torrey, H. L. Ginsberg, H. Duesberg, P. Auvray, and others with respect to the authenticity of the Cairo Geniza Hebrew may have been occasioned by the failure of the vast majority of scholars, who defended the genuineness of the Hebrew text, to consider seriously the partial retroversion hypothesis which explains much of the "hideous" and "late" diction found in our MSS.

6. Although we must concede that the Geniza text of Sir is essentially genuine, we have seen that it contains nevertheless many retroversions from Syriac. These retroversions, however, form only a part of the textual corruptions found in the Cairo MSS. We have given special notice to the retroversions, because it appears that these comprise the major part of the textual corruptions. And it seems that these have caused the opponents to dismiss the Geniza text in its entirety as retranslation from Syriac and/or Greek.

7. The opponents of the Cairo Hebrew, basing some of their arguments upon texts which could best be explained as retroversions from Syriac, have shown themselves myopic in rejecting outright the complete text of the Cairo fragments merely because some of its parts were defective. No scholar has ever attempted, with any degree of success, to prove that a major portion of the Cairo text is secondary, being based upon Persian (Margoliouth), Greek (Goodspeed, Hadas), Syriac (Torrey, Bickell, Ginsberg), or Syrohexaplar (Ginsberg). On the contrary, however, we do have complete commentaries by Lévi, Smend, Peters, Box and Oesterley, and Segal, all of whom admit the substantial genuineness of our Hebrew text.

B. CONCLUSIONS FROM THE HISTORICAL STUDY

According to the more than probable hypothesis defended in Chapter III, the history of the Hebrew text of Sir seems to go something like this:

1. During the first quarter of the second century B.C., Ben Sira writes his Book in Palestine.

2. Many copies are made and circulated. Some reach Alexandria where the grandson of Ben Sira makes his Greek translation some time after 132 B.C. Other copies remain in the Holy Land where the members of the Qumrân sect – the Essenes – who emigrated to the wilderness of Judea, cherish the Book, probably because of its emphasis upon the Ṣadoqite priesthood. Some copies of Sir are hidden away in the caves near Khirbet Qumrân.

3. In the Synod of Jamnia held at the end of the first century A.D., the rabbis suppress the Book, but a few copies keep in circulation.

4. At least one copy of the Hebrew text forms the basis of the Syriac translation, which was composed some time during the period from the second to fourth century A.D. probably by a Christian. By this late date the Hebrew behind the Syriac translation seems to have been a recension other than that preserved in the Qumrân cave.

5. The Hebrew text survives till the time of St. Jerome (died 420) who writes in his preface to the Books of Solomon (*PL*, 28, 1307 f.): "Fertur et πανάρετος Jesu filii Sirach liber, et alius ψευδεπίγραφος qui Sapientia Salomonis inscribitur. Quorum priorem Hebraicum reperi, non Ecclesiasticum, ut apud Latinos; sed Parabolas praenotatum . . ."

6. By the middle of the fifth century A.D., it seems that the Hebrew text of Sir is finally quashed. Popular recollections of and favorite proverbs from the Book survive and are often quoted by rabbinical writers. But such quotations, as we noted in Chapter III, are often inexact, proving that they were cited from memory or from poorly transmitted *florilegia*.

7. Near the end of the eighth century A.D., the Hebrew text of Sir is recovered from the Jericho cave that was accidentally found by an Arab hunter who had been looking for his dog. There are

very solid reasons for believing that this cave is one of those discovered anew near Khirbet Qumrân from 1947 onward.

8. The Qaraites who recover the MSS of Sir from this cave are happy to obtain the Book in Hebrew and make many copies of it. Perhaps, among other reasons, due to the poor preservation of some of the cave MSS and to the difficulty of reading the Qumrân script (especially such letters as *waw* and *yod*), some copyist(s) retranslated from the Syriac version passages that did not seem to make sense or that were not contained in the cave fragments. This explains many of the doublets, as we saw in Chapter IV.

9. The Qaraites and other Jews – Saadia, for example – enjoy the use of Sir in Hebrew up to the twelfth century when the Rabbanites again succeed in suppressing the Book. Hence, since the Hebrew text of the Book disappears into the Genizas, Jewish authors from the Middle Ages to almost the beginning of the present century never again use it.

10. Near the end of the nineteenth century a vast amount of material is recovered from the Qaraite Synagogue in Old Cairo. Among the thousands of Geniza fragments that reached various libraries in Europe and in America, four distinct Hebrew MSS of Sir – A, B, C, and D – are identified around the turn of the century by S. Schechter, A. E. Cowley, A. Neubauer, I. Lévi, G. Margoliouth, E. N. Adler, and M. Gaster. In 1931, J. Marcus discovers MS E, and in 1958 and 1960, J. Schirmann finds more leaves of MSS B and C.

GENERAL BIBLIOGRAPHY

The following bibliography covers studies on the Book of Sirach in general, not just the specific problems dealt with in the present book. We have examined the literature up to June, 1964. For a good Sirach bibliography up to 1909, see E. Schürer, *Geschichte des jüdischen Volkes in Zeitalter Jesu Christi*, 3, 4th ed. (Leipzig, 1909), 212–228; some of the works found in Schürer are not included below. For studies dealing with the theological problems (canonicity, inspiration, etc.) of Sirach, see L. Bigot, "Ecclésiastique (Livre de l')", *Dictionnaire de théologie catholique*, 4, 2 (Paris, 1911), 2028–2054. For a detailed list of commentators from Patristic to modern times, see A. Gelin, "Ecclésiastique (Livre de l')", *Dictionnaire de théologie catholique, Tables générales* (Paris, 1956), 1098f.

A. SOURCES

The Geniza MSS of Sirach

Adler, E. N., "Some Missing Chapters of Ben Sira [7, 29–12, 1]", *JQR*, 12 (1899 to 1900), 466–480.

Cowley, A. E.-A. Neubauer (eds.), *The Original Hebrew of a Portion of Ecclesiasticus* (Oxford, 1897).

Facsimiles of the Fragments Hitherto Recovered of the Book of Ecclesiasticus in Hebrew (Oxford-Cambridge, 1901).

Gaster, M., "A New Fragment of Ben Sira [parts of chapters 18, 19, and 20]", *JQR*, 12 (1899–1900), 688–702.

Knabenbauer, I., *Textus Ecclesiastici Hebraeus* ... (= Appendix to *Commentarius in Ecclesiasticum* [see under Commentaries]) (Paris, 1902).

Di Lella, A. A., "The Recently Identified Leaves of Sirach in Hebrew", *Bib*, 45 (1964), 153–167.

Lévi, I., *L'Ecclésiastique ou la Sagesse de Jésus, fils de Sira*, 2 parts (Paris, 1898, 1901).

——, "Fragments de deux nouveaux manuscrits hébreux de l'Ecclésiastique", *REJ*, 40 (1900), 1–30.

——, *The Hebrew Text of the Book of Ecclesiasticus (= Semitic Study Series 3)* (Leiden, 1904).

——, "Un nouveau fragment de Ben Sira", *REJ*, 92 (1932), 136–145.

Marcus, J., *The Newly Discovered Original Hebrew of Ben Sira (Ecclasiasticus xxxii, 16–xxxiv, 1): The Fifth Manuscript and a Prosodic Version of Ben Sira (Ecclesiasticus xxii, 22–xxiii, 9)* (Philadelphia, 1931). This is a corrected reprint of the article which appeared originally in *JQR*, n. s., 21 (1930–1931), 223–240.

Margoliouth, G., "The Original Hebrew of Ecclesiasticus XXXI. 12–31, and XXXVI. 22–XXXVII. 26", *JQR*, 12 (1899–1900), 1–33.

Peters, N., *Der jüngst wiederaufgefundene hebräische Text des Buches Ecclesiasticus untersucht, herausgegeben, übersetzt und mit kritischen Noten versehen* (Freiburg i.B., 1902).

——, *Liber Jesu filii Sirach sive Ecclesiasticus hebraice* (Freiburg i.B., 1905).

Schechter, S., "A Fragment of the Original Text of Ecclesiasticus", *Expositor*, 5th series, 4 (1896), 1–15.

——, "A Further Fragment of Ben Sira (= MS C: parts of chapters 4, 5, 25, and 26)", *JQR*, 12 (1899–1900), 456–465.

——, "Genizah Specimens. *Ecclesiasticus* (= original text of 49, 12–50, 22)", *JQR*, 10 (1897–1898), 197–206.

Schechter, S.-C. Taylor, *The Wisdom of Ben Sira: Portions of the Book Ecclesiasticus from Hebrew Manuscripts in the Cairo Genizah Collection Presented to the University of Cambridge by the Editors* (Cambridge, 1899).

Schirmann, J., "*Dap ḥādāš mittôk sēper ben-Sîrā' hā-ʿibrî*", *Tarbiẕ*, 27 (1957 to 1958), 440–443.

——, "*Dappîm nôsᵉpîm mittôk sēper 'ben-Sîrā'*'", *Tarbiẕ*, 29 (1959–1960), 125–134.

Segal, M. H., *Sēper ḥokmat ben-Sîrā' ha-šālēm* (Jerusalem, 1933).

——, *Sēper ben-Sîrā' ha-šālēm*, 2d ed. (Jerusalem, Israel, 1958).

Smend, R., *Die Weisheit des Jesus Sirach, hebräisch und deutsch* (Berlin, 1906).

Strack, H. L., *Die Sprüche Jesus', des Sohnes Sirachs* (Leipzig, 1903).

Vigouroux, F., *L'Ecclésiastique (= La Sainte Bible Polyglotte 5)* (Paris, 1904).

The Versions of Sirach

Greek:

Hart, J. H. A., *Ecclesiasticus: the Greek Text of Codex 248* (Cambridge, 1909).

Holmes, R.-J. Parsons, *Vetus testamentum graecum cum variis lectionibus*, 4 (Oxford, 1827).

Rahlfs, A., *Septuaginta*, 2, 5th ed. (Stuttgart, 1952).

Swete, H. B., *The Old Testament in Greek*, 2, 3d ed. (Cambridge, 1907).

Old Latin:

Biblia sacra iuxta latinam vulgatam versionem, 12: *Sapientia Salomonis, Liber Hiesu filii Sirach* (Rome, 1964).

Herkenne, H., *De veteris latinae Ecclesiastici capitibus I–XLIII* (Leipzig, 1899).

de Lagarde, P., *Die Weisheiten der Handschrift von Amiata (Mittheilungen 1)* (Göttingen, 1884), Sir pp. 283–378.

Syrohexaplar:

Ceriani, A. M., *Codex syro-hexaplaris Ambrosianus photolithographice editus* (Milan, 1874).

Syriac Peshiṭta:

Biblia sacra juxta versionem simplicem quae dicitur Pschitta, 2 (referred to as the Mosul edition) (Beirut, 1951) (Sir pp. 204–255).

Ceriani, A. M. (ed.), *Translatio Syra Pescitto veteris testamenti ex codice Ambrosiano sec. fere VI photolithographice edita*, 2, 4 (Milan, 1878).

de Lagarde, P. A., *Libri veteris testamenti apocryphi syriace* (Leipzig-London, 1861).

Walton, B., *Biblia sacra polyglotta*, 4 (London, 1657). Variants are contained in vol. 6, pp. 46f.

Arabic:

Sinai Arabic MS 155 (this translation was made from the Greek; R. M. Frank, of the Catholic University of America, is preparing an edition of this Arabic version).

Walton, B., *Biblia sacra polyglotta*, 4 (London, 1657) (this Arabic translation was made from the Peshiṭta).

Coptic:

de Lagarde, P., *Aegyptiaca* (Göttingen, 1883) (Coptic version of Sir, pp. 107 to 206).

Ethiopic:

Dillmann, A., *Biblia veteris testamenti aethiopica*, 5: *Libri apocryphi* (Berlin, 1894), 54–117.

For information concerning the other versions and editions thereof, see L. Bigot, "Ecclésiastique (Livre de l')", *Dictionnaire de théologie catholique* 4,2 (Paris, 1911), 2031ff.

B. COMMENTARIES AND ARTICLES ON SIRACH

Abbott, T. K., "Margoliouth's Essay on the Place of Ecclesiasticus in Semitic Literature", *Hermathena: A Series of Papers on Literature, Science, and Philosophy*, 16 (1890), 341–344.

Abrahams, I., "Schechter and Taylor's *Wisdom of Ben Sira*", *JQR*, 12 (1899 to 1900), 171–176.

Alfrink, B., *Het Boek Ecclesiasticus* (= *Oud Testament 4, 6*) (Bruges, 1934).

——, "Het gebed van Jesus Sirach (Eccl. 51, 1–17)", *Nederlandsche Katholieke Stemmen*, 33 (1933), 137–144.

André, T., *Les Apocryphes de l'Ancien Testament* (Florence, 1903).

Anonymous, "Ueber den liturgischen Gebrauch des Hohenliedes und des Ecclesiasticus im marianischen Cultus", *Der Katholik*, N.F., 1 (1859), 111–121.

The Apocrypha, trans. by E. J. Goodspeed, introduction by M. Hadas (New York, 1959).

The Apocrypha according to the Authorized Version, with an Introduction by R. H. Pfeiffer (London, n.d.).

Arnald, R., *Ecclesiasticus*, in *A Critical Commentary and Paraphrase on the Old and New Testament and the Apocrypha*, 3 (London, 1844), 936–1097.

Auvray, P., "Notes sur le Prologue de *l'Ecclésiastique*", in *Mélanges bibliques rédigés en l'honneur de André Robert* (Paris [1957]), 281–287.

Bacher, W., "Four Quotations from the Hebrew Ben Sira", *JQR*, 11 (1898 to 1899), 344.

——, "The Hebrew Text of Ecclesiasticus", *JQR*, 9 (1896–1897), 543–562.

——, "An Hypothesis about the Hebrew Fragments of Sirach", *JQR*, 12 (1899 to 1900), 92–108.

——, "Notes on the Cambridge Fragments of Ecclesiasticus", *JQR*, 12 (1899 to 1900), 272–290.

——, "Notes sur les nouveaux fragments de Ben Sira. I", *REJ*, 40 (1900), 253ff.

——, "Die persischen Randnotizen zum hebräischen Sirach", *ZAW*, 20 (1900), 308ff.

Baillet, M.-J. T. Milik-R. de Vaux, *Les 'Petites Grottes' de Qumrân (= Discoveries in the Judaean Desert of Jordan 3)* (Oxford, 1962), ⋆ *Textes*, ⋆⋆ *Planches*.

Bauckmann, E. G., "Die Proverbien und die Sprüche des Jesus Sirach: Eine Untersuchung zum Strukturwandel der israelitischen Weisheitslehre", *ZAW*, 72 (1960), 33–63.

Bauer, J., "'Kein Leben ohne Wein' (Jesus Sirach 31, 27): Das Urteil der Hl. Schrift", *Bibel und Liturgie*, 23 (1955–1956), 55–59.

——, "Des Vaters Segen ..., der Fluch der Mutter ... [Sir 3, 9]", *Bibel und Liturgie*, 23 (1955–1956), 295f.

Bauer, J. B., "Der priesterliche Schöpfungshymnus in Gen. 1 [Sir 15, 14]", *TZ*, 20 (1964), 1–9.

——, "Sir. 15, 14 et Gen. 1, 1", *VD*, 41 (1963), 243f.

Baumgartner, W., "Jesus Sirach", in *Die Religion in Geschichte und Gegenwart*, 3, 2d ed. (Tübingen, 1929), 169f.

——, "Die literarischen Gattungen in der Weisheit des Jesus Sirach", *ZAW*, 34 (1914), 161–198.

Bentzen, A., *Introduction to the Old Testament*, 1–2, 2d ed. (Copenhagen, 1952).

——, "Sirach, der Chronist, und Nehemia", *ST*, 3 (1949 [1951]), 158–161.

Ben Zeeb, I. L., *Ḥokmat Y^{e}hôšu'a ben-Sîrā'* (Vienna, 1828).

Bickell, G., "Ein alphabetisches Lied Jesus Sirach's", *ZKT*, 6 (1882), 319–333.

——, "Der hebräische Sirachtext eine Rückübersetzung", *WZKM*, 13 (1899), 251–256.

Bigot, L., "Ecclésiastique (Livre de l')", *Dictionnaire de théologie catholique*, 4,2 (Paris, 1911), 2028–2054.

Bissell, E. C., *The Apocrypha of the Old Testament* (= *A Commentary on the Holy Scriptures* ... vol. 15 of the Old Testament) (New York, 1880), 274–409.

Blau, L., "Quelques notes sur Jésus ben Sirach et son ouvrage. I", *REJ*, 35 (1897), 19–29.

Bonartius, O., *In Ecclesiasticum Commentarius* (Antwerp, 1634).

Box, G. H.-W. O. E. Oesterley, "Sirach", in *The Apocrypha and Pseudepigrapha of the Old Testament*, 1, ed. by R. H. Charles (Oxford, 1913), 268–517.

Bretschneider, C. G., *Liber Iesu Siracidae graece ad fidem codicum et versionem emendatus et perpetua annotatione illustratus* (Ratisbon, 1806).

Brockington, L. H., *A Critical Introduction to the Apocrypha (= Studies in Theology 61)* (London, 1961).

Brockington, L. H., *Ideas of Mediation between God and Man in the Apocrypha* (London, 1962).

De Bruyne, D., "Étude sur le texte latin de l'Ecclésiastique", *RevBén*, 40 (1928), 5–48.

——, "Le Prologue, le titre et la finale de l'Ecclésiastique", *ZAW*, 47 (1929), 257–263.

——, "Saint Augustin reviseur de la Bible", *Miscellanea Agostiniana*, 2 (Rome, 1931), 521–606 (section on Sir, pp. 578–585).

Büchler, A., "Ben Sira's Conception of Sin and Atonement", *JQR*, n. s., 13 (1922–1923), 303–335; 461–502; 14 (1923–1924), 53–83.

Burkill, T. A., "Ecclesiasticus", in *Interpreter's Dictionary of the Bible*, 2 (New York-Nashville, 1962), 13–21.

Burney, C. F., "Notes on Some Hebrew Passages. – Ecclesiasticus iv 26b., v 10.", *JTS*, 21 (1919–1920), 242f.

Cadbury, H. J., "The Grandson of Ben Sira", *HarvTR*, 48 (1955), 219–225.

Carmignac, J., "Les rapports entre l'Ecclésiastique et Qumrân", *Revue de Qumran*, 3 (1961), 209–218.

Caspari, W., "Der Schriftgelehrte besingt seine Stellung Sir 51, 12–17 (29)", *ZNW*, 28 (1929), 143–148.

——, "Über die Textpflege, nach den hebräischen Handschriften des Sira", *ZAW*, 50 (1932), 160–168; 51 (1933), 140–150.

Celada, B., "El velo del templo [Sir 50]", *Cultura Biblica*, 15 (1958), 109–112.

Chait, S., *Buddha and Sirach: A Comparative Study* (reprinted from the Hebrew Monthly *Hatoren*, 10 [1923], 1–16).

Chajes, H. P., "Notes critiques sur le texte hébreu de l'Ecclésiastique", *REJ*, 40 (1900), 31–36.

Cheyne, T. K., "Ecclus. xi. 19", *JQR*, 10 (1897–1898), 13–17.

——, *Job and Solomon, or the Wisdom of the Old Testament* (London, 1887).

——, "Note (on D. S. Margoliouth's 'The Language and Metre of Ecclesiasticus')", *Expositor*, 4th series, 1 (1890), 390f.

——, "Note on Sirach L. 9", *JQR*, 12 (1899–1900), 554.

Churton, W. R., *The Uncanonical and Apocryphal Scriptures* (London, 1884).

Cook, S. A., "An Arabic Version of the Prologue to Ecclesiasticus", in *Proceedings of the Society of Biblical Archaeology* (May 14, 1902), 173–184.

Cowley, A., "Notes on the Cambridge Texts of Ben Sira", *JQR*, 12 (1899–1900), 109ff.

——, "Review of *De Veteris Latinae Ecclesiastici capitibus i–xliii . . ., scripsit Dr. Theol. Henr. Herkenne*", *JQR*, 12 (1899–1900), 168–171.

Cronbach, A., "The Social Ideals of the Apocrypha and Pseudepigrapha", *HUCA*, 18 (1943–1944), 119–156.

Czajkowski, M., "Na tropach tradycji eschatologicznej i mesjańskiej u Ben-Syracha", *Ruch Biblijny i Liturgiczny*, 16 (1963), 87–98.

Davidson, A. B., "Sirach's Judgment of Women", *ExpT*, 6 (1894–1895), 402ff.

Desečar, E., *De conceptu stultitiae in libro graeco Jesu Sirach* (= unpublished doctoral dissertation at the Pontificium Athenaeum Antonianum) (Jerusalem, Jordan, 1963).

Douais, C., *Une ancienne version latine de l'Ecclésiastique* (Paris, 1895).

Driver, G. R., "Ben Sira, XXXIII, 4", *JJS*, 5 (1954), 177.

——, "Ecclesiasticus: A New Fragment of the Hebrew Text", *ExpT*, 49 (1937 to 1938), 37ff.

Driver, G. R., "Hebrew Notes on the Wisdom of Jesus Ben Sirach", *JBL*, 53 (1934), 273–290.

Driver, S. R., "Note (on D. S. Margoliouth's 'The Language and Metre of Ecclesiasticus')", *Expositor*, 4th series, 1 (1890), 387–390.

Dubarle, A.-M., *Les sages d'Israël* (Paris, 1946).

Duesberg, H., "Ecclésiastique (Livre de l')", *Dictionnaire de Spiritualité*, 4 (Paris, 1958), 52–62.

——, "Il est le tout, Siracide 43, 27–33", *Bible et Vie chrétienne*, 54 (1963), 29–32.

——, "Le médecin, un sage (Ecclésiastique 38, 1–15)", *Bible et Vie chrétienne*, 38 (1961), 43–48.

Duesberg, H.-P. Auvray, *Le livre de l'Ecclésiastique (La Sainte Bible de Jérusalem)*, 2d ed. (Paris, 1958).

Eberharter, A., *Das Buch Jesus Sirach oder Ecclesiasticus (= Die Heilige Schrift des Alten Testamentes übersetzt und erklärt in Verbindung mit Fachgelehrten 6,5)* (Bonn, 1925).

——, "Zu Ekkli 16, 14", *BZ*, 6 (1908), 162f.

——, "Die 'Ekklesiastikuszitate' bei Klemens von Alexandrien. Gesammelt und mit LXX und Vulgata verglichen", *TQ*, 93 (1911), 1–22.

——, "Die Ekklesiastikus-Zitate in den Pseudocyprianischen Schriften", *Bib*, 7 (1926), 324f.

——, "Exegetische Bemerkungen zu Ekkli. 16, 1–5", *Der Katholik*, 4te Folge, 37 (1908), 386–389.

——, *Der Kanon des Alten Testaments zur Zeit des Ben Sira (= Alttestamentliche Abhandlungen 3, 3)* (Münster i. W., 1911).

——, "*KŠL* in Ps 105, 3 und Ekkli 14, 9", *BZ*, 6 (1908), 155–161.

——, "The Text of Ecclesiasticus in the Quotations of Clement of Alexandria and Saint Cyprian", *Bib*, 7 (1926), 79–83.

——, "Textkritische Bemerkungen zu Ekkli. Ekkli 6, 19 IV; 8, 10 I; 13, 9 I", *BZ*, 5 (1907), 22–26.

Edersheim, A., *Ecclesiasticus*, in *Apocrypha*, 2, ed. by H. Wace (London, 1888), 1–239.

Eissfeldt, O., *Einleitung in das Alte Testament*, 2d ed. (Tübingen, 1956), 737 to 741.

Elmslie, W. A. L., *Studies in Life from Jewish Proverbs* (special reference to Prv and Sir) (London, n.d. [1917]).

Eybers, I. H., "Some Light on the Canon of the Qumran Sect", in *New Light on Some Old Testament Problems* (= Papers Read at 5th Meeting Held at the University of South Africa, Pretoria) (Pretoria, South Africa, 1962), 1–14.

Fang Che-yong, M., "Ben Sira de novissimis hominis", *VD*, 41 (1963), 21–38.

——, *De discrepantiis inter textum graecum et hebraicum libri Ecclesiastici seu Ben Sira quarum origo sensus necnon momentum theologicum investigantur* (= unpublished doctoral dissertation at the Pontifical Biblical Institute) (Rome-Munich, 1963).

——, *Quaestiones theologicae selectae libri Sira ex comparatione textus graeci et hebraici ortae* (Rome, 1963 [published in 1964]).

——, "Sir 7, 36 (Vulg 7, 40) iuxta hebraicam veritatem", *VD*, 40 (1962), 18–26.

Ferrar, W. J., *The Uncanonical Jewish Books* (London-New York, 1918).

de Flores, A., *Commentarius litteralis et moralis in c. 24 Ecclesiastici, seu conceptus praedicabiles de Christo, eius Matre, eiusque sponsa Ecclesia* (Antwerp, 1661).

Fonck, L., "'Quasi cedrus exaltata sum in Libano ...' (Eccli. 24, 17)", *VD*, 1 (1921), 226–231.

Fraenkel, S., "Zu Ben Sîrâ", *ZAW*, 21 (1901), 191f.

——, "Zur Sprache des hebräischen Sirach", *Monatsschrift für Geschichte und Wissenschaft des Judenthums*, 43 (1899), 481–484.

De Fraine, J., "Het Loflied op de menselijke Waardigheid in Eccli 17, 1–14", *Bijdragen*, 11 (1950), 10–22 (French summary on pp. 22f.).

Fritzsche, O. F., *Kurzgefaßtes exegetisches Handbuch zu den Apokryphen*, 5 (Leipzig, 1859).

Fruhstorfer, K., "Des Weisen curriculum vitae nach Sirach (39, 1–15)", *TPQ*, 94 (1941), 140ff.

Fuchs, A., *Textkritische Untersuchungen zum hebräischen Ekklesiastikus (= Biblische Studien 12, 5)* (Freiburg i. B., 1907).

Fuss, W., *Tradition and Komposition im Buche Jesus Sirach* (Tübingen, 1963).

Gallus, T., "'A muliere initium peccati et per illam omnes morimur' (Sir 25, 24 [33])", *VD*, 23 (1943), 272–277.

Gasser, J. K., *Das althebräische Spruchbuch und die Sprüche Jesu Ben Sira in Bezug auf einige wesentliche Merkmale ihrer historischen Verschiedenheit untersucht* (Gütersloh, 1903).

——, *Die Bedeutung der Sprüche Jesu Ben Sira für die Datierung des althebräischen Spruchbuches untersucht (Beiträge zur Forderung christlicher Theologie Jhrg. 8. Hft. 2, 3)* (Gütersloh, 1904).

Geiger, Dr., "Warum gehört das Buch Sirach zu den Apokryphen?" *ZDMG*, 12 (1858), 536–543.

Gelin, A., "Ecclésiastique (Livre de l')", *Dictionnaire de théologie catholique, Tables générales* (Paris, 1956), 1087–1091.

Germann, H., "Jesus ben Siras Dankgebet und die Hodajoth", *TZ*, 19 (1963), 81–87.

Gigot, F. E., "Ecclesiasticus", in *Catholic Encyclopedia*, 5 (New York, 1909), 263–269.

Ginsberg, H. L., "The Original Hebrew of Ben Sira 12 10–14", *JBL*, 74 (1955), 93ff.

——, [Sir 50, 25], *ZAW*, N.F., 14 (1937), 308f.

Ginzberg, L., "Randglossen zum hebräischen Ben Sira", *Orientalische Studien, Theodor Nöldeke gewidmet*, 2, ed. by C. Bezold (Gießen, 1906), 609–625.

Girotti, G., "Ecclesiastico", in *La Sacra Bibbia commentata da M. M. Sales e G. Girotti, Il Vecchio Testamento*, 6: *I Sapienziali* (Turin, 1938), 345–544.

Gonzalo Maeso, D., "Disquisiciones filológicas sobre el texto hebreo del Eclesiástico", *Miscelanea de estudios árabes y hebraicos*, 8, 2 (1959), 3–26.

Goodspeed, E. J., *The Apocrypha*, in *The Complete Bible, An American Translation* (Chicago, 1951).

——, *The Story of the Apocrypha* (Chicago, 1939).

Gordis, R., "The Social Background of Wisdom Literature", *HUCA*, 18 (1943 to 1944), 77–118.

Gray, G. B., "A Note on the Text and Interpretation of Ecclus. XLI. 19", *JQR*, 9 (1896–1897), 567–572.

Grimme, H., "Mètres et strophes dans les fragments du manuscrit parchemin du Siracide", *RB*, 9 (1900), 400–413.

——, "Mètres et strophes dans les fragments hébreux du manuscrit A de l'Ecclésiastique", *RB*, 10 (1901), 55–65; 260–267; 423–435.

——, "Strophenartige Abschnitte im Ecclesiasticus", *Orientalistische Litteratur-Zeitung*, 2 (1899), 213–217.

Grootaert, A., "L'Ecclésiastique est-il antérieur à l'Ecclésiaste?" *RB*, n. s., 2 (1905), 67–73.

Gutberlet, K., *Die liturgischen Lesungen im Brevier und Missale aus Jesus Sirach (Ecclesiasticus)* (Fulda, 1937).

Habermann, A. M., "*'Ālepbêtā' dᵉben-Sîrā' nūsḥāh šᵉlîšît* (= Hebrew University Hebrew MS 2203)", *Tarbiẓ*, 27 (1957–1958), 190–202.

Hadot, J., "L'Ecclésiastique ou le Siracide", in *La Bible, L'Ancien Testament* (= Bibliothèque de la Pléiade), 2 (Paris, 1959), 1708–1885.

Haire Forster, A., "The Date of Ecclesiasticus", *Anglican Theological Review*, 41 (1959), 1–9.

Halévy, J., *Étude sur la partie du texte hébreu de l'Ecclésiastique récemment découvert* (Paris, 1897).

Hall, B. G., "Ecclesiasticus iv. 26", *ExpT*, 37 (1925–1926), 526.

Hamp, V., *Das Buch Sirach oder Ecclesiasticus (= Echter-Bibel, das AT 4)* (Würzburg, 1959).

——, "Jesus Sirach (Ecclesiasticus)", in *Das Alte Testament nach den Grundtexten übersetzt und herausgegeben* (Würzburg, 1955), 820–871.

——, "Zukunft und Jenseits im Buche Sirach", in *Bonner Biblische Beiträge 1: AT Studien (= Festschrift Nötscher)* (Bonn, 1950), 86–97.

Hart, J. H. A., "[Note on] Sir. xlviii 17, a, b.", *JTS*, 4 (1902–1903), 591f.

——, "Primitive Exegesis as a Factor in the Corruption of Texts of Scripture Illustrated from the Versions of Ben Sira", *JQR*, 15 (1902–1903), 627–631.

Hartman, L. F., "Sirach in Hebrew and in Greek", *CBQ*, 23 (1961), 443–451.

Hartman, L. F.-A. van den Born, "Sirach, the Book of", in *Encyclopedic Dictionary of the Bible* (= A Translation and Adaptation of A. van den Born's *Bijbels Woordenboek*, 2d rev. ed. [1954–1957], by L. F. Hartman) (New York, 1963), 2247–2250.

Hartum, A. S., *Ben-Sîrā' (= Ha-sᵉpārîm ha-ḥîṣônîm)* (Tel-Aviv, 1963).

Hatch, E., "On the Text of Ecclesiasticus", in *Essays in Biblical Greek* (Oxford, 1889), 246–282.

Herkenne, H., *Die Textüberlieferung des Buches Sirach (= Biblische Studien 6, 1–2)* (Freiburg i. B., 1901), 129–140.

Herz, N., "Dr. Ryssel on the Origin of the Doublets in the Hebrew 'Ben Sira'", *ExpT*, 19 (1907–1908), 189f.

——, "The Hebrew Ecclesiasticus", *JQR*, 10 (1897–1898), 719–724.

Hogg, H. W., "Another Edition of the Hebrew Ecclesiasticus", *AJSLL*, 15 (1898–1899), 42–48.

Holkot, R., *In librum Ecclesiasticum Jesu filii Sirach expositio subtilissima* (Venice, 1509).

Holzmeister, U., "Pro morte defluente deprecatus (-a) sum (= Eccli. 51, 13 [9])", *VD*, 9 (1929), 30.

Höpfl, H.-A. Miller-A. Metzinger, *Introductio specialis in vetus testamentum*, 5th ed. (Rome, 1945).

Hughes, H. M., *The Ethics of Jewish Apocryphal Literature* (London, n. d. [1909]).

Husslein, J., "Wisdom and the Toiler", *HPR*, 22 (1922), 1299–1302.

Isaack, M., *Die Pädagogik des Jesus Sirach (= Sammlung pädagogischer Vorträge 12, 12)* (Bonn [1900]).

Jacob, E., "L'Histoire d'Israel vue par Ben Sira", in *Mélanges bibliques rédigés en l'honneur de André Robert* (Paris [1957]), 288–294.

Jacobs, J., "A Romance in Scholarship (= the discovery of Hebrew Sirach)", *Fortnightly Review*, 72 (1899), 696–704.

Jansen, A., "Einige textkritische und exegetische Bemerkungen zum Buche Ekklesiastikus: Eccli 33, 3; 50, 1–5; 50, 24a", *BZ*, 4 (1906), 20–24.

Jansen, H. L., *Die spätjüdische Psalmendichtung ihr Entstehungskreis und ihr "Sitz im Leben"* (Oslo, 1937).

Jenni, E., "Jesus Sirach", in *Die Religion in Geschichte und Gegenwart*, 3, 3d ed. (Tübingen, 1959), 653ff.

Kaatz, S., *Die Scholien des Gregorius Abulfaragius Bar Hebraeus zum Weisheitsbuch des Josua ben Sira* (Halle, 1892).

Kahana, A., *Ha-s^{e}pārîm ha-ḥîsônîm: dibrê Šim'ôn ben-Sîrā'* (Tel-Aviv, 1937).

Kaiser, O., "Die Begründung der Sittlichkeit im Buche Jesus Sirach", *ZKT*, 55 (1958), 51–63.

Kaufmann, D., "Notes to Sirach XLIII. 20 and XL. 12", *JQR*, 11 (1898–1899), 159–162.

——, "Sirach L. 5–8", *JQR*, 10 (1897–1898), 727f.

——, "Das Wort *tḥlyp* bei Jesus Sirach", *Monatsschrift für Geschichte und Wissenschaft des Judenthums*, 41 (1897), 337–340.

Kearns, C., *The Expanded Text of Ecclesiasticus: Its Teaching on the Future Life as a Clue to Its Origin* (= unpublished doctoral dissertation at the Angelicum) (Rome, 1951).

Kearns, C. J., "Ecclesiasticus", in *A Catholic Commentary on Holy Scripture* (London, 1953), 512–526.

——, "La vie intérieure à l'école de l'Ecclésiastique", *VieSp*, 82 (1950), 137–146.

Keel, L., *Sirach. Das Buch von der Weisheit, verfaßt von Jesus, dem Sohne Sirach's erklärt für das christliche Volk* (Kempten, 1896).

Kilpatrick, G.D., "προσανοικοδομηθήσεται Ecclus. iii. 14", *JTS*, 44 (1943), 147f.

Klawek, A., "Slowa Boże-pieśń ku czci Stworzyciela z księgi Ecclesiasticus 42, 15–43, 33", *Ruch Biblijny i Liturgiczny*, 4 (1951), 329–332.

Knabenbauer, I., *Commentarius in Ecclesiasticum (= Cursus Scripturae Sacrae, Commentariorum in vet. test. pars II, in libros didacticos VI)* (Paris, 1902).

Knabenbauer, J., "Einiges über die neuentdeckten hebräischen Stücke des Buches Sirach", *Stimmen aus Maria-Laach*, 62 (1902), 526–539.

König, E., *Die Originalität des neulich entdeckten hebräischen Sirachtextes* (Freiburg i. B., 1899).

——, "Professor Margoliouth and the 'Original Hebrew' of Ecclesiasticus", *ExpT*, 10 (1898–1899), 512–516; 564–566; 11 (1899–1900), 31f.

Krauss, S., "Notes on Sirach: 1. The name Sirach; 2. The Author; 3. Sayings of Sirach in Rabbinic Literature; 4. The word *tḥlyp*", *JQR*, 11 (1898 to 1899), 150–158.

Kroon, J., "'Qui spernit modica, paulatim decidet' [Eccli. 19, 1]", *VD*, 5 (1925), 210f.

Kuhn, G., "Beiträge zur Erklärung des Buches Jesus Sira", *ZAW*, 47 (1929), 289–296; 48 (1930), 100–121.

A Lapide, C., *In Ecclesiasticum (= Commentaria in Scripturam Sacram 9–10)*, 9th ed. (Paris, 1868).

Lefèvre, A., "Les livres deutérocanoniques: L'Ecclésiastique (ou Siracide)", in *Introduction à la Bible*, 1, 2d ed., ed. by A. Robert-A. Feuillet (Tournai, Belgium, 1959), 771–776.

Le Frois, B. J., "Our Lady and the Wisdom Passage from Sirach", *AER*, 135 (1956), 1–8.

——, "Las lecciones Litúrgicas del Libro de Sirac", *Revista Biblica con Seccion Litúrgica*, 19 (1957), 72f.

Lehmann, M. R., "Ben Sira and the Qumran Literature", *Revue de Qumran*, 3 (1961), 103–116.

——, "'Yom Kippur' in Qumran [and Ben Sira]", *Revue de Qumran*, 3 (1961), 117–124.

Di Lella, A. A., "Authenticity of the Geniza Fragments of Sirach", *Bib*, 44 (1963), 171–200.

——, "Qumrân and the Geniza Fragments of Sirach", *CBQ*, 24 (1962), 245–267.

Leloir, L., "Orientales de la Bible (Versions): II. Versions arméniennes", *VDBS*, 6 (Paris, 1960), 810–818.

Lesètre, H., *L'Ecclésiastique: Introduction critique, traduction française et commentaires* (= *La Sainte Bible avec commentaires*, ed. by P. Drach-A. Bayle), 2d ed. (Paris, 1896).

Lévi, I., "Le chapitre III de Ben Sira", in *Festschrift zu Ehren des Dr. A. Harkavy*, ed. by D. v. Günzburg and I. Markon (St. Petersburg, 1908), 1–5.

——, "Découverte d'un fragment d'une version hébraïque de l'Ecclésiastique de Jésus, fils de Sirach", *REJ*, 32 (1896), 303f.

——, *L'Ecclésiastique ou la Sagesse de Jésus, fils de Sira*, 2 parts (Paris, 1898, 1901).

——, "Notes sur les ch. VII. 29–XII. 1 de Ben Sira édités par M. Elkan N. Adler", *JQR*, 13 (1900–1901), 1–17.

——, "Notes sur les nouveaux fragments de Ben Sira. II. III.", *REJ*, 40 (1900), 255ff.

——, "Les nouveaux fragments hébreux de l'Ecclésiastique de Jésus fils de Sira", *REJ*, 39 (1899), 1–15; 177–190.

——, "Quelques notes sur Jésus ben Sirach et son ouvrage, II", *REJ*, 35 (1897), 29–47.

——, "La Sagesse de Jésus, fils de Sirach: découverte d'un fragment de l'original hébreu", *REJ*, 34 (1897), 1–50.

——, "Sirach, The Wisdom of Jesus, the Son of", *The Jewish Encyclopedia*, 11 (New York-London, 1905), 388–397.

Liebermann, S., "Ben Sira à la lumière du Yerouchalmi", *REJ*, 97 (1934), 50–57.

Lods, A., *Histoire de la littérature hébraïque et juive* (Paris, 1950).

Luzzi, G., "Ecclesiastico", in *Apocrifi dell'Antico Testamento (= La Bibbia tradotta dai testi originali e annotata da G. Luzzi)* (Florence, 1930), 345–504.

McHardy, W. D., "The Arabic Text of Ecclesiasticus in the Bodleian MS. Hunt[ington]. 260", *JTS*, 46 (1945), 39ff.

——, "Ben-Ze'eb's Edition of the Peshitta Text of Ecclesiasticus", *ZAW*, 61 (1945/1948), 193f.

McRae, C. A., *The Hebrew Text of Ben Sira* [39, 15–43, 33] (Toronto, 1910).

Mader, J., "Zu Sir 51, 13", *BZ*, 11 (1913), 24f.

Maertens, T., *L'Eloge des Pères (Ecclésiastique XLIV–L) (= Collection Lumière et Vie 5)* (Bruges, 1956).

Mancini, G., *Ecclesiastico di Gesù figliuolo di Sirach volto in terza rima ... con la traduzione e note di Monsig. A. Martini* (Siena, 1845).

Marbach, C., *Carmina Scripturarum, scil. Antiphonas et Responsoria ex sacro Scripturae fonte in libros liturgicos S. Ecclesiae Romanae derivata* (Straßburg, 1907) (use of Sir in liturgy pp. 288–302).

Marcus, R., *Law in the Apocrypha* (New York, 1927).

Margoliouth, D. S., "The Date of Ben-Sira", in *Occident and Orient ... Gaster Anniversary Volume* (London, 1936), 403–408.

——, "The Destruction of the Original of Ecclesiasticus", *ExpT*, 16 (1904 to 1905), 26–29.

——, "Ecclesiastes and Ecclesiasticus", *Expositor*, 7th series, 5 (1908), 118–126.

——, "Ecclesiasticus in Arabic Literature", *ExpT*, 18 (1906–1907), 476f.

——, "The Language and Metre of Ecclesiasticus", *Expositor*, 4th series, 1 (1890), 295–320; 381–387.

——, "Note on Ecclus. vii. 25", *ExpT*, 23 (1911–1912), 234f.

——, "Observations on the Fragment of the Original of Ecclesiasticus Edited by Mr. Schechter", *Expositor*, 5th series, 4 (1896), 140–151.

——, *The Origin of the 'Original Hebrew' of Ecclesiasticus* (London-Oxford, 1899).

——, "Three Notes on Ecclesiasticus", *ExpT*, 13 (1901–1902), 331f.

Margolis, M. L., "Ecclus. 3, 27", *ZAW*, 25 (1905), 199f.

——, "Ecclus. 6, 4", *ZAW*, 25 (1905), 320ff. [As regards this article, cf. I. Lévi, *ZAW*, 26 (1906), 142; and Margolis' answer in *ZAW*, 27 (1907), 276f.].

——, "Ecclus. 7, 6d", *ZAW*, 25 (1905), 323.

——, "Mr. Hart's 'Ecclesiasticus' (= Review of J. H. A. Hart's *Ecclesiasticus. The Greek Text of Codex 248* [Cambridge, 1909])", *JQR*, n. s., 1 (1910 to 1911), 403–418.

——, "A Passage in Ecclesiasticus [34, 16–17]", *ZAW*, 21 (1901), 271f.

Mari, F., "L'originale ebraico dell'Ecclesiastico recentemente scoperto", *Studi religiosi*, 3 (1903), 63–82; 170–182.

Marmorstein, A., "Jesus Sirach 51, 12ff.", *ZAW*, 29 (1909), 287–293.

Matthes, J. C., "Bemerkungen zu dem hebräischen Texte Jesus Sirachs und seiner neuesten Übersetzung", *ZAW*, 29 (1909), 161–176.

——, "Das Buch Sirach und Kohelet in ihrem gegenseitigen Verhältniß. Die Prioritätsfrage", *Vierteljahrsschrift für Bibelkunde*, 2 (1904–1905), 258 to 263.

Merguet, K. H. V., *Die Glaubens- und Sittenlehren des Buches Jesus Sirach*, 1–2, (Königsberg, 1874, 1901).

Metzger, B. M., *An Introduction to the Apocrypha* (New York-Oxford, 1957).

Michaelis, D., "Das Buch Jesus Sirach als typischer Ausdruck für das Gottesverhältnis des nachalttestamentlichen Menschen", *TLZ*, 83 (1958), 601 to 608.

Minocchi, S., "La découverte du texte hébreu original de l'Ecclésiastique", in *Congrès scientifique des Catholiques, 1897. II: Sciences exégétiques* (Fribourg, Swiz., 1898), 283–296.

Moffatt, J., "Literary Illustrations of the Book of Ecclesiasticus", *Expositor*, 7th series, 4 (1907), 279–288; 473–480; 8th series, 1 (1911), 84–96.

Moran, W. L., "Ugaritic *ṣîṣûma* and Hebrew *ṣîṣ* (= Sir 43, 19; Jer 48, 9)", *Bib*, 39 (1958), 69ff.

Morenz, S., "Eine weitere Spur der Weisheit Amenopes in der Bibel (Sir 33, 13 [Greek])", *Zeitschrift für Ägyptische Sprache*, 84 (1959), 78f.

Moulton, R. G., *Ecclesiasticus (= The Modern Reader's Bible)* (New York, 1896).

——, *The Modern Reader's Bible: The Books of the Bible with Three Books of the Apocrypha* (New York, 1919).

Mowinckel, S., "Die Metrik bei Jesus Sirach", *ST*, 9 (1955), 137–165.

Nestle, E., "Ecclus. xii. 10, 11", *ExpT*, 11 (1899–1900), 143.

——, "Jesus Sirach Neffe oder Enkel des Amos Sirach", *ZAW*, 23 (1903), 128ff.

——, "Zum Prolog des Ecclesiasticus", *ZAW*, 17 (1897), 123f.

——, "Sirach (Book of)", in *A Dictionary of the Bible*, 4, ed. by J. Hastings (New York-Edinburgh, 1902), 539–551.

Nicolaus Lyranus, *Biblia sacra cum glossa interlineari, ordinaria*, 3 (Venice, 1588), folios 387–439.

Nöldeke, T., "Bemerkungen zum hebräischen Ben Sīrā", *ZAW*, 20 (1900), 81–94.

——, "The Original Hebrew of a Portion of Ecclesiasticus", *Expositor*, 5th series, 5 (1897), 347–364.

Octavianus de Tufo, *In Ecclesiasticum commentaria nunc primum in Germania edita* (Cologne, 1630).

Oesterley, W. O. E., *An Introduction to the Books of the Apocrypha* [1st publ. 1935] (London, 1953).

——, *The Wisdom of Ben-Sira (Ecclesiasticus)* (London, 1916).

——, *The Wisdom of Jesus the Son of Sirach or Ecclesiasticus* (Cambridge, 1912).

Pacchi, D., *Il Libro dell'Ecclesiastico illustrato con toscana parafrasi*, 2 (Modena, 1792).

Pautrel, R., "Ben Sira et le Stoïcisme", *Recherches de Science Religieuse*, 51 (1963), 535–549.

Peters, N., *Das Buch Jesus Sirach oder Ecclesiasticus (= Exegetisches Handbuch zum Alten Testament 25)* (Münster i. W., 1913).

——, "Ekklesiastes und Ekklesiastikus", *BZ*, 1 (1903), 47–54; 129–150.

——, *Die sahidisch-koptische Uebersetzung des Buches Ecclesiasticus auf ihren wahren Werth für die Textkritik untersucht (= Biblische Studien 3, 3)* (Freiburg i. B., 1898).

——, "Sirach", in *Lexicon für Theologie und Kirche*, 9, 2d ed. (Freiburg i. B., 1937), 594f.

Pfeiffer, R. H., *History of New Testament Times with an Introduction to the Apocrypha* (New York, 1949).

——, "The Literature and Religion of the Apocrypha", in *The Interpreter's Bible*, 1 (New York, 1952), 391–419.

Pisani, V., "Acqua e fuoco [Sir 15, 17–18]", *Acme*, 1 (1948), 94.

Power, A. D., *The Wisdom of Jesus the Son of Sirach Commonly Called Ecclesiasticus* (Chelsea, England [Ashendene Press], 1932).

Prelipceanu, V., "Actualitatea învăţăturilor moral-sociale dîn cartea lui Iisus fiul lui Sirah", *Studii Teologice*, 7 (1955), 582–599.

Procter, W. C., *The Value of the Apocrypha* (London, n.d. [1926?]).

Rácz, Z., *Józsua Ben Szirach* (Budapest, 1930).

Ring, E., *Det sedliga handlandets motiv enligt Siraks bok* (Stockholm, 1923).

Rivkin, E., "Ben Sira and the Nonexistence of the Synagogue: A Study in Historical Method", in *In the Time of Harvest: Essays in Honor of Abba Hillel Silver* (New York, 1963), 320–354.

Roth, C., "Ecclesiasticus in the Synagogue Service", *JBL*, 71 (1952), 171–178.

Rothstein, J. W., "Ein Spezimen criticum zu hebräischen Texte des Sirachbuches", *Orientalische Studien, Theodor Nöldeke gewidmet*, 1, ed. by C. Bezold (Gießen, 1906), 583–608.

Rudnitzky, N., *Die Apokryphen und Pseudepigraphen des Alten Testaments* (Pforzheim, 1926).

Rydén, L., "LXX Sirach 37, 2", *Eranos*, 59 (1961), 40–44.

Ryssel, V., "Die neuen hebräischen Fragmente des Buches Jesus Sirach und ihre Herkunft", *Theologische Studien und Kritiken*, 73 (1900), 363–403; 505–541; 74 (1901), 75–109; 269–294; 547–592; 75 (1902), 205–261; 347–420.

——, "Die Sprüche Jesus', des Sohnes Sirachs", in *Die Apokryphen und Pseudepigraphen des Alten Testaments*, 1, ed. by E. Kautzsch (Tübingen, 1921), 230–475.

Sabatier, P., *Bibliorum sacrorum latinae versiones antiquae seu Vetus Italica*, 1 (Paris, 1751), Preface i–lxxv.

da S. Marco, E., "Ecclesiastico", in *La Sacra Bibbia, Il Vecchio Testamento*, 2 (Turin, 1960), 467–566.

Santoro, L., "L'inno al Creatore di Gesù Ben Sirac", *Città di Vita*, 2 (1947), 253–261.

Scazzocchio, L., "Ecclesiastico, Tobia, Sapienza di Salomone alla luce dei testi di Qumran", *Rivista degli Studi Orientali*, 37 (1962), 199–209.

Schechter, S., "The British Museum Fragments of Ecclesiasticus", *JQR*, 12 (1899–1900), 266–272.

——, "A Glimpse of the Social Life of the Jews in the Age of Jesus the Son of Sirach", in *Studies in Judaism, Second Series* (Philadelphia, 1908), 55–101.

——, "A Hoard of Hebrew Manuscripts I", in *Studies in Judaism, Second Series* (Philadelphia, 1908), 1–11.

——, "The Quotations from Ecclesiasticus in Rabbinic Literature", *JQR*, 3 (1890–1891), 682–706.

——, "Review of *The Origin of the 'Original Hebrew' of Ecclesiasticus*", *The Critical Review*, 9 (1899), 387–400.

Schiffer, S., "Le Paragraphe 40, 13–17 de l'Ecclésiastique de Ben Sira", in *Oriental Studies Dedicated to Paul Haupt* (Baltimore, 1926), 106–110.

Schildenberger, J., "Die Bedeutung von Sir 48, 24f. für die Verfasserfrage von Is 40–66", in *Bonner Biblische Beiträge 1: AT Studien (= Festschrift Nötscher)* (Bonn, 1950), 188–204.

Schilling, O., *Das Buch Jesus Sirach (= Herders Bibelkommentar. Die heilige Schrift 7/2)* (Freiburg i. B., 1956).

Schlatter, A., *Das neu gefundene hebräische Stück des Sirach. – Der Glossator des griechischen Sirach und seine Stellung in der Geschichte der jüdischen Theologie (= Beiträge zur Förderung christlicher Theologie 1, 5–6)* (Gütersloh, 1897).

Schlögl, N., "Das Alphabet des Siraciden (Eccls. 51, 13–29), eine textkritische Studie", *ZDMG*, 53 (1899), 669–682.

Schlögl, N., *Ecclesiasticus (39, 12–49, 16) ope artis criticae et metricae in formam originalem redactus*, (Vienna, 1901).
Schmidt, N., *Ecclesiasticus (= The Temple Bible)* (London, 1903).
Schmitt, E., *Leben in den Weisheitsbüchern Job, Sprüche und Jesus Sirach (= Freiburger Theologische Studien 66)* (Freiburg i. B., 1954).
Schürer, E., *Geschichte des jüdischen Volkes im Zeitalter Jesu Christi*, 3, 4th ed. (Leipzig, 1909).
Segal, M. H., "Ben-Sîrā'", in *'Enṣîqlôpēdyāh miqrā'ît*, 2 (Jerusalem, Israel, 1954), 162–169.
——, "'*Dappîm nôs^{e}pîm mittôk sēper ben-Sîrā*' *(H. Šîrman, Tarbîṣ, kṭ, 'm' 125–134)*", *Tarbiẕ*, 29 (1959–1960), 313–323.
——, "The Evolution of the Hebrew Text of Ben Sira", *JQR*, n. s., 25 (1934 to 1935), 91–149.
——, "*ḥqr, nḥqr b^{e}s[ēper] ben-Sîrā*'", *Lĕšonénu*, 21 (1957), 143.
——, "*K^{e}tab-ha-yād ha-ḥămîšî šel ben-Sîrā' hā-'ibrî*", *Tarbiẕ*, 2 (1930–1931), 295–307.
——, "*Sēper ben-Sîrā' b^{e}qûmrân*", *Tarbiẕ*, 33 (1963–1964), 243–246.
——, *Sēper ben-Sîrā' ha-šālēm*, 2d ed. (Jerusalem, Israel, 1958).
——, *Sēper ḥokmat ben-Sîrā' ha-šālēm* (Jerusalem, 1933).
Seligmann, C., *Das Buch der Weisheit des Jesus Sirach (Josua ben Sira) in seinem Verhältniß zu den salomonischen Sprüchen und seiner historischen Bedeutung* (Halle a. d. Saale, 1883).
Selmer, C., "A Study of Ecclus. 12: 10–19", *CBQ*, 8 (1946), 306–314.
——, "Traces of the 'Sayings of the Seven Sages' in the *Liber Ecclesiasticus*", *CBQ*, 5 (1943), 264–274.
Siebeneck, R. T., "May Their Bones Return to Life! – Sirach's Praise of the Fathers", *CBQ*, 21 (1959), 411–428.
Silverstone, H. S., *A Guide to the Prophets and the Apocrypha* (Baltimore, 1942 [1945?]).
Sionnet, A., *Le livre de l'Ecclésiastique*, in *Sainte Bible expliquée et commentée*, 8: *Livres sapientiaux* (Paris, 1844), 243–427.
Skehan, P. W., "*Didache* 1, 6 and Sirach 12, 1", *Bib*, 44 (1963), 533–536.
——, "They shall not be found in parables (Sir 38, 33)", *CBQ*, 23 (1961), 40.
——, "Tower of Death or Deadly Snare? (Sir 26, 22)", *CBQ*, 16 (1954), 154.
Smend, R., *Das hebräische Fragment der Weisheit des Jesus Sirach (= Abhandlungen der königlichen Gesellschaft der Wissenschaften zu Göttingen. Philologisch-Historische Klasse. N.F. 2, 2)* (Berlin, 1897).
——, "Nachträgliches zur Textüberlieferung des syrischen Sirach", *ZAW*, 27 (1907), 271–275.
——, *Die Weisheit des Jesus Sirach erklärt* (Berlin, 1906).
Snaith, J. G., "The Importance of Ecclesiasticus (The Wisdom of Ben Sira)", *ExpT*, 75 (1963–1964), 66–69.
Sović, A., "Enkomij liječnicima u Svetom Pismu [Sir 38, 1–15]", *Bogoslovska Smotra*, 26 (1938), 165–179 (Latin summary on p. 165).
Spadafora, F., "Ecclesiastico", in *Enciclopedia Cattolica*, 5 (Vatican City, 1950), 40–45.
Spicq, C., "L'Ecclésiastique", in *La Sainte Bible*, 6, ed. by L. Pirot-A. Clamer (Paris, 1951), 529–841.
——, "Le Siracide et la structure littéraire du prologue de Saint Jean", *Mémorial Lagrange* (Paris, 1940), 183–195.

Squillaci, D., "La preghiera missionaria dall'Ecclesiastico (36, 1–19)", *Palestra del Clero*, 41 (1962), 260–263.

Steinhardt, J., *Neun Holzschnitte zu ausgewählten Versen aus dem Buche Jeschu ben Elieser ben Sirah mit einer Einleitung von Arnold Zweig* (Berlin, 1929).

Storr, R., "Einige Bedenken gegen die Echtheit des hebräischen Jesus Sirach", *TQ*, 106 (1925), 203–231.

Strauss, D., "Sprachliche Studien zu den hebräischen Sirachfragmenten", *Schweizerische Theologische Zeitschrift*, 17 (1900), 65–80.

Stummer, F., "'Via peccantium complanata lapidibus' (Eccli 21, 14)", in *Colligere Fragmenta – A. Dold* (Beuron in Hohenzollern, 1952), 40–44.

Swete, H. B., *An Introduction to the Old Testament in Greek*, 2d ed. (Cambridge, 1902).

Szczygiel, P., "Daniel i Judyta w księdze Siracha", *Przegląd Biblijny*, 1 (1937), 117–147.

Taylor, A. F., "Meditations in the Apocrypha [Ecclus]", *ExpT*, 37 (1925–1926), 40ff.; 91ff.

——, *Meditations in Ecclesiasticus* (London, 1928).

Taylor, C., "The Alphabet of Ben Sira", *JQR*, 17 (1904–1905), 238f.

——, "The Alphabet of Ben Sira", *Journal of Philology*, 30 (1907), 95–132.

——, "Studies in Ben Sira", *JQR*, 10 (1897–1898), 470–488.

——, "The Wisdom of Ben Sira", *JQR*, 15 (1902–1903), 440–474; 604–626.

——, "The Wisdom of Ben Sira", *JTS*, 1 (1899–1900), 571–583.

Taylor, C.-J. H. A. Hart, "Two Notes on Enoch in Sir. xliv 16", *JTS*, 4 (1902 to 1903), 589ff.

Taylor, W. R., *The Originality of the Hebrew Text of Ben Sira in the Light of the Vocabulary and the Versions* (Toronto, 1910).

Tedesche, S. S., *Prayers of the Apocrypha and Their Importance in the Study of Jewish Liturgy* (reprinted from Yearbook, vol. 26, Central Conference of American Rabbis, 1916).

Tennant, F. R., "The Teaching of Ecclesiasticus and Wisdom on the Introduction of Sin and Death", *JTS*, 2 (1900–1901), 207–223.

Thielmann, P., "Die europäischen Bestandteile des lateinischen Sirach", *Archiv für lateinische Lexikographie und Grammatik*, 9 (1896), 247–284.

——, "Die lateinische Übersetzung des Buches Sirach", *Archiv für lateinische Lexikographie und Grammatik*, 8 (1893), 501–561.

Thomas, D. W., "The LXX's Rendering of *šnwt lb twb* in Ecclus. XXXIII 13", *VT*, 10 (1960), 456.

Tobac, E., *Les cinq livres de Solomon* (Brussels, 1926), 173–214.

Torrey, C. C., *The Apocryphal Literature* (New Haven, 1945).

——, "The Hebrew of the Geniza Sirach", in *Alexander Marx Jubilee Volume* (New York, 1950), 585–602.

Touzard, J., "Ecclésiastique", in *Dictionnaire de la Bible*, 2, 1 (Paris, 1899), 1543–1557.

——, "Nouveaux fragments hébreux de l'Ecclésiastique", *RB*, 9 (1900), 45–62; 525–563.

——, "L'original hébreu de l'Ecclésiastique", *RB*, 6 (1897), 271–282; 547–573; 7 (1898), 33–58.

——, *Traduction française du texte hébreu de l'Ecclésiastique avec les variantes du grec et du latin* (Paris, 1909) (Appendix to F. Vigouroux, *La Sainte Bible polyglotte, Ancien Testament 5*, 885–970).

Toy, C. H., "Ecclesiasticus", in *Encyclopaedia Biblica* (London, 1904), 1164 to 1179.

——, "Remarks on the Hebrew Text of Ben-Sira", *JAOS*, 23 (1902), 38–43.

——, "Sirach", in *Encyclopaedia Biblica* (London, 1904), 4645–4651.

Treves, M., "Studi su Gesù ben Sirach", *La Rassegna mensile di Israel*, 22 (1956), 387–397; 464–473.

Trinquet, J., "Ecclésiastique (Livre de l')", in *Catholicisme*, 3 (Paris, 1952), 1244–1249.

——, "Les liens 'sadocites' de l'Écrit de Damas, des manuscrits de la Mer Morte et de l'Ecclésiastique", *VT*, 1 (1951), 287–292.

Tyler, T., "Ecclesiasticus: The Retranslation Hypothesis", *JQR*, 12 (1899 to 1900), 555–562.

Vaccari, A., "Il concetto della Sapienza nell'Antico Testamento", *Gregorianum*, 1 (1920), 218–251.

——, "Ecclesiastici hebraice fragmentum nuper detectum", *VD*, 11 (1931), 172–178.

——, "Eccli. 24, 20s. de Beata Virgine", *VD*, 3 (1923), 136–140.

——, *L'Ecclesiastico (= La Sacra Bibbia tradotta dai testi originali con note a cura del Pontificio Istituto Biblico 5)* (Florence, 1952), 177–289; 295–297.

——, *L'Ecclesiastico (= La Sacra Bibbia tradotta dai testi originali con note, a cura del Pontificio Istituto Biblico di Roma)* (Rome, 1961), 1179–1258.

——, "Ecclesiastico, 37, 10. 11: critica ed esegesi", *EstEc*, 34 (1960), 705–713.

——, "'Oratio Iesu, filii Sirach' (Eccli. 51, 1–17)", *VD*, 2 (1922), 71f.

——, "'Quasi plantatio rosae in Iericho' (Eccli. 24, 18)", *VD*, 3 (1923), 289 to 294.

Vargha, T., "De Psalmo hebraico Ecclesiastici c. 51", *Anton*, 10 (1935), 3–10.

Vattioni, F., "Genesi 1, 1 ed Eccli. 15, 14", *Augustinianum*, 4 (1964), 105–108.

——, "Nuovi fogli ebraici dell'Ecclesiastico", *Rivista Biblica*, 8 (1960), 169–179.

Vawter, B., *The Book of Sirach with a Commentary* (= *Pamphlet Bible Series*, 40–41), 2 Parts (New York, 1962).

Vogt, E., "Novi textus hebraici libri Sira", *Bib*, 41 (1960), 184–190.

——, "Novum folium hebr. Sir 15, 1–16, 7 MS B", *Bib*, 40 (1959), 1060ff.

Volz, P., *Hiob und Weisheit (Das Buch Hiob, Sprüche und Jesus Sirach, Prediger) (= Die Schriften des Alten Testaments 3, 2)*, 2d ed. (Göttingen, 1921).

Wellhausen, J., "Reis im Buch Sirach [39, 13]", *ZDMG*, 64 (1910), 258.

Wicks, H. J., *The Doctrine of God in the Jewish Apocryphal and Apocalyptic Literature* (London, 1915).

Wilmart, A., "Nouveaux feuillets Toulousains de l'Ecclésiastique", *RevBén*, 33 (1921), 110–123.

Wilson, R. D., "Ecclesiasticus", *The Presbyterian and Reformed Review*, 11 (1900), 480–506.

Winter, P., "Ben Sira (33 [36] 7–15) and the Teaching of 'Two Ways'", *VT*, 5 (1955), 315–318.

——, "Lukanische Miszellen: I. Lc 1, 17 und Ben Sira 48, 10c Heb", *ZNW*, 49 (1958), 65f.

The Wisdom of the Apocrypha (= The Wisdom of the East Series), with an introduction by C. E. Lawrence (London, 1910).

Zenner, J. K., "Ecclesiasticus 38, 24–39, 10", *ZKT*, 21 (1897), 567–574.

——, "Zwei Weisheitslieder [Sir 24, Bar 3, 9–4, 4]", *ZKT*, 21 (1897), 551–558.

Ziegler, J., "Hat Lukian den griechischen Sirach rezensiert?" *Bib*, 40 (1959), 210–229.

——, "Die hexaplarische Bearbeitung des griechischen Sirach", *BZ*, N.F., 4 (1960), 174–185.

——, *Die Münchener griechische Sirach-Handschrift 493: Ihre textgeschichtliche Bedeutung und erstmalige Edition durch den Augsburger Humanisten David Hoeschel (1604)* (*Bayerische Akademie der Wissenschaften, Philosophisch-Historische Klasse Sitzungsberichte* [1962], Heft 4).

——, "Die Vokabel-Varianten der *O*-Rezension im griechischen Sirach", in *Hebrew and Semitic Studies Presented to Godfrey Rolles Driver* (Oxford, 1963), 172–190.

——, "Zum Wortschatz des griechischen Sirach", Beihefte *ZAW*, 77 (1958), 274–287.

Zöckler, O., *Die Apokryphen des Alten Testaments (= Kurzgefaßter Kommentar zu den heiligen Schriften Alten und Neuen Testamentes sowie zu den Apokryphen)* (Munich, 1891), 255–354.

Zorell, F., "Canticum Ecclesiastici. (Sir. 36)", *VD*, 7 (1927), 169–171.

C. CONCORDANCES, DICTIONARIES, AND GRAMMARS

Arndt, W. F.-F. W. Gingrich, *A Greek-English Lexicon of the New Testament and Other Early Christian Literature* (A translation and adaptation of W. Bauer's *Griechisch-Deutsches Wörterbuch zu den Schriften des Neuen Testaments und der übrigen urchristlichen Literatur*, 4th rev. and augmented ed., 1952) (Chicago-Cambridge, 1957).

Barth, J., *Die Nominalbildung in den semitischen Sprachen*, 2d ed. (Leipzig, 1894).

Bauer, H.-P. Leander, *Historische Grammatik der hebräischen Sprache des Alten Testaments*, 1 (Halle a. S., 1922).

Ben Yehuda, E., *A Complete Dictionary of Ancient and Modern Hebrew* [in Hebrew], 1–16 (Jerusalem, Israel, 1911–1959).

Blass, F.-A. Debrunner, *A Greek Grammar of the New Testament and Other Early Christian Literature*, trans. by R. W. Funk (Chicago, 1961).

Brockelmann, C., *Grundriß der vergleichenden Grammatik der semitischen Sprachen*, 1–2 (Berlin, 1908, 1913).

——, *Lexicon Syriacum*, 2d ed. (Halle, 1928).

Brønno, E., *Studien über hebräische Morphologie und Vokalismus auf Grundlage der Mercatischen Fragmente der zweiten Kolumne der Hexapla des Origenes* (Leipzig, 1943).

Brown, F.-S. R. Driver-C. A. Briggs, *A Hebrew and English Lexicon* (Oxford, 1959).

Gesenius, W. E.-E. Kautzsch, *Hebrew Grammar*, trans. by A. E. Cowley, 2d ed. (Oxford, 1910).

Gordon, C. H., *Ugaritic Manual (=Analecta Orientalia 35)* (Rome, 1955).

Grossman, R.-M. H. Segal, *Compendious Hebrew-English Dictionary* (Tel-Aviv, 1956).

Hatch, E.-H. A. Redpath, *A Concordance to the Septuagint and the Other Greek Versions of the Old Testament (Including the Apocryphal Books)*, 1–2 (Oxford, 1897).

Jastrow, M., *A Dictionary of the Targumim, The Talmud Babli and Yerushalmi, and the Midrashic Literature*, 1–2 (London-New York, 1903).
Joüon, P., *Grammaire de l'hébreu biblique*, 2d ed. (Rome, 1947).
Koehler, L.-W. Baumgartner, *Lexicon in veteris testamenti libros*, with *Supplementum* (Leiden, Holland, 1958).
Kuhn, K. G. (ed.), *Konkordanz zu den Qumrantexten* (Göttingen, 1960).
Levy, J.-H. L. Fleischer, *Neuhebräisches und Chaldäisches Wörterbuch über die Talmudim und Midraschim*, 1–4 (Leipzig, 1876–1889).
Liddell, H. G.-R. Scott-H. S. Jones-R. McKenzie, *A Greek-English Lexicon*, a new ed., revised and augmented throughout (Oxford, 1953).
Mandelkern, S., *Veteris testamenti concordantiae hebraicae atque chaldaicae*, 1–2, new printing (Graz, 1955).
Nöldeke, T., *Compendious Syriac Grammar*, trans. from the 2d and improved German ed. by J. A. Crichton (London, 1904).
——, *Kurzgefaßte syrische Grammatik*, 2d and improved ed. (Leipzig, 1898).
Redpath, H. A., *Supplement* to *A Concordance to the Septuagint*, ed. by E. Hatch-H. A. Redpath (Oxford, 1906).
Segal, M. H., *A Grammar of Mishnaic Hebrew* (Oxford, 1958).
Smend, R., *Griechisch-syrisch-hebräischer Index zur Weisheit des Jesus Sirach* (Berlin, 1907).
Smith, J. Payne, *A Compendious Syriac Dictionary* (Oxford, 1903).
Smith, R. Payne, *et al.* (eds.), *Thesaurus syriacus*, 1–2 (Oxford, 1879, 1901).
Smyth, H. W., *Greek Grammar*, rev. by G. M. Messing (Cambridge, Mass., 1956).
Zorell, F. (ed.), *Lexicon hebraicum et aramaicum veteris testamenti* (only the Hebrew part is published thus far) (Rome, 1963).

D. OTHER BOOKS AND ARTICLES

Audet, J.-P., *La Didachè: Instructions des Apôtres (Études Bibliques)* (Paris, 1958).
Bacher, W., "Qirqisāni, the Karaite, and His Work on Jewish Sects", *JQR*, 7 (1894–1895), 687–710.
Badrān, M. (ed.), *Kitāb al Milal wan-Niḥal*, 1–2, (Cairo, 1910, 1955).
Baillet, M., "Fragments du Document de Damas. Qumrân, Grotte 6", *RB*, 63 (1956), 513–523.
——, "Le travail d'édition des fragments manuscrits de Qumrân. Communication de M. Baillet", *RB*, 63 (1956), 54f.
Baron, S. W., *A Social and Religious History of the Jews*, 1–8, 2d ed. (New York, 1952–1960).
Barthélemy, D., "Notes en marge de publications récentes sur les manuscrits de Qumrân", *RB*, 59 (1952), 187–218.
Barthélemy, D.-J. T. Milik, *Qumran Cave I (= Discoveries in the Judaean Desert 1)* (Oxford, 1955).
Bidawid, R. S., *Les lettres du Patriarche nestorien, Timothée I (= Studi e Testi 187)* (Vatican City, 1956).
Bloch, J., "The Printed Texts of the Peshitta Old Testament", *AJSLL*, 37 (1920 to 1921), 136–144.
Boilot, D. J., "Al-Bīrūnī (Bērūnī) Abu'l-Rayḥān Muḥammad b. Aḥmad", *The Encyclopaedia of Islam*, 1, new ed. (Leiden-London, 1960), 1236ff.

Braun, O., "Ein Brief des Katholikos Timotheos I über biblische Studien des 9 Jahrhunderts", *Oriens Christianus*, 1 (1901), 299–313.

——, "Der Katholikos Timotheos I und seine Briefe", *Oriens Christianus*, 1 (1901), 138–152.

Brockelmann, C., *Geschichte der arabischen Literatur, Supplement*, 1 (Leiden, 1937).

Brown, R. E., "The Messianism of Qumrân", *CBQ*, 19 (1957), 53–82.

Broydé, I., "Ḳirḳisani, Abu Yusuf Ya'ḳub al-", *The Jewish Encyclopedia*, 7 (New York-London, 1904), 509f.

——, "Moses Ben Naḥman Gerondi", *The Jewish Encyclopedia*, 9 (New York-London, 1905), 87–92.

Broydé, I.-R. Gottheil, "David (Abu Sulaiman) Ibn Merwan al-Muḳammaṣ (or al-Miḳmaṣ) al-Raḳḳi", *The Jewish Encyclopedia*, 4 (New York-London, 1903), 466f.

Burrows, M., *The Dead Sea Scrolls* (New York, 1955).

——, "*Waw* and *Yodh* in the Isaiah Dead Sea Scroll (DSIa)", *BASOR*, 124 (1951), 18–20.

Carra de Vaux, B., "Al-S̲h̲ahrastānī, Muḥammad b. 'Abd al-Karīm", *Encyclopédie de l'Islām*, 4 (Leiden-Paris, 1934), 272f.

Charles, R. H., "Fragments of a Zadokite Work", in *The Apocrypha and Pseudepigrapha of the Old Testament in English*, 2, ed. by R. H. Charles (Oxford, 1913), 785–834.

Cowley, A. E., "Seadiah, Ben Joseph", *Encyclopaedia Britannica*, 20 (Chicago, 1947), 239f.

Cowley, A. E.-R. H. Charles, "An Early Source of the Testaments of the Patriarchs", *JQR*, 19 (1906–1907), 566–583.

Cross, F. M., *The Ancient Library of Qumran and Modern Biblical Studies* (New York, 1958).

——, "The Development of the Jewish Scripts", in *The Bible and the Ancient Near East* (Essays in honor of William Foxwell Albright, ed. by G. E. Wright) (New York, 1961), 133–202.

Cureton, W. (ed.), *Book of Religious and Philosophical Sects, by Muhammad al-Sharastani*, 2 parts, (London, 1892).

Devreesse, R., *Introduction à l'étude des manuscrits grecs* (Paris, 1954).

Driver, G. R., "New Hebrew Manuscripts", *JQR*, n. s., 40 (1949–1950), 359 to 372.

Drubbel, A., "Le conflit entre la Sagesse profane et la Sagesse religieuse", *Bib*, 17 (1936), 45–70; 407–428.

Eissfeldt, O., "Der gegenwärtige Stand der Erforschung der in Palästina neu gefundenen hebräischen Handschriften", *TLZ*, 74 (1949), 595–600.

Filson, F. V., "Some Recent Study of the Dead Sea Scrolls", *BA*, 13 (1950), 96–99.

Gardthausen, V., *Griechische Palaeographie*, 2. Band: *Die Schrift, Unterschriften und Chronologie im Altertum und im byzantinischen Mittelalter*, 2d ed. (Leipzig, 1913).

Gaster, T. H., *The Dead Sea Scriptures* (New York, 1957).

Geers, F. W., "The Treatment of Emphatics in Akkadian", *JNES*, 4 (1945), 65–67.

Gordis, R., "Saadia ben Joseph", *Universal Jewish Encyclopedia*, 9 (New York, 1943), 289ff.

Gordon, C. H., "Review of *Publications of the Alexander Kohut Memorial Foundation*, Vol. VIII", *JBL*, 56 (1937), 413–416.

Greenberg, M., "The Stabilization of the Text of the Hebrew Bible, Reviewed in the Light of the Biblical Materials from the Judean Desert", *JAOS*, 76 (1956), 157–167.

Grelot, P., "Notes sur le Testament araméen de Lévi", *RB*, 63 (1956), 391–406.

de Harkavy, A., "Karaites", *The Jewish Encyclopedia*, 7 (New York-London, 1904), 438–446.

Humbert, P., *Recherches sur les sources égyptiennes de la littérature sapientiale d'Israël* (Neuchatel, 1929).

De Jonge, M., *The Testaments of the Twelve Patriarchs. A Study of Their Text, Composition and Origin* (Assen, 1953).

Kahle, P. E., "The Age of the Scrolls", *VT*, 1 (1951), 38–48.

——, *The Cairo Geniza*, 2d ed. (Oxford, 1959).

Kenyon, F., *Our Bible and the Ancient Manuscripts*, rev. by A. W. Adams, 5th ed. (London, 1958).

Kittel, R., *Biblia Hebraica*, 10th ed. (Stuttgart, 1951).

Knudsen, E. E., "Cases of Free Variants in the Akkadian *q* Phoneme", *JCS*, 15 (1961), 84–90.

Lambert, G., "Les manuscrits du désert de Juda: IV, Tient-on un nouveau chapitre de l'histoire de la grotte?" *NRT*, 72 (1950), 199–202.

Malter, H., *Saadia Gaon: His Life and Works* (Philadelphia, 1921).

Mann, J., *Texts and Studies in Jewish History and Literature*, 2: *Ḳaraitica* (Philadelphia, 1935).

Mansoor, M., *The Thanksgiving Hymns* (Grand Rapids, Mich., 1961).

Marchal, L., "Esséniens", *VDBS*, 2 (Paris, 1934), 1109–1132.

Marx, A., "An Aramaic Fragment of the Wisdom of Solomon", *JBL*, 40 (1921), 57–69.

——, "Rab Saadia Gaon", in *Essays in Jewish Biography* (Philadelphia, 1947), 3–38.

Milik, J. T., *Ten Years of Discovery in the Wilderness of Judaea*, trans. by J. Strugnell (London, 1959).

——, "Le Testament de Lévi en araméen", *RB*, 62 (1955), 398–406.

Moore, G. F., *Judaism in the First Centuries of the Christian Era*, 1–3 (Cambridge, Mass., 1927–1930).

Murphy, R. E., "*Yēṣer* in the Qumran Literature", *Bib*, 39 (1958), 334–344.

Nemoy, L., "Al-Qirqisānī's Account of the Jewish Sects and Christianity", *HUCA*, 7 (1930), 317–397.

——, "Karaites", *Universal Jewish Encyclopedia*, 6 (New York, 1942), 314–319.

——, "Kirkisani, Jacob", *Universal Jewish Encyclopedia*, 6 (New York, 1942), 397f.

——, (ed.), *Yaʿqūb al-Qirqisānī, Kitāb al-Anwār wal-Marāqib*, 1–5 (New York, 1939–1943).

Newman, A. A., "Saadia and His Relation to Palestine", *JQR*, n. s., 33 (1942 to 1943), 109–132.

Pass, H. L.-J. Arendzen, "Fragment of an Aramaic Text of the Testament of Levi", *JQR*, 12 (1899–1900), 651–661.

Pinkuss, H., "Die syrische Uebersetzung der Proverbien", *ZAW*, 14 (1894), 65–141; 161–222.

Poznanski, S., "Philon dans l'ancienne littérature judéo-arabe", *REJ*, 50 (1905), 10–31.

Rabin, C., *The Zadokite Documents: I. The Admonition. II. The Laws*, 2d rev. ed. (Oxford, 1958).

Ratzaby, Y., "Remarks concerning the Distinction between *Waw* and *Yodh* in the Habakkuk Scroll", *JQR*, n. s., 41 (1950–1951), 155ff.

Rowley, H. H., *The Zadokite Fragments and the Dead Sea Scrolls* (Oxford, 1952).

Sachau, C. E. (ed.), *Chronologie orientalischer Völker von Albērūnī*, 2 parts (Leipzig, 1876, 1878).

——, *The Chronology of Ancient Nations. An English Version of the Arabic Text of the Athār-ul-Bâkiya of Albīrūnī* (London, 1879).

Schechter, S., *Fragments of a Zadokite Work (= Documents of Jewish Sectaries 1)* (Cambridge, 1910).

——, *Saadyana: Geniza Fragments of Writings of R. Saadya Gaon and Others* (Cambridge, 1903).

Siebeneck, R. T., "The Messianism of Aggeus and Proto-Zacharias", *CBQ*, 19 (1957), 312–328.

Skehan, P. W., "Communication: Professor Zeitlin and the Dead Sea Scrolls", *CBQ*, 20 (1958), 228f.

——, "Exodus in the Samaritan Recension from Qumran", *JBL*, 74 (1955), 182–187.

——, "The Period of the Biblical Texts from Khirbet Qumrân", *CBQ*, 19 (1957), 435–440.

——, "Qumran and the Present State of Old Testament Text Studies: The Masoretic Text", *JBL*, 78 (1959), 21–25.

——, "The Qumran Manuscripts and Textual Criticism", *VT Supplement*, 4 (1957), 148–160.

Stern, S. M., "Abū ʿĪsā Muḥammad b. Hārūn al-Warrāḳ", *The Encyclopaedia of Islam*, 1, new ed. (Leiden-London, 1960), 130.

Teicher, J. L., "The Dead Sea Scrolls – Documents of the Jewish-Christian Sect of Ebionites", *JJS*, 2 (1951), 67–99.

Van Puyvelde, C. "Manuscrits bibliques. I. Manuscrits hébreux. Les manuscrits de la geniza du Caire", *VDBS*, 5 (Paris, 1957), 798–800.

de Vaux, R., "A propos des manuscrits de la Mer Morte", *RB*, 57 (1950), 417–429.

——, "Exploration de la région de Qumrân", *RB*, 60 (1953), 540–561.

Zeitlin, S., *The Zadokite Fragments. Facsimile of the Manuscripts in the Cairo Genizah Collection in the Possession of the University Library, Cambridge, England (= JQR Monograph Series 1)* (Philadelphia, 1952).

INDEX OF NAMES AND SUBJECTS

INDEX OF HEBREW WORDS

INDEX OF SYRIAC WORDS

INDEX OF BIBLICAL REFERENCES